T0349422

**More Praise for *Ghosts of Iron Mountain***

"THOUGHTFUL, PROVOCATIVE, UNIQUE, AND SMART are just a few of the adjectives that describe Phil Tinline's engrossing and highly readable *Ghosts of Iron Mountain*. You have to read this book to understand the roots of Trumpism in America today."

—**Steven M. Gillon, *New York Times* bestselling author of *America's Reluctant Prince* and *10 Days That Unexpectedly Changed America***

"A BRILLIANTLY RESEARCHED HISTORY that has the acid kick of a well-mixed gimlet. Tinline tell us, in a way we've never heard before, about the era of JFK and Vietnam—and the dark tendrils reaching out from then to now."

—**Rana Mitter, S. T. Lee Chair in U.S.-China Relations at the Harvard Kennedy School and author of *Forgotten Ally: China's World War II, 1937–1945***

"PERSPECTIVE-SHIFTING. *Ghosts of Iron Mountain* tells a story that subverts expectations of a perfectly polarized left-wing and right-wing mindset in the U.S. The fabricated document at this narrative's center has, since the 1960s, felt true to both sides, helping to explain why it continues to ping between satire and gospel across the political spectrum—and to this day remains distressingly relevant."

—**Whitney Phillips, coauthor of *The Shadow Gospel: How Anti-Liberal Demonology Possessed U.S. Religion, Media, and Politics***

"A GRIPPING, BEAUTIFULLY WRITTEN, REAL-LIFE HISTORICAL THRILLER. Roller-coasting from past to present, *Ghosts of Iron Mountain* reveals why many among us clutch at yarns about evil cabals and shadowy power brokers, and it finally answers the crucial question: Why do so many Americans cling to the stubborn belief that if something *feels* real, it *is* real?"

—**Brian Klaas, contributing writer at *The Atlantic* and author of *Fluke: Chance, Chaos, and Why Everything We Do Matters***

"DEEPLY INSIGHTFUL. The conspiratorial narratives that threaten society often come without warning, like a shock weather event. Or so it seems. Here, Phil Tinline reveals the actual truth—that fears about colluding forces are a quite predictable reaction to the centralization of state power and abuses by those who wield it. *Ghosts of Iron Mountain* is a masterly account of how post–World War II America succumbed to a paranoia that still has many of its citizens chasing extremes."

—**James Ball, author of *Post-Truth: How Bullshit Conquered the World***

"A PAGE-TURNING, RIPPING GOOD READ. It is, in fact, a true story about us, our beliefs and fears, our political choices, and our paranoia about power. Read it and be awakened."

—**Michael Shermer, publisher of *Skeptic* magazine and author of *Conspiracy: Why the Rational Believe the Irrational***

"PACEY AND ENGAGING. Both the immediate response to the *Report* and its enduring legacy reveal the extent of Americans' suspicions of and alienation from their government and help make sense of the apparent insanity of QAnon and other deep-state conspiracy theories."

—**Laura Beers, author of *Orwell's Ghosts: Wisdom and Warnings for the Twenty-First Century***

"UNPUTDOWNABLE. This superb story of a runaway hoax peels back like an onion. By the time you get to the deepest layer, everything you thought you knew about politics is transformed."

—**Bradley Garrett, author of *Bunker: What It Takes to Survive the Apocalypse***

# REPORT FROM IRON MOUNTAIN ON THE POSSIBILITY AND DESIRABILITY OF PEACE

WITH INTRODUCTORY MATERIAL
BY LEONARD C. LEWIN

"The unwillingness of [The Special Study Group] to publicize their findings [is] readily understandable. . . . They concluded [that] lasting peace, while not theoretically impossible, is probably unattainable; even if it could be achieved it would almost certainly not be in the best interests of a stable society to achieve it . . . ."

# GHOSTS OF
# IRON MOUNTAIN

## THE HOAX OF THE CENTURY,
## ITS ENDURING IMPACT, AND
## WHAT IT REVEALS ABOUT AMERICA TODAY

# PHIL TINLINE

SCRIBNER

New York   Amsterdam/Antwerp   London
Toronto   Sydney/Melbourne   New Delhi

*For my family*

# CONTENTS

# GHOSTS OF IRON MOUNTAIN

# FOREWORD

It was a left-wing conspiracy—and I happened to be in a position to know four of the plotters: Victor Navasky, Richard Lingeman, E. L. Doctorow, and Ping Ferry. They were mischievous merry pranksters who, with no inkling of the ultimate scale of what they were creating, managed to pull off what Phil Tinline rightly calls the hoax of the century.

I first met Victor Navasky in the spring of 1978 when he walked in to take over *The Nation*, the country's oldest political weekly. I was a twenty-six-year-old assistant editor, and he seemed terribly intimidating—even humorless. But as I learned over the years, this first impression was quite mistaken. Victor had an impish, even mischievous sense of humor. At forty-six-years of age, he'd already had quite a career. He'd published a serious biography of Bobby Kennedy—and he was about to publish *Naming Names*, a definitive history of the McCarthy era and the Hollywood Ten case, "a conspiracy so immense," as the communist-hunting senator once inveighed. But Navasky had also been the publisher and editor of a biting satirical magazine, *Monocle*, that he'd founded while studying law at Yale.

Navasky brought with him to *The Nation* his *Monocle* buddy, Richard Lingeman, a reserved, ever so soft-spoken Midwesterner who'd written much of the copy for *Monocle*. By the late 1970s, E. L. Doctorow was already an acclaimed novelist, but he would occasionally drop off his essays at *The Nation*'s offices. The very rich Ping Ferry rarely entered the magazine's run-down lair, but it was assumed he always came with a sizable check.

At the time, I had a vague knowledge that these middle-aged men had been comrades from *Monocle*, the now wholly forgotten and defunct political satire magazine. I had no idea of their dark secret. Once or maybe twice I heard the phrase "Iron Mountain"—and someone would lift their eyebrows and emit a soft chuckle. I shrugged it off as ancient history.

By 1981, I was ready to embark on my first book project, a biography of John J. McCloy, the powerful Wall Street Rockefeller family lawyer—the man whom John Kenneth Galbraith had named as the mysterious "chairman of the U.S. Establishment." In college I'd read *The Power Elite* by C. Wright Mills, and my ambition with McCloy was to use his life to explore how power works in our complicated democracy. McCloy was the chairman of the Council on Foreign Relations, chairman of the Ford Foundation, a director of the Rockefeller Foundation, and a member of both the Bilderberg Group and the Trilateral Commission. And, of course, he allegedly ran naked with other powerful members of the Establishment each summer in the elite Bohemian Grove club near San Francisco.

Needless to say, Victor thought this was a terrific project, and he shepherded my way to a literary agent and a somewhat modest book advance from Alice Mayhew at Simon & Schuster.

I spent ten years on *The Chairman: John J. McCloy and the Making of the American Establishment.* It was a serious biography, by which I mean it had thousands of source notes. And, yes, I wrote about McCloy's involvement with elite institutions as a vehicle to understand the workings of power and how decisions are made, particularly in the field of foreign affairs. And yet, I was always wary of being labeled a conspiratorialist. McCloy, for example, was a member of the Warren Commission to investigate John F. Kennedy's assassination. Early in the commission's deliberations, Allen Dulles asserted that most presidential assassins typically were misfits and loners. To which McCloy retorted, "The Lincoln assassination was a plot."

Still, McCloy understood that it was going to be hard to prove the absence of a plot. "The Commission," he said in its very first meeting, "is going to be criticized . . . no matter what we do." Indeed, the Warren Commission rightly concluded that Oswald had acted alone—but this wholly reasoned conclusion to their investigations only planted the seeds for a growth industry in myriad conspiracy theories.

All of this is to confess that as a biographer and historian I have wrestled with the attractions of a conspiratorial narrative in history. I have spent decades writing about elite players and the culture of the Establishment. But I remain a skeptic of any particular conspiracy as an explanation of how power is exercised by these elites. Those who reflexively fall for a conspiratorial narrative, often convoluted, slip into thinking that nothing is an accident. But from our daily experience, we all know that life is often a series of accidents.

---

What we have here in Phil Tinline's astonishing book is something altogether unique—an account of a brilliantly conceived spoof that has quite unintentionally changed the course of history, feeding a frenzy of conspiratorially minded narratives that have poisoned the electorate and threaten our civic discourse. The spoof would be hilarious if it were not so dangerous.

What was Navasky thinking when he opened this door on the deep state? Well, Victor and his comrades were only having good fun—and trying to get people to wake up to the mad nature of what Dwight Eisenhower called the military-industrial complex and the tragedy of Lyndon Johnson's endless Vietnam War. When Victor persuaded struggling writer Leonard Lewin to write a parody of a top-secret government study exploring what would happen if "peace" suddenly broke out, Navasky was just trying to get people to think. The *Report from Iron Mountain* was an anti-war spoof, that's all.

But the hoax was too successful. When published, it made news on the front page of the *New York Times*. It became a bestseller. Lewin's prose, echoing the deadpan, amoral language of nuclear war strategists like Herman Kahn at the Hudson Institute, convinced all too many people, left and right, that *Report from Iron Mountain* was authentic. And some continued to believe it was the real thing even when Lewin and Navasky owned up to the hoax five years later.

As Tinline documents, the *Report from Iron Mountain* became "a satire on the thinking of the real power elite that was purloined by fascists."

The unintended consequences have been both knee-slappingly ludicrous and quite deadly. *Iron Mountain* spawned so much conspiracy thinking: Oliver Stone's blockbuster 1991 film *JFK*. The anti-Semitic trash of Liberty Lobby's *Spotlight* publications. And perhaps even Timothy McVeigh's April 19, 1995, truck bomb attack on the federal building in Oklahoma City that killed 168 people. There were also the hateful ravings of radio host Alex Jones. The activities of various right-wing state militias that published pirated editions of *Iron Mountain*. And one could argue that even former president Donald Trump's exhortations against the "deep state" ultimately trace back to Navasky's hoax.

*Iron Mountain* has had a very strange life. It has even fed left-wing hallucinations. As Tinline writes, "The horrible irony is that *Report from Iron Mountain* was crafted with such ingenuity and insight that Lewin, Doctorow, and Navasky accidentally created another multipurpose, undying conspiracy theory that could be used to substantiate the craziest claim about the elite's schemes." *Iron Mountain* has been used to explain why we should not believe the science of climate change. Or why we should distrust vaccines. Or, even more often, why we should distrust the federal government and our elected leaders.

Tinline's history of the hoax is fascinating and hilarious. But it is also a serious intellectual history that illuminates our times. In part, Tinline relies on the thinking of the late, great historian Richard Hofstadter, the author of the influential essay "The Paranoid Style in American Politics." Understanding the role of elites, he points out, doesn't mean viewing history as just a secret plot. "There is a great difference between . . . locating conspiracies in history and saying that history *is*, in effect, a conspiracy."

If Victor were still with us today he would emphatically agree. But I think the mischief-maker in him would still be delighted with his prank—even as he would be worried that so many people continue to misunderstand his serious intentions.

Kai Bird

# INTRODUCTION: WHAT HAPPENED?

How do you know that someone in power isn't plotting right now to do you harm?

How did we get to the point where many of us, on all sides of politics, are convinced that our opponents are evil and mean to destroy us?

And how did America, the last best hope of earth, the beacon of democracy, the shining city on a hill, find its Capitol under attack by its own citizens? Why, nearly four years later, in November 2024, did a majority of Americans vote for a former president who did not exactly seem displeased that that attack had happened? Many voters clearly felt, based on everyday experience, that the government did not have their best interests at heart. But at least for some people, Donald Trump's appeal appeared to go beyond the problems of high prices or illegal migration. At rally after rally, he told a story about how the state had become a malign, even demonic force.

One way to make sense of this is to look back to the forging of the United States in the firestorm of popular revolt. The mob that gathered in the heart of Washington, DC, on January 6, 2021, certainly had that history of resistance in mind; it's a vital part of the story. But the independent United States's new capital city was meant to symbolize the inauguration of government of, by, and for the people. It takes its name from the leader of the revolt against tyranny. By what strange sequence of events has *Washington* come to be seen as tyranny's command center?

This book is about the stories we tell ourselves about power, and how today's nightmares about deep states and dark conspiracies were formed:

specters that were ready and waiting to be summoned and pressed back into service once America lurched back into crisis.

To make sense of the latest reawakening of long dormant fears, we need to go back first not all the way to 1776, but to the time when American power as we think of it today really took shape—an era when most of its recent leaders were also forged. Joe Biden was born in 1942, the first full year of America's involvement in the Second World War, as the war machine was gearing up. Trump—like Bill Clinton and George W. Bush—was born in the summer of 1946, as America emerged to find its global standing transformed. The United States in which they grew up really did seem to be a shining city. So what happened?

As we'll see, it was in that confident postwar world—when the United States was at the zenith of its power—that many people stopped trusting the government and started worrying about whether it was still possible to tell the difference between truth and deception—between fact and fiction. This really took off in the mid-1960s,[1] but even before that, voices on both the left and right feared how powerful the center had become, how secretive, how easily it told lies. And that powerful center lied not only to the public but to itself, to the point where it sometimes seemed lost in a maze of delusions. It was in that era that today's fears of what some now call the deep state crystalized.

The descent into a kind of omnipresent paranoia—crucially, a paranoia tinged with truth—is best captured in the true story of a hoax. A hoax that shocked the nation in the late 1960s, and that, once created, seemed impossible to extinguish.

Most hoaxes, of course, are eventually revealed, and that's the end of their run. But this one endured, infinitely metastasizing because it captured all too well those fears of power, whether one stood on the left or right. The fabricated document at the hoax's center purported to sum up a top secret government investigation into what would happen if permanent global peace broke out. The government investigators—referred to only as "the Special Study Group"—predicted that if America's vast war machine had to be dismantled, terrible consequences would follow. They recommended horrifying alternative methods that the state would have to use to keep control of the population.

The notion that such a study group actually existed raised the fear of a cabal within the government that secretly pulls on puppet strings, manipulating the course of our lives. This belief that what the hoax revealed was real persisted for years and years—long after the fabrication was exposed. Its influence spread to Hollywood and to the extreme right. It's still alive right *now*.

The man at the heart of this story—a writer named Leonard Lewin—understood very well what haunted people, and he proved masterly in creating a false document that would be taken for the truth. But before we follow him to a mysterious place called Iron Mountain we must journey back to the fifties and early sixties, to meet two other men of his generation.

C. Wright Mills was a radical maverick who developed a hugely influential left-wing critique of how American power worked. John F. Kennedy embodied that power—and found himself facing attacks from the far right. Each played a crucial, if unwitting, role in laying the conspiratorial kindling that allowed this hoax to catch fire in the popular imagination.

# 1

# THE POWER ELITE

In the wake of the Second World War, the United States suddenly found itself the most powerful nation in history. America was suddenly, aggressively *big*: big new factories and shipyards, big cars and big cities, big growth figures, big budgets, big corporations and big unions, a few big computers. At the heart of it all, big government with grand ambitions; a newly gigantic military; and, overshadowing everything, the most colossal and destructive weapons ever made.

The atomic bomb was terrifying in itself, but it raised another fear: that this apocalyptic new weapon handed immense power to a handful of American technocrats. The once-lean American state had been transformed into a vast war machine that now drafted young men into the military in peacetime.

Those in command, meanwhile, were even more apprehensive, because the postwar world had brought a series of unnerving shocks and defeats. Stalin's Soviet Union, lately America's ally, had swallowed half of Europe; it looked as though Greece would be next. France and Italy seemed vulnerable. And communism was armed not just with tanks but invisible, insidious ideas that had penetrated America's homeland, especially among the kind of bright young people now rising into positions of influence. In 1948, Czechoslovakia fell to a stealth communist coup. Then the Soviets blockaded West

Berlin, forcing the United States to lead a year-long airlift to feed a city of more than two million. At home, defectors and the FBI were exposing spies inside the government. In 1949, the communist tide engulfed China, and it emerged that Stalin had the Bomb. In 1950, communist North Korea invaded South Korea, and a third world war, fought with atomic weapons, seemed imminent. Three weeks later, a man named Julius Rosenberg was arrested on suspicion of passing atom bomb secrets to Moscow.

Many Americans saw the global communist threat as the overriding danger. But not everyone. For some on the left, the progressive impetus of President Roosevelt's government-expanding New Deal in the 1930s had vanished, leaving a much bigger, stronger state—but one which now saw them as the enemy. They watched as a single law—the 1947 National Security Act—entrenched the federal government's new Cold War powers in three forbidding new institutions. First, the National Security Agency: a secretive inner circle at the heart of the executive branch; in time, this would place a powerful unelected figure at the president's side: the national security adviser. Second, in the immense new Pentagon building—another product of the war—the old War and Navy Departments and the newly independent air force came together as the Department of Defense. And third, the act inaugurated America's first peacetime foreign espionage organization, the Central Intelligence Agency. From 1950, under the Internal Security Act, the president was authorized, in an internal security emergency, to detain anyone deemed a spy, saboteur, or subversive. And then there were the loyalty oaths and the blacklists, and the firings and forced resignations.

For leftists looking over their shoulders, there seemed no serious difference between the centers of government and the baying hounds of the far right, led by the terrifying Republican senator Joseph McCarthy. His indiscriminate hunt for supposed communists to haul before his investigations committee and drive from public life was making him immensely popular.

But McCarthy was just as distrustful of powerful centrist elites as his opposite numbers on the left. He was a Wisconsin farm-boy populist, aggressively suspicious of the high-born liberals who ran America's big government machine. He accused the State Department, the CIA, and eventually the army of being riddled with traitors who despised the real America.

Here—on the left, the right, and in the center of government—were three competing visions of power. All three visions were overblown, but it was McCarthy's wild talk of the "immense" communist "conspiracy"[1] that went furthest into fiction. He began with the narrative he wanted to push, then had his staff scrabble for evidence to back it up. One journalist wrote that McCarthy behaved like a private eye in a movie; a Senate committee report on the communist hunter's early accusations denounced them as "a fraud and a hoax."[2]

In 1954, McCarthy's Establishment enemies finally faced him down, when he directly challenged the U.S. Army, but in the years that followed, both the left and the right kept struggling to come to terms with the federal government's sinister, secretive new concentration of power, and how to resist it. In many ways, they were right to be wary of the threat. But at times, in their attempts to fight the power, they built the state up into an overwhelming, omnipotent force at the heart of a vast web of conspiracy.

―――――――――

In the timid world of American academia in the mid-1950s, Charles Wright Mills was a very unusual sort of scholar: a Texan who tore around on a motorcycle, built his own houses, and took great pride in having once kicked a racist in the face. With both feet. He was born in Waco, went to high school in Dallas, and seemed on course to be an engineer in the booming Texas economy. He did not leave his home state until he was twenty-three. Even as a fast-rising sociologist, he remained an "outlander."[3] He once praised a friend for being "like the cowboy and detectives in the movies, an autonomous man."[4] His fellow academic sociologists at Columbia University tended to confine themselves to narrow, highly focused research projects, which they strove to make as objective as possible. But Mills was aiming far higher, and wider.

Driven by the image of the little man against the system, C. Wright Mills variously declared himself a socialist and an anarchist. As a teenager, he'd rebelled against the harshness of military school. He saw the Second World War as a pointless "bloodbath"[5] and was relieved that, for medical reasons, he was rejected for military service. The war, he wrote, "made a radical of me."[6] He'd planted his flag on the left, but lauded that hero of hard-right libertarians, the American Revolutionary icon Patrick Henry: another autonomous man who'd stood up against centralized power.

Amid the postwar boom and Cold War paranoia, Mills saw an America in which ordinary citizens felt that power had been sucked out of their lives and relocated to far-off rooms where tight-knit groups of men, with endless funds and infinite ambition plotted . . . who knew what? This was the country he set out to understand.

In 1956, he published a book called *The Power Elite*: a data-rich, deeply researched assault on the new establishment that had developed since the war. "Historically," Mills argued, "democracy in America has been underpinned by the militia system of armed citizens at a time when the rifle was the key weapon and one man meant one rifle as well as one vote." The Constitution was "constructed in fear of a powerful military establishment."[7] But now, there was the Pentagon, that gargantuan death star, symbolizing how "the American means of violence have been enlarged and centralized."[8] Corporations, politicians, and the military, he argued, were inextricably intertwined: generals went to work for defense companies, which funded congressmen, who lobbied for more money for the military. This was a fearsome centralization of power.

The status quo was sustained by a "permanent war economy" which had extended that intertwining of state, military, and corporations into peacetime. Or rather, into the era of Cold War. The permanent war economy kept a 1930s-style slump at bay, but at a price: "war or a high state of war preparedness," Mills wrote, "is felt to be the normal and seemingly permanent condition of the United States."[9] Under the supposedly permanent threat of attack, the military had unprecedented influence on political decisions.

The generals, businessmen, and politicians—as well as defense intellectuals, Pentagon-funded scientists, and media cheerleaders—all behaved as if their Cold War world view was calm, grown-up common sense. Mills attacked the way they sought to manipulate the masses into accepting that there was no alternative to "the military definition of reality." He attacked the warlords' no-expense-spared public relations onslaught, which they'd deployed ever since the Second World War to "sell their ideas and themselves to the public and to the Congress." This, he complained, extended to a Pentagon newsroom with at least thirty-six journalists and "the largest motion-picture studio in the East."[10] In the face of this, too many Americans had lost "the desire to be independent."[11] They were becoming "cheerful robots,"[12] helplessly apathetic and cynical about what the powerful did in their name.

Mills's ideas chimed with lurid fears expressed by many in the early years of the Cold War regarding the manipulative power of brainwashing, subliminal advertising, and Madison Avenue's "hidden persuaders." But the sociologist took care to chart the limits of the power elite's capacity to bend the masses to their will. In the face of rising public distrust, he wrote, the media couldn't simply persuade them as if by "magic,"[13] much as it might want to.

And crucially, he argued that the dreamworld the power elite sought to impose on the public was one they lived in themselves, in which war had "become seemingly total and seemingly permanent" and was "the only reality."[14]

In 1958, to the consternation of his studiously empirical colleagues, Mills set out his ideas in a polemical paperback aimed at the mass market. *The Causes of World War Three* denounced the powerful men stuck in this militaristic mindset as deluded "crackpot realists" who were dragging the world toward destruction. The book sold in large numbers. It argued that, since the end of the Second World War, "many in elite circles have felt that economic prosperity in the US is immediately under-pinned by the war economy and that desperate economic—and so political—problems might well arise should there be disarmament and genuine peace."[15] At times, he made a more alarming assertion: that to a "considerable extent, militarism has become an end in itself."[16]

Mills was desperate to break the suffocating elite consensus. The bipartisan approach to foreign policy. The way real decisions were made in secret by executives and the military, not openly in Congress. Journalists' willingness to "disseminate the official definitions of world reality."[17] He wanted America to get back to thrashing political issues out in open public argument. He wanted to show what the economy would look like "with the economics of war subtracted,"[18] to take private profit out of war preparations and "replace the permanent war economy by a permanent peace economy." And above all, he wanted a break with the "military metaphysic"—the whole mindset spawned by America's vertiginous ascent to superpower status, which maintained that the arms race and the permanent war economy were the only rational approaches. It was vital to "move towards making possible alternative definitions of reality."[19]

All these ideas—of the power elite, mass manipulation, and the need to break through official reality to an alternative—came close to conspiracy theory. But Mills was careful to avoid taking that further step. He tested his analysis with his long-time friend and colleague, a historian named Richard Hofstadter. Mills stressed that the "conception of the power elite . . . does *not* rest upon the assumption that American history since the origins of World War II must be understood as a secret plot, or as a great and coordinated conspiracy of the members of this elite. The conception rests upon quite impersonal grounds":[20] on often-visible similarities of world view and interest. He invoked Hofstadter's caution that "there is a great difference between locating conspiracies *in* history and saying that history *is*, in effect, a conspiracy."[21]

But when more shocks came, others wouldn't be quite so careful.

————————

If anyone embodied Mills's triangle of military, business, and politics, it was his contemporary John F. Kennedy: war hero, son of a multimillionaire, and a senator before he was forty. As a fast-rising Irish-American banker and businessman, his father, Joseph P. Kennedy, would doubtless have been happy with the idea of the power elite, provided he could break into it. He hated the First World War, but was ready to use it to boost his ascent. He was a conservative, isolationist tycoon, but in the 1930s he saw that it was interventionist government that was on the rise, so he made sure he hitched himself to President Franklin Roosevelt and his New Deal. As he rose with it, he prepared to pull his sons up with him—despite his relentless support for appeasement and, once war broke out in 1939, for American neutrality.

John—or "Jack," as the family called him—grew up in such a bubble that he didn't notice the Great Depression. As he later admitted, "I read about it at Harvard."[22] When war broke out, he was determined to serve despite his various illnesses, which included chronic back pain and Addison's disease. Joe scratched the necessary backs to ensure that, despite his health, Jack was enlisted in the navy. This was self-promotion as well as self-sacrifice, but young Kennedy ended up displaying genuine heroism, rescuing his men when their torpedo boat was cut in half by a Japanese destroyer. He earned his write-up in the New Yorker. In 1946, John F. Kennedy ran for Congress, and his father paid for one hundred thousand copies of a shortened version of the New Yorker article to be distributed across the district.

To a great extent, John's views were just what you might expect from an apprentice member of the power elite. He was much more militaristic than his isolationist father, though this was tempered by empathy for fellow veterans and robust contempt for the military's higher-ups. He was a fairly conventional cold warrior, uncritical of hard-line anti-communists' conspiratorial frame of mind. He voted for the 1950 Internal Security Act and its new powers to intern so-called subversives in a national emergency. He was no fan of Joseph McCarthy, but when, in 1954, the Wisconsin demagogue finally faced a censure vote from fellow senators, Kennedy avoided participating.[23] His father had links with McCarthy; his brother Bobby had worked for him.

On one important Cold War question, Kennedy's stance was more distinctive—for the moment, at least. President Eisenhower was investing in ever-greater U.S. military aid to South Vietnam, with the aim of ensuring it didn't fall under communist control. This buildup accorded with the so-called domino theory that insisted that if South Vietnam fell, neighboring countries would soon follow. Kennedy won praise for arguing *against* U.S. military intervention. But he did so on the grounds that it "would be dangerously futile and destructive," not that the goal was wrong.[24] He remained in the political center; he wasn't challenging the basic logic of the Cold War.

In *The Power Elite*, Mills referred to Kennedy only once—in a footnote. He pointed to the young senator's rise to show how "today, the politician must rely on the mass media, and access to these media is expensive." He also suggested that such access wasn't always truthfully accounted for. Kennedy, Mills explained, was the "son of multimillionaire Joseph P Kennedy." He "was reported to have spent $15,866 in his 1952 campaign," but curiously enough "committees on his behalf . . . spent $217,995."[25] Joe paid for a blizzard of ads across every available medium, and even bought the support of a whole newspaper. No one fought their way to power without a little trickery.

As Kennedy's undeclared run for president geared up through 1959, this expensive promotion began to become a public relations problem, particularly given who was doing the spending. During the Wisconsin primary, a hopelessly outgunned Hubert Humphrey complained: "We are not selling corn flakes or some Hollywood production."[26] As Kennedy clinched the nomination and prepared to take on Republican Richard Nixon, he could rely on the media to keep his incessant promiscuity to themselves. Stories about his chronic health problems were reflexively, and successfully, denied.

One key plank of Kennedy's campaign sprang straight from the "military definition of reality" that Mills said the power elite both embraced and pushed onto everyone else. America, Kennedy warned, faced a terrifying "missile gap." Despite having once been the country's top general, President Eisenhower had supposedly let the United States fall dangerously behind the USSR in intercontinental ballistic missile production. Since 1956, Khrushchev had been boasting that the Soviet Union was pumping out ICBMs like sausages. Then, on October 4, 1957, news had broken that the Soviets had managed to launch a satellite. The unnerving success of Sputnik seemed to confirm that Soviet missiles could strike America. A few weeks later, the *Washington Post* revealed that the top secret Gaither report on the nation's defenses against nuclear attack had leaked—and was terrifying. It portrayed "a United States in the gravest danger in its history"; only "an enormous increase in military spending" would save the day.[27]

Which was all very compelling, but there was no missile gap. Or rather, there *was*, but it was in America's favor. The Soviet leader had been making it all up—and the hardened anti-communist cold warriors in the air force had chosen to believe him. The historian Sharon Ghamari-Tabrizi has charted the enthusiastic credulity of air force analysts and their fellow experts at the affiliated think tank, the RAND Corporation, who saw what they wanted to see in blurred photographs and misinterpreted an absence of tests not as evidence that the Soviet program had stalled, but that it had moved to a terrifying new phase.

This was the military definition of reality Mills had identified—the demands of managing the incomprehensible stakes of the arms race had led intelligent men to demand maximum rearmament on the back of guesswork and self-delusion. Kennedy was all too keen to seize on the gap for political advantage. Eventually, exasperated by the Democratic candidate's claims about the missile gap, President Eisenhower instructed the Joint Chiefs of Staff to show the ambitious young senator the real picture. But either this sharing of information was so restricted by continuing secrecy that Kennedy was shown too little to convince him, or Kennedy *was* persuaded but, regardless, chose to keep shaking his fist at the nonexistent gap.

One force driving the desperation for unachievable certainty was the series of shocks America had endured, ever since the start of the Cold War, as countries from Czechoslovakia to China had been taken over by communists. No wonder that, like many in the late 1950s power elite, Kennedy was an advocate of the domino theory. And now it had happened again, far closer to home. In Cuba, just ninety miles off the coast, on New Year's Day, 1959, a revolutionary socialist guerrilla leader, Fidel Castro, had seized power, nationalizing U.S.-owned businesses. To the power elite, this posed a political and military threat, especially if revolution caught fire across Latin America. At the height of his battle for the White House, Kennedy made an incendiary call for America to "strengthen" and "support" exiled Cuban "fighters for freedom" who wanted to overthrow Castro. Even Nixon, who'd made his name as a hard-line anti-communist, accused Kennedy of risking a Third World War.

C. Wright Mills, meanwhile, was making himself the loudest, most outspoken defender of Castro in the United States. Days before Kennedy called for American support for the exiles, Mills had finished hammering out a book in six weeks flat: *Listen, Yankee: The Revolution in Cuba*. It had soon sold more than a hundred thousand copies. Mills had moved a long way from the scholarly approach of *The Power Elite*. His new book's argument was based on a visit to Cuba in August 1960, during which he recorded interviews with "soldiers, intellectuals, government officials, and citizens,"[28] questioned most of the revolutionary leaders, including Che Guevara, and spent more than three days with Castro himself—and it was written in the voice of a Cuban revolutionary.

Shortly before he set off, Mills had been told by Cuba's alternate representative to the United Nations that Castro had read *The Power Elite* during the revolutionary struggle, and discussed it with his followers. And now

Mills sought to give a voice to a valiant small nation struggling to free itself from the long shadow of its colossal neighbor. The Texan in New York, the champion of the little man against big power, was escalating his crusade to a geopolitical scale.

Early in *Listen, Yankee*, Mills takes aim at the two presidential candidates whom he sees as much the same, each as belligerent and ignorant of Cuba as the other. "What are we to suppose," his imaginary revolutionary asks, "when Mr. Nixon speaks openly about bringing us to our knees whenever he decides to, and Mr. Kennedy 'takes the hard line' and calls us a 'Communist satellite.' . . . All the Kennedys and Nixons can see in the world is an imagined military scene, and both see that with all the vision of the hysteric."[29]

Days before he left for Cuba, Mills read a piece in the *New York Times* called "The Managerial Revolution Hits Politics," which noted approvingly that neither candidate "is burning with ideological zeal, which is what bothers the extremists of Right and Left. They are the organization men of politics."[30] This liberal centrism, to Mills, was exactly the problem.

He was not the only American public figure prepared to speak up for Cuba—he was involved with a body called the Fair Play for Cuba Committee (FPCC), which had been launched that April with a declaration in the *New York Times*, signed by the novelists Norman Mailer, James Baldwin, and Truman Capote; the French philosopher Jean-Paul Sartre; and the English theater critic Kenneth Tynan. Reportedly, it was at the behest of one of the organization's founders that Mills wrote *Listen, Yankee* in the first place. But he was now going further than any of them in railing against the power elite.

He agreed to take on his Cold War liberal foes in a debate on live television before an audience of millions. His opponent was to be Adolf Berle, who'd been assistant secretary of state for Latin American Affairs during the war, and ambassador to Brazil. He'd also been an early critic of *The Power Elite*.

Like the autonomous man going up against the system he so admired in detective novels and movies, the moral maverick up against "immoral society,"[31] Mills had left himself open to attack from multiple angles. The FBI was on his case; he received a death threat, telling him "an American agent disgused as a South American" would assassinate him when he went to Cuba in the New Year.[32] Mills said he could believe it—according to an FBI report, he assumed "the Federal Bureau of Investigation and other similar U.S. organizations do not approve of his activities."[33] He started finding out how to buy a gun.

His press clippings agency was sending him the reviews of *Listen, Yankee*, which charged him not just with spite, claptrap, and childishness but with spreading distortions, lies, and propaganda paid for by Havana. *Listen, Yankee* pushes back at the idea that America's "catastrophes around the world are caused by a mere handful of conspirators stirring up trouble." But now he stood accused of peddling the converse conspiracy theory: that the masses were unknowingly under the thumb of "shadowy directors who sit around polished tables in Manhattan."[34] He was trying to replace a phantom cabal of cackling communists with a phantom cabal of cackling capitalists. And while all this was coming his way, an ever more exhausted Mills was stressing over the preparations for the debate on live TV. As he told a British friend, "the pressure on me because of Cuba, official and unofficial, is mounting. It is very subtle and very fascinating. But also worrisome and harassing."[35] The night before the debate, Mills suffered a severe heart attack.

In the drawer next to his hospital bed, he kept a pistol.

———

Not that he could have known, but in his lonely crusade against Kennedy and the power elite Mills had a surprising ally. In the White House, President Eisenhower's chief speechwriter was a political scientist—and ex-journalist—named Malcolm Moos. According to the historian James Ledbetter, Moos had "certainly" read C. Wright Mills.[36] He'd also taken to leafing through the aerospace journals in which the defense industry busily retailed its wares to the Pentagon. It was, he remembered, "astounding to go through them, and see some 25,000 different kinds of related companies."[37]

Between Kennedy's Cuba speech and the publication of *Listen, Yankee*, Moos met with a colleague to discuss what their boss should say when he left office at the start of 1961. What if Eisenhower said farewell by addressing "the problem of militarism"? As never before, they agreed, "the United States has a permanent war-based industry." On top of that, they were becoming increasingly aware of the sheer number of officers who were retiring in their forties, then mysteriously reappearing as directors "in the war-based industrial complex, shaping its decisions and guiding the direction of its tremendous thrust."[38]

You might think Eisenhower, supreme Allied commander in Europe during the Second World War, would balk at saying any such thing. In fact, he had a long-standing concern with the size of the military and an old-school belief in balancing the government's books. He was irritated by the phony "missile gap" attacks and Kennedy's performative hawkishness in the election. And he was "outraged at the antics of the cabal consisting of air force officers, aviation industry lobbyists and trade associations, and congressmen promoting arms programs beneficial to their districts who regularly fed ammunition to his critics."[39] Business, military, politicians in cahoots, using tall tales to make their permanent war economy self-interest palatable. As Moos and his colleagues prepared the speech for Eisenhower, Kennedy narrowly won the election.

On January 17, 1961, America watched as its genial old president looked directly into the camera and bid his country farewell. He included in his remarks this startlingly bleak warning: "In the councils of government, we must guard against the acquisition of unwarranted influence, whether sought or unsought, by the military-industrial complex. The potential for the disastrous rise of misplaced power exists and will persist."[40]

Left-wingers reacted with delighted surprise. As Mills recovered from his heart attack, he read the maverick journalist I. F. Stone's stop-the-presses reaction to the speech in his weekly newsletter. Under the headline "The

Monster We Can No Longer Control," Stone connected the speech to Eisenhower's State of the Union jibe a few days before that the missile gap was a "fiction." "We wonder," wrote Stone,

> whether a civilian president, without Mr. Eisenhower's prestige as a military commander, will dare challenge myths of this kind. . . . How is the ordinary citizen to know the truth when it takes time even for a military man as President to see behind bloated intelligence estimates?[41]

But perhaps Kennedy didn't want to challenge these myths at all. In Mills's papers there is an intriguing article marked up with his underlinings. It's from an unnamed journal, dated December 10, 1960—the day Mills was supposed to have been on TV debating Cuba, had he not had a heart attack. It suggested that Kennedy's victory had "aroused new hopes in the breasts of the armament interests" in anticipation of a healthy boost in military spending. Indeed, the author speculates drily, the "enormous vested interest in armaments" is such that, "if the Soviet Union should announce its intention to disarm unilaterally, there would be enormous pressure on Washington to force military aid on the former enemy and re-establish it as a menace."[42]

---

Kennedy's big "New Frontier" pitch to Americans was youth, efficiency, and vigor—and into the heart of power on his coattails came a fresh generation of smart young "defense intellectuals." In the *New York Times*, James Reston wrote admiringly that "These men are not bound to an established set of policies. They are not talking in ideological terms or traditional terms. They are reviewing the problems facing the country quite analytically and it is obvious that they are perfectly willing to follow the facts wherever they may lead."[43] Some of these men, pristine in their horn-rims, bow ties, and short-sleeved white shirts, were associated with the U.S. Air Force–affiliated think tank the RAND Corporation. Like the CIA, this enterprise was a product of the Second World War: it had sprung from scientists' cooperation with the military and was leading the transformation of "war" into something beyond the comprehension of the public, and even of the generals.

The whiz kid of whiz kids was the dauntingly clever ex-president of Ford Motor Company Robert McNamara, who'd made his name transforming the efficiency of America's bombing forces during the Second World War. Once installed in the Pentagon, the new secretary of defense and his bright young men were going to do the same for the whole of the U.S. military. Their primary weapons would be "systems analysis" and "operations research." These innovative methods used computers to conduct holistic, coolly objective measurements of cost and need, with precisely zero care for the finer feelings of the blustering top brass. This was all dazzlingly scientific. But did these men's belief that they could order the world, and their reliance on future projections, lend their methods just a hint of science fiction?

———

Within weeks of Kennedy's idealistic inaugural, Castro was complaining that the Pentagon and the CIA were conducting daily air drops of weapons to guerrillas in Cuba's mountains. Meanwhile, the New York Times was reporting that Kennedy was increasingly talking about the problem of tyranny on the island.

Mills was at home in rural New York, following the news as he tried to recuperate under the eye of the FBI. And now he was being sued for millions of dollars by a finance company over a passage in Listen, Yankee alleging unlawful activity in prerevolutionary Cuba. He wrote to an English friend, a Marxist academic named Ralph Miliband: "I'm afraid there is going to come about a very bad time in my country for people who think as I do." He feared he was "in for it,"[44] but wouldn't say why. And he was worried about his heart.

By March 18, 1961, less than three months after its publication, Listen, Yankee had sold four hundred thousand copies, and Mills was receiving letters every day from across the world, some asking how the senders could back Castro. Mills told his parents that he felt "a big responsibility to thousands of people all over the world to tell the truth as I see it and to tell it exactly and with drama."[45] Some of his old friends and colleagues thought he was letting the drama overwhelm the exactitude. But a new source of support had emerged. *The Militant*, house newsweekly of a tiny Trotskyist group, the Socialist Workers Party, had been praising *Listen, Yankee* to the skies.

To be fair, Mills had doubts about Castro, not least over his increasing centralization of power. But as tensions between the Cuban leader and the new American administration intensified, Mills's break from his old liberal colleagues was becoming total. He despised the "moral cowardice" of an American intelligentsia who refused to face the "moral ambiguity . . . which any violence involves."[46] He read of Che Guevara telling a rally of Cuban workers that their country was about to face a fight to the death with the "immense hyena" across the water.[47] On April 11, as sales of *Listen, Yankee* pushed toward half a million, Mills insisted it was "still right on the ball."[48]

———————

Historically, since its establishment in 1947, those who have run the CIA have often been caricatured as creatures of the far right, but the agency's founding fathers were highborn Cold War centrists. These men were Ivy League alumni, brought up in British-style boarding schools, despised by McCarthy-style nativist right-wingers. One typical figure was a fairly liberal Democrat who'd taught economics at Yale; among his former students was Kennedy's supersharp, born-to-rule new national security adviser McGeorge Bundy. The Kennedy men were suitably awed by the agency's high command, while the spooks hailed the new administration as full of zest for action and impatience with red tape. What could possibly go wrong?

Something had to be done, they told each other, about Cuba. The CIA had been trying to assassinate Castro for months; within weeks of Kennedy's coming to power, the agency was focusing on its more grandiose plan:

an invasion by Cuban exiles. But when the men from the CIA apprised Kennedy of the plan in the White House Cabinet Room, the commander in chief declared it "too spectacular."[49] American involvement had to be deniable. This would be challenging, given that the press had been reporting for months about rumors of U.S. camps training Cuban exiles in Guatemala.[50] Worse, as the historian Evan Thomas observes, deniability meant failure: instead of aiming for the mountains where a small band of anti-Castro rebels was holding out, the exiles would have to land at the Bahía de Cochinos— the Bay of Pigs—then cross a nearly impassable swamp. Later in the 1960s, some of these Washington officials would land America in a metaphorical quagmire in Vietnam; in April 1961, they landed their doomed Cubans in a real one.

The operation was at once dangerously aggressive and self-defeatingly cautious. Here was the centrist's tragicomic flaw—trying to have it both ways, and ending up antagonizing left and right alike. As Castro's troops squelched the invasion, Mills added his name to a telegram to the president. The message charged that the invasion preparations had "the obvious sympathy and active support of your administration" and urged Kennedy to "Instruct the CIA and other secret agencies to stop all activities in support of the invaders."[51] Mills worked with the Fair Play for Cuba Committee to place a full-page ad in the New York Times. Appearing on April 21, it declared that the United States had effectively been "caught lying to the world," and Congress had "surrendered its functions to conspirators." The FPCC would "do all in our power to safeguard the integrity of the legitimate government of Cuba. If this be treason," the ad announced, "we stand condemned."[52] At this, the FBI started investigating Mills again.

That Saturday, the FPCC held a rally in San Francisco. Hundreds of the committee's supporters stood in the rain chanting "Hands Off Cuba," while about seventy-five students held up placards saying "Beats are Dupes" and "Russians Go Home," and demanded they "Back Jack."[53] And then someone read out a telegram from Mills. "Kennedy and company have returned us to barbarism," he proclaimed. "Sorry I cannot be with you. Were I physically able to do so, I would at this moment be fighting alongside Fidel Castro."[54] This prompted the FBI to start monitoring—though not opening—his mail.

Ill or not, Mills departed the United States for Europe, viewing it as an escape from all the "unmanageable pressures"[55] he faced at home in the United States. There, he wrote a long denunciation of the power elite's intervention in Cuba as an illegal invasion based on delusions and lies. Yet he was laboring under illusions about Cuba of his own. He seriously considered exile in England, where he was being offered professorships. But at last, in January 1962, he decided to go back and fight in America.

At just this point, Castro threw in his lot with the Soviets once and for all. Bridges burned, disillusioned with his great cause, a target of the FBI, and attracting growing political hostility and a lawsuit that couldn't be dodged much longer, Mills was cornered. On March 20, he had another heart attack, which killed him. His grieving friend Ralph Miliband wrote that C. Wright Mills had never been "a regular soldier." He'd been a "deliberately lone guerrilla."[56]

---

Here and there, Mills's attack on the power elite and its "crackpot realists" was beginning to take hold. In his last year at the University of Michigan, beginning in the fall of 1960, a student named Tom Hayden took to reading Mills's work. He'd grown up in the Detroit suburbs, raised by middle-class parents who were comfortably divorced. In his teens, he was a scrawny prankster, reading *Mad* magazine's send-ups of the Cold War and beginning to think there must be more to life than the boring conformism he saw all around. And then he came to Mills's warning about people turning into cheerful robots. Here, Hayden realized, was his dad, "proud in his starched white collar, occupying his accountant's niche above the union work force and below the real decision makers, penciling in numbers by day, drinking in front of the television at night, muttering about the world to no one in particular."[57] Hayden's father, and millions like him, had "only an illusion of reason and freedom, existing in an isolated personal context divorced from the larger structures where his destiny was being determined."[58]

Hayden was all too conscious of those larger structures determining his destiny: of growing up in the shadow of the Bomb; of being old enough to be drafted before he was old enough to vote; and of the fact that, in the South, his Black fellow Americans often couldn't vote at all. He seized on *The Power Elite* as both a scathing attack on how things were and a glimpse of how they could be changed. By the end of 1961, he was in the Deep South. He was beaten up in Mississippi for supporting the campaign for civil rights. He took the train across Georgia to fight segregation by breaking its racist rules, for which he was thrown in jail. He didn't want to think that he was risking his life for a mere illusion of democracy. He didn't buy the happy liberal vision of postwar America, but nor did he accept the hopeless Marxist message that government was just the "executive committee of the ruling class."[59] He was becoming one of the leaders of an emerging young New Left and of an organization called Students for a Democratic Society (SDS). Mills, he remembered, "quickly became the [movement's] oracle . . . combining the rebel life-style of James Dean and the moral passion of Albert Camus, with the comprehensive portrayal of the American condition we were all looking for."[60]

But what could the New Left do to overcome the power elite and its "megadeath intellectuals"?[61] Some activists protested outside the White House with picket signs that tried to hurl Kennedy's slogans back at him—and the president had a butler take them coffee. A few managed to secure meetings with some of the administration's Cold War liberals—and met a polite stone wall. A handful of more senior New Leftists even secured jobs in government and pushed for the creation of a national peace agency—only to watch as a rather more anodyne body, the Arms Control and Disarmament Agency, emerged instead. Those disillusioned young staffers in the Kennedy administration finally resigned and set up a kind of anti–think tank, the Institute for Policy Studies. The organization set out to revive democracy by fighting apathy—providing the public with information to counter the "mostly invented or colored view"[62] of government experts.

To Hayden, learning from Mills, the challenge was "to prevent the coming of the cheerful robot by transforming these drifting individuals into self-aware citizens, the amorphous masses into an educated public." The military-industrial complex might be delivering prosperity through vast defense spending, but it was turning America into a dangerously militaristic society.[63] Hayden and his allies had to find ways to shake the American public to see through the official narrative that made it seem as though there was no alternative.

In June 1962, still grieving for Mills and the loss of the chance to meet his guru, Hayden joined his fellow New Leftists at Port Huron, Michigan, to thrash out a formal statement of their political mission, based on a draft by Hayden. They agreed that they needed to attack the official claim that the Soviet Union was bent on world domination. That as a result, the Cold War had to override everything. That the threat of conflict meant the government must spend vast sums on equipping for warfare, not welfare. And that the population must accept the loss of their civil liberties. Their manifesto contended that this set of untruths was sold to the public through manipulative persuasion techniques, with the help of scare stories: the supposed Soviet threat; the fear that political involvement would get you in trouble. A big part of the problem was what was *not* talked about: where power lay in America and how it worked.

As with *The Power Elite*, this view of the world veered close to conspiracy theory with its depiction of helpless sheeple manipulated by shadowy forces peddling tall tales. Part of the difficulty of challenging a conspiracy theory was that you could end up sounding like a conspiracist yourself. Arguing that there was no monolithic Moscow-directed plot to tyrannize Americans might lead you to contend that there *was* a monolithic Washington-directed plot to do much the same thing.

The seedbed of conspiracism, however, is humiliation and despair; and in 1962, Hayden and his comrades were still full of hope. They didn't see the power elite's supposed hold on Americans as absolute or unbreakable. Their manifesto merely challenged the dominant idea that the ordinary person was "a thing to be manipulated."[64]

And so the techniques they used to take on that dominant narrative were not lurid accusations about sinister cabals. Indeed, they followed Mills in disavowing the idea that concentrated wealth and power operated by "conscious conspiracy."[65] Instead, they sought to break its hold by pointing out how the Cold War narrative was being exploited to block change, tracing the growth of the military-industrial complex. They set out to tackle people's "feelings of helplessness and indifference" by revealing "the political, social, and economic sources of their private troubles."[66] Hayden wrote later that, "We attempted to show that the power elites were to blame for seemingly individual troubles, and communicated that they had to take back power and responsibility over their lives."[67]

---

Inside the apparently monolithic power elite, however, all was not well. Kennedy and the military chiefs were locked in a struggle for . . . power. On March 28, 1961, the president warned Congress that America and its economy must not become "dependent upon the permanent maintenance of a large military establishment." This sounded like Eisenhower's speech about the military-industrial complex. But Kennedy wasn't turning against the eye-wateringly high levels of military spending—unlike Eisenhower, he was recommending that *more* tax dollars should be spent on weaponry. Peace had to come through military strength, whatever the cost. The "Free World" had to be defended—just more effectively. Kennedy was picking a fight with the military over who decided what all that money would be spent on, and what would be done with the weaponry thus purchased.

Less than three weeks later, the exiles backed by Kennedy's "peace-loving" America tried and failed to invade Cuba at the Bay of Pigs and the recriminations that followed just intensified the internal battle for control. Reviewing the president's first hundred days, *Newsweek* reported that "The sad attempt of the anti-Castro landings . . . shook [Kennedy's] faith in the Joint Chiefs of Staff setup, which had approved the Cuban plan."[68] The chiefs felt much the same about their wet-behind-the-ears new commander in chief, who they thought had chickened out of sending planes to back the Cuban invaders. In June, Kennedy reluctantly appointed a new air force chief of staff, Curtis LeMay—the mastermind behind the 1944 firebombing of Tokyo, which had killed one hundred thousand people in three hours. LeMay thought nuclear war was coming before the end of 1961, and did not seem especially upset at the prospect. That summer, a crisis blew up over Soviet objections to the ongoing presence of Western troops in West Berlin. While Kennedy strove to face down Khrushchev without war, LeMay "wanted to go nuclear from the get-go."[69]

Kennedy's defense secretary, Robert McNamara, was issuing computerized, systems analysis-driven reports that brought to light the waste, obsolescence, and duplication caused by the three services' flagrant exercise of their vested interests. McNamara was aghast at the air force's hunger for as many bombers as possible, particularly since it dovetailed with its long-standing nuclear strategy of "massive retaliation": fire everything at once, nuking Russian cities until the rubble was gravel. The air force didn't take kindly to the idea that a more restrained doctrine based on fewer weapons might be both more efficient and less provocative. Or the argument that intercontinental ballistic missiles made their bombers obsolete. Or that it might be more worthwhile to fight global communism and its many guerrilla armies with counterinsurgency, led by the Green Berets of the Special Forces. The air force fought back with its own formidable array of allies, not least congressmen whose voters' jobs depended on all those Pentagon contracts.

The fierce nature of this power struggle was clear from the other casualty of the Bay of Pigs: Kennedy's relationship with the CIA. He was incandescent at the agency's failures but not with its end goal: more badly than ever he wanted the snake Castro dealt with. So he wrenched power away from them and put his hyperaggressive brother Robert, the attorney general, in effective charge of a new Operation Mongoose. Dead set on avenging Jack's humiliation, Bobby hounded the CIA to "get rid of"[70] the Cuban dictator by any covert means necessary. But, try as they might, the spooks couldn't find anything that worked.

Finally, Cuba's maddening defiance pushed the divisions in the administration to the breaking point. In October 1962, Khrushchev had nuclear missiles installed in bases in Cuba—to protect the island, he later claimed, from a U.S. invasion. As a countermove, Kennedy's preference was for a naval blockade while a political solution could be found. He feared that attacking Cuba would provoke the Soviets to attack West Berlin, with nuclear war to follow. LeMay objected that such a mild response was "almost as bad as the appeasement at Munich." To Kennedy's astonishment, LeMay said he didn't think the Soviets would retaliate, and he insisted that the United States had to destroy not just the Soviet missiles in Cuba and any enemy planes but also "the air, the radar, the communications, the whole works!"[71]

Even after the extreme jeopardy of the missile crisis, the Kennedy brothers, especially Bobby, remained fixated on ousting Castro. A new operational structure was set up, led once more by the CIA, which kept up their efforts in the hope that, just maybe, a successful assassination might trigger a coup.

———

At the same time that these cracks were spreading through the power elite, there came the sound of thunder on the right. To civil rights campaigners and New Left activists like Tom Hayden, Kennedy's attempt to support Black civil rights was maddeningly timid. But for a rising phalanx of rightwingers, it was treasonous betrayal. And that was just part of the evil they thought they spied, lurking in the heart of power. During the first months of Kennedy's presidency, a swarm of ultraright groups seemed to be on the warpath against Washington. And while Mills and the New Left tried to stay clear of conspiracy theories about the nature of the power elite, these people harbored no such inhibitions. In 1961, they found themselves a leader.

Like Mills, General Edwin Walker was a Texan, but Walker was from an old frontier town. Where Mills rebelled against military school and fled to academia, Walker rose through the army for thirty years, from special forces daredevil to decorated officer. And, like Mills, Walker spent the 1950s growing more and more radically critical of America's power elite, and finally rebelled against the timidities of his home institution. But the general's vision of the elite and its aims was utterly different.

He was an enthusiastic conspiracy theorist, who saw himself locked in deadly combat with a malignant "control apparatus" that lurked deep inside the state. The Kennedy administration's preference for the army to focus more on counterinsurgency techniques was really a cover to "train the military to crack down on the people."[72] The armistice that had closed the Korean War in 1953, during which Walker served with distinction, had really been in the service of "an invisible scheme—global conquest."[73] The integration of schools, mandated by the treacherous Supreme Court, was just part of the plot by the communists and the United Nations to undermine the United States. His biographer Peter Adams notes that Walker repeatedly referred to the ease with which American prisoners of war in Korea had apparently been "brainwashed by enemy propaganda because they lacked sufficient understanding of communism and the values of their own country."[74] Back home, he detected mind-control techniques everywhere, from the communist media pushing race mixing to the school textbooks that peddled un-American immorality.

One of the main influences on Walker's nightmarish world view was the John Birch Society, which he had joined in 1959, soon after its creation. The Birchers' leader, an ex–candy executive named Robert W. Welch Jr., preached that America's institutions were riddled with communists, intent on destroying it from within. One leading Bircher warned that the Council on Foreign Relations, an elite New York think tank, and its associated groups formed "an amazing web which is the invisible government of the United States," which was working to "convert America into a socialist nation and then make it a unit in a one-world socialist system."[75] Walker feared that Chinese troops lurked in Mexico, waiting to invade and subjugate Americans.

In April 1961, Walker was commander of the 24th Infantry Division in Augsburg, Germany. And then the press exposed his urgent attempts to indoctrinate his troops with hard-line propaganda provided by the John Birch Society. Walker had also denounced past presidents to his troops as "definitely pink."[76] Kennedy demanded Walker be immediately relieved of his post. This was the day the Cuban exiles landed at the Bay of Pigs, which did very little to improve the president's opinion of the military, or vice versa. Kennedy told a press conference that Walker should focus on the external communist threat and stop worrying about "the loyalty of President Eisenhower, President Truman, or Mrs. Roosevelt, or myself."[77] Liberal columnists and mainstream politicians backed Kennedy; hard-line conservative senators backed Walker, as did the many members of the public who wrote to the White House to say so.

Finally, Walker resigned from the army and marched into politics, proclaiming that he wanted to be free of the "executive power" that subjected members of the armed forces "to arbitrary and ruthless treatment for daring to speak the truth."[78] He joined forces with the Birchers and declared rhetorical war on Kennedy's supposedly tyrannical, Red-ridden regime. In the far right's crusade against the liberal center, the general was the most promising figure to emerge since the fall of Joe McCarthy.

As Walker's implacable face stared out from the cover of *Newsweek*, Kennedy shot back. Before an audience of Democrats in the Hollywood Palladium, he took aim at the conspiracist logic that drove his opponents, always responding to shocks and crises by looking for "a simple solution, an appealing slogan or a convenient scapegoat." One by one, he mocked the right's long history of wild theories:

Financial crises could be explained by the presence of too many immigrants or too few greenbacks. War could be attributed to munitions makers or international bankers. Peace conferences failed because we were duped by the British, or tricked by the French, or deceived by the Russians. It was not the presence of Soviet troops in Eastern Europe that drove it to communism, it was the sellout at Yalta. It was not a civil war that removed China from the Free World, it was treason in high places. . . . They find treason in our churches, in our highest court, in our treatment of water.[79]

Walker set up his headquarters in Dallas, where he had plenty of support from right-wing business leaders. Men like the editor of the *Dallas Morning News*, who'd just told Kennedy to his face that the country needed "a man on horseback"—a military savior—but that many people thought he was riding round on his daughter's tricycle. Now it looked as though the man on horseback had arrived.

The renegade general found himself in high demand, appearing before cheering, flag-waving crowds as he charged that "the subversion of United States interests is accomplished by a class of men who believe that, in 'one world' of 'peace' and 'internationalism,' United States sovereignty and independence are obsolete."[80] He snarled that "we won't fight a boasting, bragging Communist goon on our own doorstep in Cuba."[81] By early 1962, he was running for the Democratic nomination for Texas governor.

That April, Walker was called before a Senate committee, and had the chance to set out his theory of how power worked in America. But the gap between the heroic leadership qualities his followers had projected onto him and his actual capacities made observers cringe. Despite all the notes his increasingly frantic aides passed him, he struggled to articulate his notions about "the real control apparatus." "You mean there is a direct connection between the State Department and high schools?" asked one senator.[82] In the primary, he finished last.

But he *had* won 138,387 votes—and as tensions over civil rights rose, Walker had no shortage of support. That September, a Black air force veteran, James Meredith, won a Supreme Court case compelling the state of Mississippi to allow him to study at the University of Mississippi, or "Ole

Miss," in the small city of Oxford. The state dragged its feet. Accompanied though he was by federal marshals, Meredith was repeatedly blocked from registering; at one point the state's governor came to refuse him in person. Once Meredith was finally holed up on campus, he was blocked by a crowd from entering the administration building to register. The mob grew to at least two thousand strong, some in Confederate uniforms, and pelted the marshals guarding the building with bricks and Molotov cocktails.

As Kennedy federalized the state's National Guard, Walker rushed to Mississippi, calling for "violent vocal protest" against the Supreme Court's "conspiracy from within."[83] At the university, he took up position at the base of a Confederate monument opposite the besieged administration building and led the rioting crowd in fresh charges against the marshals, who fought back with tear gas. When the National Guard arrived, the rioters attacked with a fire truck and a bulldozer. Cars burned. Shots were fired. Kennedy sent the army. By the time the troops finally reached campus, two people were dead. Walker was arrested and charged with insurrection.

The radical right saw Kennedy and the "control apparatus" as in league with the radical left, just as the radical left, such as it was, saw Kennedy and the "power elite" as in league with the radical right. But where the right was on the march, the left had long been in retreat. On the face of it, it seemed clear which side posed the real threat.

---

All his life, Lee Harvey Oswald was one of those little guys C. Wright Mills had written about, dwarfed by the powers that be. Not the cheerful robot, but the would-be autonomous man, trying to break free. Oswald had withdrawn from his unaffectionate mother as they moved from New Orleans to Dallas to New York and back again. Bright but starved of love, he'd stirred up trouble at school and been marked down as a juvenile delinquent. At seventeen, he'd fled into the marines—and complained that it was like living in Orwell's *Nineteen Eighty-Four*. He'd been court-martialed twice, for possession of an unauthorized gun and for fighting with a sergeant; he'd also learned to be a sharpshooter. His string of dead-end jobs barely ever reached white-collar level—but he saw himself as much more than an ordinary worker.

As a teenager he'd found an angle that validated his struggle with the world. On the street one day, around 1953, someone handed him a handbill about the controversial execution of Julius and Ethel Rosenberg for spying: two more small people crushed by the big malignant power structure. Oswald started reading Marxist texts and developed a crude form of the insight the New Left wanted people to grasp—that their plight was the fault of high powers; in the marines, one of his fellows recalled, Lee would denounce "American capitalist warmongers."[84] He became a fiery believer in the fight against capitalist exploitation and racial bigotry, even if he didn't much like actual people.

From a very young age, he found another way to fill the aching chasm between his self-image and how his life really was. He devoured a TV series called *I Led Three Lives*, about an FBI mole in the Communist Party. A psychiatrist said he had a "vivid fantasy life, turning around the topics of omnipotence and power, through which [he] tries to compensate for his present shortcomings and frustrations."[85] As an adult, he took to using false names and forged IDs; he read James Bond novels and talked about wanting to be a spy. Norman Mailer wrote that Oswald was certainly a "secret agent"; the only question was "whether he was working for any service larger than the power centers in the privacy of his mind."[86]

By the end of 1962, he'd spent the first three years of his twenties in exile in the Soviet Union. But, after the authorities had failed to give him the kind of work he felt he deserved, he'd come back to Dallas. Even before he fled the United States, in 1959, he'd been an enthusiastic supporter of Fidel Castro; now, disillusioned with the Soviets, Oswald clung to Cuba as his one remaining beacon of revolutionary hope: a "tiny country surrounded by enemies," up against the colossal power of the hated United States. He already subscribed to the Communist Party weekend paper *The Worker*. Shortly after the Cuban missile crisis, he subscribed to *The Militant*—the Trotskyist newsweekly that once championed Mills's *Listen, Yankee*. In it he read of Kennedy's welcoming home the just-released Bay of Pigs invaders and expressing his hope for the restoration of "freedom" in Cuba. Oswald bought Socialist Workers Party pamphlets, including one called *The Coming American Revolution*, which promised that though the "Yankee colossus" was now "the strongest power in the world," it could be overthrown by a "new, even greater, power"[87]—the American working class. At a party in February 1963, he denounced the continuing acts of sabotage and terror against the Castro regime.

By this time, Oswald had decided to strike back against malignant political power. His target was a man he called "the leader of a fascist organization".[88] Edwin Walker. Freshly acquitted of insurrection, the general was touring the United States on his Operation Midnight Ride, "to alert the country to the enemy within and without." The Communist Party's *Daily Worker* had warned of a conspiracy by "military-monopolist-pro-fascist plotters"; they were concocting a mass movement, and Walker was the "first open candidate for leadership."[89] On March 6, 1963, the *Dallas Times Herald* reported Walker's demand that Kennedy send the 82nd Airborne Division to "liquidate the scourge that has descended upon the island of Cuba."[90] Six days later, Oswald used a false name to order a rifle through the mail. One sunny Sunday afternoon, he asked his wife, Marina, to photograph him in their tiny, scrappy, West Neely Street backyard: dressed in black, brandishing his gun as well as copies of *The Militant* and *The Worker*. The lead in that edition of *The Militant* was about a Black civil rights activist murdered in Mississippi. Oswald sent the photo to the newspaper, to show that he was "ready for anything." He'd run repeated missions to scout out Walker's grand five-bedroom house on upscale Turtle Creek Boulevard—six miles north of West Neely Street, in another world. On April 10, through the fence at the back of the house, he shot at Walker through a ground floor window. He missed, by millimeters.

A man who knew Oswald remembered him setting out his world view at a dinner, a week before he tried to kill Walker. He seemed to think that "all the working class was exploited, and he also thought they were brainwashed, and . . . thought that churches were all alike . . . they were all apparatus of the power structure to maintain itself in power." Anyone who disagreed was "spouting the line that was fed to them by the power structure."[91]

So shooter and target had something in common. Each was chafing against the supposed oppressions of a power structure that was too strong to overthrow and that kept itself in power through brainwashing the cheerful robots. In the month before the shooting, Walker was in Alabama lambasting the president's "dictatorship"; Oswald stood alone in downtown Dallas, handing out a pamphlet that accused Kennedy et al. of acting "as a tight little group of conspiratorial bureaucrats" and pursuing "a policy of undemocracy" toward the press.[92]

Oswald obtained that pamphlet from Mills's old allies in the Fair Play for Cuba Committee, which he joined, as best he could. The New York office remained wary of his involvement, partly for his own sake, warning him about the right-wing "lunatic fringe." There's a hint, in his foray into peaceful activism, that Oswald's radical antagonism toward power might have taken a less violent path. A few weeks before he tried to kill Walker, he wrote to *The Militant*, urging them to pay more attention to campaigns like the independent 1962 Senate run of H. Stuart Hughes, a liberal Harvard professor, nuclear disarmer, and ally of the New Left.[93]

That summer, he moved back to his birthplace, New Orleans, and set up what he made out to be a proper chapter of the FPCC. His crusade for Castro and his zest for deception came together. He tried to infiltrate the city's plentiful Cuban exile networks by offering training as an ex-marine. No one was fooled. When he heard that an aircraft carrier that had been involved in the missile crisis was coming into port, he went down to the streets near the wharves to hand out FPCC literature, including *The Crime Against Cuba*, two Castro speeches, and a "Hands Off Cuba" handbill. Since New Orleans was at that time one of the most anti-Castro cities in the country it was no surprise that Oswald was harassed and arrested, and saw his literature thrown into the air. How many passers-by, watching those leaflets flutter back to earth, picked one up and read its question: "WHAT IS THE GOVERNMENT HIDING?" Or noticed that the handbill recommended reading Mills's *Listen, Yankee* for the "side of the story you haven't been told"?[94]

The hullabaloo in the street won Oswald an invitation to a radio studio, where he was questioned respectfully and at length about the FPCC's positions. He seized his chance to show off his knowledge, rattling off answers about media bias, and arguing—like Mills—that the United States had forced Cuba into the arms of the Soviet Union. At one point, he defended his politics by invoking the British National Health Service. But days later, he was summoned again for a more hostile grilling; the station had learned from the FBI that he had lived in the USSR, which he'd avoided revealing. However bruising, the encounter helped Oswald build up his case for what he'd decided to do. He would find his way to Cuba via Mexico and join Castro's volunteer army of revolutionaries. But when at last he arrived in Mexico City, he hit a wall of bureaucracy at the Cuban embassy, and was sent to the Soviet embassy, which wasn't inclined to help.

There, he finally broke down in despair.

———

Outraged that Dallas was to celebrate October 23 as "United Nations Day," General Walker organized a "United States Day" in the city for the day before. That evening, members of the John Birch Society and the Minutemen, a right-wing group stockpiling guns for the counterrevolution, turned out to hear Walker declare that the United States was now the primary battleground. Oswald was back in Dallas, stuck in a dead-end job in a school book depository, and he went along to the general's rally, too, to watch the fascist he'd failed to stop. All summer, the struggle over civil rights had grown more violent. Kennedy federalized another southern state's national guard, this time in Alabama, to integrate a university by force—then sent a sweeping civil rights bill to Congress. In Mississippi that night, civil rights activist

Medgar Evers was gunned down in his driveway; Walker visited the killer. In September, four young Black girls were killed when a bomb exploded in a Birmingham church. For Dallas's United Nations Day, Kennedy's UN ambassador, Adlai Stevenson, came to town, and was beaten with placards by right-wingers; Walker told the press the "invisible government" had brought Stevenson to Dallas, and he'd got what was coming. The next day, in Jackson, Mississippi, Walker told a White Citizens' Council meeting that the Kennedys had "liquidated the government of the United States. It no longer exists. . . . The best definition I can find today for Communism is Kennedy liberalism."[95] To the radical right, the center was on the same side as the radical left, just as for the much weaker radical left, the center was on the same side as the radical right. As that pamphlet Oswald had handed out declared: "our Government has given new heart and hope to every right-wing chauvinist in the U.S.A., and to every frenetic, anti-freedom group in the land, from the American Legion to the John Birch Society."[96]

---

On November 18, Kennedy was in Miami and made a speech in which some heard a call for rapprochement with Cuba. But others interpreted it as a call for Castro's overthrow—the president condemned the "small band of conspirators" who'd poisoned Cuba's revolution. His next major trip was to Dallas. A study he'd privately commissioned warned that the radical right was now a "formidable force." A Texan political ally warned him not to go to Dallas. On the morning of his visit, a handbill printed by one of Walker's close associates appeared on windshields along the president's route. On it were the words "WANTED FOR TREASON" printed beneath photos of Kennedy's face. Around 12:30 p.m., the presidential motorcade finally reached the end of Main Street, all glittering windows and cheering crowds, and turned right onto Houston. When Kennedy arrived at the grand luncheon at the Trade Mart a few minutes later, he was going to call on his audience to ignore the extremist "voices preaching doctrines wholly unrelated to reality." And he would reassure them that, in its pursuit of peace through strength, America had expanded its strategic nuclear arsenal by 100 percent, its conventional forces by 45 percent, and its special forces by nearly 600 percent.

And then the limousine turned sharp left onto Elm Street, by the Texas School Book Depository, where Lee Harvey Oswald was waiting on the sixth floor, an autonomous man, a lone guerrilla with a rifle bought by mail order for $21.45.[97] Poised to seize his chance to take aim at capitalist exploitation, or Castro's enemy, or his own infuriating obscurity. Or perhaps, simply, at American power.

-----

The night before Kennedy arrived in Dallas, C. Wright Mills's old friend and Columbia University colleague Richard Hofstadter was at Oxford University to give a lecture. In a truly eerie coincidence, his theme was "The Paranoid Style in American Politics."

Hofstadter was reacting against the rise of the extreme anti-communists of the John Birch Society, whom he cast as the successors to Joseph McCarthy. He argued that the Birchers' fear of an immense communist conspiracy had long roots in American political thinking, often starting from a reasonable concern about invisible power, from secret societies of "influential men"[98] to the spies who gave the secrets of the Bomb to Stalin. The problem with thinking in the paranoid style, he suggested, was not a lack of facts but "the curious leap of imagination that is always made at some critical point in the recital of events."[99] This was exacerbated when people were "shut out of the political process," could not see power's "actual machinery," and so found "their original conception of the world of power as sinister and malicious fully confirmed."[100] This led to the fallacy that nothing is accidental: "if for every error and every act of incompetence one can substitute an act of treason, we can infer how many points of fascinating interpretation are open to the paranoid imagination"; there follow "heroic strivings for evidence to prove that the unbelievable is the only thing that can be believed."[101] He mockingly quoted the Birchers' leader, Robert Welch, chattering about cover-ups and the "accumulation of detailed evidence so extensive and so palpable" that it seemed to put Welch's conviction that Eisenhower was a communist "beyond any reasonable doubt."[102]

Hours later, when the news broke that the president had been shot dead, it seemed obvious that the killer, or killers, must have been from the Dallas far right—the people who'd been branding Kennedy a traitor. But the man the police arrested was a leftist: Lee Harvey Oswald, a member of the Fair Play for Cuba Committee.

Moderate politicians sought to dissolve the apparent contradiction by suggesting that Kennedy had somehow been killed by the general "miasma of hatred" on left and right alike.[103]

*The Militant*, Oswald's favored paper, talked in similar terms. But General Walker, one of the initial suspects, seized on Oswald's arrest to argue that, given the president was shot by a "communist," the blame lay with those who'd stymied Joe McCarthy's battle with the great Red conspiracy.

A frightened federal administration commissioned an investigation under the chief justice of the Supreme Court, Earl Warren, tasked with maintaining trust in government and confirming that there was no conspiracy, particularly not a communist one.[104] It wanted to smooth away Oswald's fervent support for Castro. It also sought to obscure its own government's murderous campaign against the Cuban leader. If that came out, it might make the assassination look like the revenge attack that Castro had appeared to threaten two months earlier. A year after the missile crisis, the idea that the Cubans had killed the American president would produce tremendous pressure for military retaliation, and with it the danger of nuclear war. And so the secrecy and deception endemic to the Kennedy administration continued under his successor, Lyndon Johnson.

In time for the presidential election in November 1964, the Warren Commission concluded that Oswald wasn't part of a conspiracy. But many couldn't believe that the commander in chief of the United States could be killed by one young loser, especially a left-wing one. On top of that, Oswald had protested he was just a "patsy"—and was himself murdered on live television two days after his arrest, making his trial and any embarrassing revelations that might arise from it impossible. The "lone gunman" theory seemed too convenient—the invincible power elite was surely not so vulnerable. Some element in the power elite itself must be behind it all.

Many of the early Kennedy conspiracy theorists had been victims, not long before, of McCarthyism, when so many innocent people had been tarred as guilty. Was that not simply happening all over again?

The New Left had learned from Mills to be very skeptical of "the official line," the "official version" of events.[105] Tom Hayden spent three days glued to the TV, watching Oswald's murder "over and over."[106] Looking back, he wrote:

> C. Wright Mills had described American society as fundamentally stable, a mass society in the hands of a powerful elite with shared interests. But the "lone assassin" Oswald had single-handedly shattered this stability and determined the presidency with a single bullet. . . . I thought and wrote of him as a "lurker," a member of a floating "lurking class" dissociated from bureaucratic rationality, capable of turning hallucinations into history.
>
> But if he was not alone, if he was, in his own words, a "patsy," then we were dealing with a violent conspiracy perhaps reaching into the power elite itself. Either notion was enough to unsettle my world.[107]

Hayden thought Kennedy was moving toward embracing the civil rights movement and "toward disengagement of US military forces in Vietnam" and dialogue with Castro, and détente with the Soviets. "He was accumulating, in short, a long list of enemies who might seek the survival of their interests in his death."[108] Mills's disciples were edging over the border between critical thinking and conspiracy theory. As America descended into the depths of the late 1960s, the military-industrial complex would be reimagined as a malignant, omnipotent force, responsible for killing Kennedy and much else.

Mills was not around to caution against this, but his fellow pro-Castro radical, I. F. Stone, was. Stone was a veteran of the McCarthyite blacklist, a man who'd branded the military-industrial complex "the monster we can no longer control," another man who'd taught the New Left that "the government lied." Nevertheless, in 1964, he accused fellow left-wingers of generating narratives based on the same kind of dubious connections McCarthy had once made:

> All my adult life as a newspaperman I have been fighting, in defense of the Left and of a sane politics, against conspiracy theories of history, character assassination, guilt by association and demonology. Now I see elements of the Left using these same tactics in the controversy over the Kennedy assassination and the Warren Commission Report.[109]

Few seemed ready to listen. Suspicions weren't eased by the fact that the new president, Lyndon Johnson, won congressional support for escalating the war in Vietnam, based on an incident in the Gulf of Tonkin which almost certainly never happened—as I. F. Stone had been one of the first to point out. On August, 2, 1964, a U.S. Navy destroyer, the USS *Maddox*, while engaged in electronic eavesdropping off the North Vietnamese coast, was attacked by an enemy gunboat. Arguably, it had been in North Vietnam's territorial waters,[110] but the Johnson administration cast this as an "unprovoked attack,"[111] and sent the *Maddox* back to bait the North Vietnamese. On August 4, captain and crew concluded they were under attack, but within hours, serious doubts set in—not least because atmospheric conditions had made their radar unreliable. But by that evening, Johnson was on television claiming that the United States had been subject to "deliberate attack." At his request, Congress passed a resolution—near unanimously—authorizing the use of force. By the time Johnson spoke, the first U.S. bombing raids on North Vietnam were already under way.

This process had begun with the massive expansion of the American state to fight the Second World War, culminating in the dropping of the atom bomb. Now once again, war—not the shadowboxing of the nuclear standoff, but real *war*—had become integral to how America functioned.

At the time of Mills's death in early 1962, America's role in Vietnam wasn't yet a pressing issue. There was far more focus on Cuba and even on Vietnam's western neighbor, Laos. But the escalation of America's presence in Vietnam was perhaps the gravest consequence of the mindset Mills had tried to challenge. The United States had decided that it had to protect its ally South Vietnam not just from the communist north but from guerrilla forces in the south. Yet Washington was reluctant formally to declare war. Kennedy didn't begin the process, but he significantly increased the number of U.S. military "advisers" on the ground.

So the U.S. public was tricked by the U.S. government. Tricked first, about whether America was involved militarily in Vietnam at all. Then tricked into thinking that the North Vietnamese had launched an unprovoked attack on a U.S. ship, which necessitated sweeping war powers. Then that troops sent to Vietnam wouldn't be going on the offensive. Then that they were at least fighting to save a functioning democracy. Then tricked about how much it was all costing—and then that the bombing of North Vietnam was working while leaving civilians miraculously unharmed.

At the same time, the U.S. government itself was being tricked by its own commanding officers (who were being tricked by lower-ranking officers) and by the South Vietnamese government, whose factions were tricking each other while being tricked by North Vietnamese spies.

Most of all, though, the government was tricking itself—deluding itself into believing that because withdrawal was "unthinkable," victory must be just around the corner, if only they applied more businesslike efficiency, more computational power. And, as Mills would have wanted to tell them, the need to win derived from yet another delusion: that the most obscure civil war involving communists anywhere at all was part of a vast, global Moscow- (or Peking-) directed conspiracy to take over the world. And so young Americans were sent to fight an enemy who was indistinguishable from the civilian population, putting them at permanent, nerve-shredding risk of being tricked by ambush and booby trap, with horribly predictable consequences.

Mills might as well never have bothered. "Crackpot realism" ruled. As the undeclared American war in Vietnam expanded, tax dollars poured out of the Pentagon into Boeing's aerospace plant in Wichita; and the McDonnell Douglas factory at Long Beach; and the General Dynamics missile plant at San Diego and its plane factory at Fort Worth (which was also home to Bell Helicopter); and Dow Chemical's napalm production line in Midland, Michigan; and Colt's M16 factory in Hartford, Connecticut; and Monsanto's plant at Nitro, West Virginia, which pumped out the defoliant Agent Orange; and from there into the pockets of assembly-line operatives and lab technicians and engineers and heads of academic institutes, and out into the American economy.

The New Left took to staging more and more radical acts of protest, with no visible success. The contracts and computer printouts and shipments of the military-industrial complex kept moving smoothly through the system, as if none of its critics had ever existed.

And then a strange document emerged, which cast the real motives driving the war machine in a frightening new light.

# 2

# THE UNTHINKABLE

America, winter, 1966. Nearly four hundred thousand soldiers in Vietnam. Underground bomb tests in the desert. The Monkees' "I'm a Believer" at number one.

In his apartment on Riverside Drive, on the cold edge of Manhattan, a downcast, middle-aged writer named Leonard Lewin is agonizing over whether he should just give up and go back to Indianapolis.

Lewin is of exactly the same generation as the dead rebel sociologist and the dead president: born just over a month after Mills and eight months before Kennedy, in October 1916—shortly before the United States, for the first time ever, went to war in Europe. Lewin completed his university studies in the Great Depression: like Kennedy, he went to Harvard, but his politics are closer to Mills's. After years stuck working in his late father's sugar refinery in Indianapolis, he has finally escaped to New York to make a living as a writer. But here he is, deep in middle age, worrying that he is a failure with nothing to say. He wants to be remembered "for good reasons,"[1] but cannot find a big project to sink his teeth into.

Then he gets a call. It's an old contact, a social sciences professor from back in the Midwest, whom Lewin hasn't heard from for years. The professor is in New York and wants to meet. Urgently.

Over lunch the next day, in a restaurant in midtown, the professor is on edge; finally he spills the beans. Just over three years ago, in early August 1963, he was contacted by an anonymous man in Washington, who told him that he'd been chosen to serve on a commission "of the highest importance." The idea was initiated by the defense secretary Robert McNamara and like minds in the Kennedy administration. Its task was "to determine, accurately and realistically, the nature of the problems that would confront the United States if and when a condition of 'permanent peace' should arrive." Having done so, the "Special Study Group" would have to "draft a program for dealing with this contingency."[2]

The professor tells Lewin that he felt he had no choice but to sign up. For one thing, the man from Washington seemed to know a troubling amount about his personal life.

———————

In the mid-1960s, this kind of mind-bogglingly ambitious project is fairly standard. This is the high noon of Cold War think tanks like the RAND Corporation and the Hudson Institute. The vast expansion of American wealth and power since 1945 means the nation has grave dilemmas to think through, and plenty of money to pay people to do that—but these attempts to answer huge, unfathomable questions with remorseless logic can sometimes produce strange effects on *how* people think. The think tanks' chillingly logical "defense intellectuals" are the same kind of people drafted into the Kennedy administration. Those bright young men who were going to review "the problems facing the country quite analytically," and were "perfectly willing to follow the facts wherever they may lead."[3]

Nothing encapsulates the question of what America should do with its military might more sharply than the Bomb. And no one has been following the facts about it wherever they may lead with more gusto than a man named Herman Kahn, a RAND Corporation physicist turned systems analyst who exploded into American minds in 1960. In a book called *On Thermonuclear War*, Kahn explained that, approached coolly and rationally, nuclear war was not unthinkable. He'd thought about it, and it could be fought, and won. Even if the bedraggled remnants of America had to survive for a time in bunkers deep underground.

Ever since, Kahn has been denounced as callous. He has been lampooned as a crazed scientist—he was one of the inspirations for *Dr. Strangelove*, the satirical 1964 movie about how the power elite might accidentally let lunatics blow up the world. He has even been compared to the Nazi bureaucrat Adolf Eichmann. How could any decent person calmly discuss the destruction of tens of millions of their fellow human beings? Kahn defends himself by insisting that someone has to think through the real implications of a nuclear war: Would people who accuse him of "icy rationality" prefer "a warm, human error"?[4] Is it not worth trying "to reduce casualties from, say, 100 million to 50 million Americans"?[5] But to many, this is what Mills called crackpot realism. You cannot have a "value-free" discussion about mass killing, and trying to do so just winds up rationalizing slaughter, as Vietnam shows.

There is another criticism, too: the "unthinkable" notions Kahn is thinking about are not just intolerable but *unknowable*. How can he and his colleagues be "realistic" about how nuclear war might unfold when they have no precedents to draw on? Computer modelling can only take them so far. They have to use their imaginations. One way they do so is through "war games": a fusion of computing and theater, in which generals and officials get to act out high-stakes scenarios. But these are a form of fiction, neater and cleaner than any real crisis. One war game designer would later describe his work as "more akin to writing an historical novel than proving an algebraic theorem."[6]

By 1966, Kahn has left RAND and set up a new think tank—the Hudson Institute, based in Croton-on-Hudson, in upstate New York. And he has expanded his methods beyond nuclear war, piling up more and more government contracts. However much he has spooked the public about how those in government think, Kahn's imaginative capacities are still highly valued by those same people, as they continue to grapple with the fearsome possibilities of America's newfound power.

There is a second kind of precedent for the Special Study Group: a series of studies and articles asking: "Can We Afford a Warless World?" This began with a 1962 report, *Economic Impacts of Disarmament*, by "a task force of economic experts drawn from the universities, Government, business, and the labor unions."[7] These analyses acknowledge the fear that turning off military spending will trigger a depression. They agree that it could impose "significant drag" and disruption; that it would hit defense industry–dependent regions hard. Worse, they warn there is likely to be fierce opposition to any such change. Many companies haven't been preparing for disarmament, since their leaders can't believe the Cold War will ever end. The most recent of these reports has criticized the U.S.'s plans for general disarmament, warning that "relying on an international police force" would have "deep implications for the existence of states and for the character of authority within them."[8] One report, by a Senate subcommittee, has been suppressed, apparently for fear of handing propaganda to the enemy.

These reports usually conclude, however, that, with enough planning and government support, the economy could adjust to disarmament. And, they argue hopefully, all that spending and expertise, no longer sunk into the war machine, could boost productivity and positively transform education and public health, pollution and urban decay.[9] The Special Study Group, however, was "expected to extend its scope far beyond that of any previous examination of these problems."[10] What if the real function of war is not simply keeping the economy in balance?

———

The professor tells Lewin how the group first met at a resonant location: Iron Mountain, about a hundred miles north of Manhattan. This is one of the vast underground vaults to which members of the power elite—in this case, company executives—will flee in the event of nuclear war. The professor discovered that the group included an industrialist, scientists, a systems analyst, and war planner. But most of his new colleagues were, like him, from the social sciences: an economist, a sociologist, a cultural anthropologist, a psychologist, a psychiatrist. Many of these men—they were, of course, all men—had worked with government before. Some were "very well known."[11] This is the kind of co-opting of supposedly independent experts to which the New Left objects. The radical magazine *Ramparts* has recently exposed how academics at Michigan State University spent years secretly collaborating with the CIA.

The group met around once a month for three years, all over the United States, before returning for a final session to Iron Mountain. But when they submitted their final report, it was judged too shocking for public consumption. Like that earlier study by a Senate subcommittee, it has been suppressed.

And that is why the professor has come to see Lewin. He stands by the Study Group's findings, and after "months of agonizing," he has finally decided that its report must be published, and wants Lewin's help making that happen. The public has a right to know what is "being done on its behalf."[12]

When he reads the report, Lewin sees why it has been buried. The group was charged with following its analysis, without moral or cultural value assumptions, right through to its logical conclusions. And those conclusions leave Lewin horrified. He agrees to try to find a publisher.

Meanwhile, he persuades the professor to record a series of interviews. On the tapes, the professor reveals that the idea for the study first surfaced in 1961, prompted by Kennedy's moves to reallocate military spending more efficiently. Its guiding lights, apparently, along with Secretary of Defense Robert McNamara, were another of Kennedy's bright young men—National Security Adviser McGeorge Bundy—and the Secretary of State Dean Rusk. (When Kennedy was assassinated, President Johnson kept these men in their posts.) All three were "impatient" with the absence of any "long-range planning"[13] exploring the "permanent peace" contingency.

The project took shape in the wake of the Cuban missile crisis. This was the period when those other studies were being carried out on the economic consequences of disarmament, but as the professor tells Lewin, "it was exactly that *narrowness* of approach that we were supposed to get away from."

Instead, "what they wanted from us was a different kind of *thinking*": something more akin to the bold, broad, imaginative method pioneered by Herman Kahn, following the logic of the facts without "moral posturing." The task was "to give the same kind of treatment to the hypothetical problems of peace" as Kahn had given to "a hypothetical nuclear war."[14]

Echoing the idea of the "permanent war economy," the group's assessment is that war is "the essential economic stabilizer of modern societies,"[15] allowing for the disposal of surpluses, the generation of demand, the boosting of growth. This is why, when there is news of possible peace, the stock market tends to fall. But the group's fundamental insight goes well beyond this. War, it concludes, has a much wider range of uses than all those "disarmament scenarios and reconversion plans"[16] have identified. It is not just economically useful, or strategically necessary: it is "the basic social system." This has been true for most of human history, and still is.

The report's analysis explains a lot of things that seem strange about Cold War America, from the "'unnecessary' size and power of the world war industry"[17] to the way military institutions are exempted from normal standards. And why the state sometimes has to effectively invent threats and conflicts. Without war, the Group's report explains, there is no real basis for national sovereignty. Major military threats are vital for fostering "allegiance to a society and its values."[18] The need to be ready to resist attack, and the state's capacity to protect the population, is basic to its "right to rule," and this—not least in late 1960s America—has domestic applications. As the report has it: "On a day-to-day basis, [state authority] is represented by the institution of police, armed organizations charged expressly with dealing with 'internal enemies' in a military manner."[19]

Military service itself underpins political stability by giving "antisocial elements" a role,[20] especially in periods of upheaval when they might be attracted to fascism. The evidence even suggests that the focus on war allows states to maintain the class system, including the incentives instilled by continuing poverty. And that war keeps the population level under control. On top of all that, it has done much to spur scientific advances. Were war to end, the change would disrupt all these processes and a range of substitute functions would be required.

This, the report warns, will not be straightforward. Diverting spending to health care, education, housing, and infrastructure projects, as optimistically proposed by those earlier reports, would simply not use up enough of the surplus that war currently absorbs. This would actually worsen over time, as the population's improving health would steadily reduce the costs involved. Converting the army into a "giant military Peace Corps"[21] wouldn't work. The report maintains that one purpose of war is to stabilize America's booming economy by ridding it of excess wealth; turning the army into a huge international welfare program would not achieve that, because the money would find its way back into the normal economy. The space program might provide a more sustainable alternative drain on excess resources.

Politically, to sustain the public's acceptance of its leaders' "political authority,"[22] the threat of nuclear attack would have to be replaced by a similar threat to human survival, such as "massive global environmental pollution,"[23] but this is advancing too slowly and deliberately accelerating it is unlikely to be "politically acceptable." It may be necessary to "invent a threat to prevent peace [from] causing social disintegration." This, however, is not easy. "Experiments have been proposed to test the credibility of an out-of-our-world invasion threat,"[24] but this idea seems unworkable, too.

If hundreds of thousands of young men are suddenly released from the armed forces, it could trigger serious disorder. Logically, therefore, the state might instead need to convert the "code of military discipline" into what would effectively be a "sophisticated form of slavery," adapted to "advanced forms of social organization," perhaps beginning with the introduction of military service for all. As for alternative ways to channel all that young male aggression, the report notes that "Games theorists have suggested, in other contexts, the development of 'blood games'"[25] as a method of controlling this. Without the role of war in reducing population levels, it might in theory be beneficial to introduce eugenic artificial insemination.

Much of which might sound crazy, but in the think tank world of game theory and scenario planning, doubtless another such study group has come up with worse. Having followed its logic to all these alarming conclusions, as instructed, the group concludes that "no program or combination of programs yet proposed for a transition to peace has remotely approached meeting the comprehensive functional requirements of a world without war." On that basis, "the war system cannot responsibly be allowed to disappear until . . . we know exactly what it is we plan to put in its place."[26] Further research on what would be needed to maintain acceptable levels of stability is required.

---

It does not take Lewin long to find a publisher. The Dial Press is upmarket and adventurous, a Third Avenue publisher favored by radical, taboo-breaking literary superstars like James Baldwin, author of *The Fire Next Time*, and Norman Mailer, author of *Why Are We in Vietnam?* In autumn 1967, in its new nonfiction list, Dial announces a volume called *Report from Iron Mountain: On the Possibility and Desirability of Peace*, with an introduction by Leonard C. Lewin, and waits for the media to respond. Or most of the media. The book has already grabbed the attention—and the spending power—of the one of the biggest, brashest, smartest magazines around.

A few blocks uptown and west from Dial's office, in a skyscraper on Madison Avenue, lies the headquarters of what the British *Sunday Times* calls one of "the world's great magazines."[27] In 1967, *Esquire* rules, and not just for splashing succulent Hollywood color into a print world full of black and white. Its circulation has topped a million; in 1966, its advertising revenue leapt 25 percent. *Esquire*'s superstar editor is a man named Harold Hayes—a North Carolina geek sharpened up by military service, Harvard, and years of fighting with colleagues to win the editorship. From his curved-glass corner office, he's thrown off the caution of the 1950s and now comes at things from surprising, jarring, irreverent new angles. He commissions diagrams charting America's power networks—which might look like a conspiracist's pin board if they weren't so obviously provocative. When the president was shot, Hayes ran a piece called "Kennedy Without Tears." He sent reporters to follow marines into battle in Vietnam, and turned the whole cover black, save for a quote in white from a soldier: "Oh my God—we hit a little girl."

Hayes's leadership has helped produce something that will come to be called the "New Journalism." An *Esquire* writer doesn't hack out a story; he (it's nearly always he) composes it with the care and flair of a novelist. Not least because that's what a lot of them are. James Baldwin writes about Norman Mailer; Norman Mailer writes about John F. Kennedy. Tom Wolfe hangs out with Muhammad Ali. Gay Talese chases Frank Sinatra. Two of Hayes's staffers have written the year's totemic movie, transfiguring a sordid old news story about shambolic Depression gangsters into *Bonnie and Clyde*: an achingly hip, generation-dividing celebration of fighting authority with guns.[28]

*Esquire*'s December issue is the most important of the year, packed with twice the ads. Given the clunky technology of the day, it has to be done in August. This year, not for the first time, Hayes has a Christmas bomb to set off for his million readers, to shake them up and to make them think about the impact of war. Alongside a piece by Candice Bergen on the burning of the old order, and an image of film star Sharon Tate seductively eating a pear, Hayes has decided to run what he proclaims "an important piece"[29]: a condensed version of *Report from Iron Mountain*. Condensed, as in fully twenty thousand of the *Report*'s twenty-eight thousand words.

In Washington, meanwhile, rumors of a suppressed report have been coursing through government circles, triggering "a severe case of jitters."[30] Journalists are picking up talk that it will "soon see the light of day and shock the nation."[31] One official passes the galley proofs to the next, generating what *Newsweek* calls "megatons of speculation."[32] Can this document be real?

———

Even before the *Report* and its incendiary revelations are made public, Americans are rapidly losing trust in their government: How is it really using its power, and *why*? Less than three years ago, they gave President Johnson a spectacular mandate to transform the country, from boosting civil rights and university budgets to creating Medicare and declaring a "War on Poverty." But now they see an administration pouring more and more resources, and hundreds of thousands of young men, into a war it has never officially declared, and can't find a way to win, while constantly insisting that everything is proceeding to plan. The endless bombing of North Vietnam has inflicted three-hundred-million dollars' worth of damage, but it has cost America three times that much, and that's just a fraction of what the war is costing every month. The left sees a government bent on smashing a small, defenseless nation; the right sees a government too cautious to pulverize the enemy. As occurred with Kennedy, Johnson's centrism has produced the worst of both worlds. For the first time, more Americans now think the war is a mistake than support it.

A new buzz phrase has crept into the discourse: the "credibility gap." It catches the rising frustration of reporters and politicians trying to squeeze straight answers from the Johnson administration about what is really going on in Vietnam.[33] *Life* magazine quits twisting its journalists' dispatches to fit administration guidance and comes out against the war. The *New York Times* sends a man to North Vietnam, where he exposes the fiction that U.S. bombs don't hit civilians. The *Ladies' Home Journal* runs a piece on the true horrors inflicted by Dow Chemical's napalm when it sticks to children's skin. Political magazines are advertising CREDIBILITY GAP—the board game.[34]

And so more and more Americans feel they need to push back, however hopelessly, against a government they can't trust. Hundreds of thousands march through Manhattan. Mothers horrified by those reports of napalmed kids join groups like Women Strike for Peace. Other revolts are springing up: angrier, more radical. Through the summer, anti-police riots break out in Negro neighborhoods, pitting improvised rebellion against the armed force of the state. In Newark, armed police treat Black children and seniors with all the restraint of troops "pacifying" a Vietnamese village; in Detroit, the National Guard turns up with tanks and does much the same. It fits with

*Report from Iron Mountain*'s argument that in daily life, the police represent the war power, "dealing with 'internal enemies' in a military manner."[35] The Black Power activist H. Rap Brown reacts in kind, crisscrossing the country to preach a Viet Cong–style fight back "in all the cities."[36] Students for a Democratic Society announces it's setting up "a guerrilla force" to operate "in an urban environment."[37] The *New York Review of Books* shows how to make a Molotov cocktail on its front page. On October 11, 1967, photos reach the American papers: the corpse of Che Guevara, hero of the Cuban revolution, offed in Bolivia by the power elite in the shape of the CIA. Days later, in Stop the Draft Week, thousands of police attack thousands of protesters outside Oakland's military induction center with tear gas and clubs. The demonstrators fight back with rocks and bricks. At the University of Wisconsin, SDS activists try to obstruct a recruiter from Dow Chemical, and it all happens again. Lurid rumors spread: *the government is preparing concentration camps for Black people. Or for anti-war protesters.*

On October 21, the attempt to confront the government and its lies comes to a head, with a protest against the "power elite" in Washington.[38] At first, the organizers plan to march on the Capitol, but they decide that Congress is merely "a servant of the real power in America."[39] Instead, they aim for the Pentagon: the headquarters of the war, the nerve center of the military-industrial complex. Nonetheless, two days before the protest, Congress legislates to make it a federal crime to carry guns and bombs into the Capitol; the Speaker denies that this is because of the march.[40]

Among the many journalists present is Raymond Heard, working out of the Washington Bureau of the *Montreal Star*: a young liberal exile from South Africa. Back home, he reported on the aftermath of the apartheid state's massacre of protesters at Sharpeville. The mood in the U.S. capital as the march approaches is, he reports, "exceptionally tense."[41] Thousands of federal marshals, military police, and soldiers—many veterans of Vietnam— assemble to defend the Pentagon from perhaps a hundred thousand demonstrators, some of whom are determined to shut the building down. Heard sees an ex-marine in a business suit smash a hippie demonstrator in the mouth, sending his "teeth flying in the air."[42] Heard's colleagues denounce the demonstrators as a mob that spreads myths and distorts or ignores facts, but he is more sympathetic. He sees in young Americans' refusal to fight in Vietnam the battle lines of a "generational war":[43]

> Those who made up the vanguard of the march, those who actually won territory from the troops for a few giddy hours, were young college students—bright and intelligent campus leaders who should become "opinion-makers" when they grow up and shave their beards and beatle-hairdos. Tragically, they see no place for themselves in the America of Lyndon Johnson; and there won't be a place for them until the Viet Nam tragedy is resolved.

Heard fears that the march and the violence in response mark "the point of no return." Come "the acts of mass civil disobedience, sabotage and terrorism which can now be expected," there will be a " 'new McCarthyism.' "[44]

Norman Mailer shows up, too, and turns what he finds into an *Esquire*-style "New Journalism" classic: a book called *The Armies of the Night*. The subtitle is *History as a Novel/The Novel as History*: he is obsessed with the line between fact and fiction. He opens with a block quote from *Time*'s report on his own drunken speech to demonstrators in a Washington theater. Then he promptly aims a Mills-style left hook at the magazine's lies: "Now we may leave *Time* in order to find out what happened."[45] He merrily recounts how, in the middle of his speech, he demanded that the guilty men of the news media stand up and show themselves.

He attacks his own side's fictions, too. He points out how delusional it is to attack the power elite by trying to take over the Pentagon. He recounts how around twenty-five protesters managed to push their way into the building, before rapidly being expelled. How, he asks, do you take over a building with "twenty miles"[46] of corridors? The building, the biggest in the world, is invincible, Mailer realizes, because it embodies the bigness of the new America: "High church of the corporation, the Pentagon spoke exclusively of mass man and his civilization; every aspect of the building was anonymous, monotonous, massive, interchangeable."[47]

———

The last protesters are removed from outside the Pentagon on Monday, October 23. By the end of the week, the director of the Office of Emergency Planning has caught wind that Dial Press is about to publish "a book dealing with the transition from war to peace that might be an attack on Administration policy." The book alleges, rumor has it, that the administration "purposely fosters the maintenance of the economy through war."[48] In a memo, the director warns President Johnson's hard-faced Texan chief of staff, tipping him off that extracts are going to be published in *Esquire*. And, they understand, in *Ramparts*—the daring New Left magazine with a track record of exposing government secrets.

It appears the chief of staff is concerned enough to bring this to the attention of Johnson himself: the president is already on edge about leaks. At the bottom of the memo, a scrawled note reads "To Walt/Call me" in what looks like Johnson's handwriting.[49] "Walt" is the president's national security adviser, Walt Rostow; it seems Johnson asks him to investigate whether *Report from Iron Mountain* is authentic.

But the administration's own grip on reality is slipping. Not for the last time, an American president is starting to lose touch with what is true. Besieged by rising public discontent, Johnson is exhausted by the constant enormity of the decisions he is taking about the war and by the reality that, no matter how hard he works—or how much blood and money he expends—nothing seems to improve. He is convinced he must win in Vietnam, come what may, because "the Communists want to rule the world." And he keeps trying to convince the public, and himself, that his policy is making "progress."[50] In thwarted desperation, the most powerful man on the planet is getting caught up in conspiracy theories. *The media is manipulating the public to oppose me. Bobby Kennedy is plotting to bring me down.*

This is why the president relies so heavily on his national security adviser. Walt Rostow genuinely believes that the bombing is working. This isn't surprising: it was largely his idea. At twenty-six, Rostow was in wartime London, picking targets in Germany for destruction from the air. This might have weighed heavily on some, but it made the young Rostow an evangelist for strategic bombardment. Yet he is far from an extremist. As a hugely influential academic economist, he has focused on helping the Third World prosper: he believes the Cold War can be won economically. When President Kennedy made an idealistic speech promising a "Decade of Development," he was implementing Rostow's ideas, in Rostow's words. This is a man equally at ease directing the distribution of aid or bombs. Finally, his hawkishness alienated Kennedy, but Johnson has pulled him back into the heart of power.

Rostow is a real-life crackpot realist. His intellectual self-confidence gives him the unerring ability to peer through his Perspex-framed glasses and see exactly what he wants. When it seemed, however tenuously, that a U.S. ship may have been attacked by a North Vietnamese gunboat in the Gulf of Tonkin, Rostow was poised to seize the pretext to help push sweeping war powers through Congress. "You know the wonderful thing is we don't even know if this thing happened at all," he remarked, according to a former colleague. "Boy, it gives us the chance to really go for broke on the bombing."[51] By May 1967, James C. Thomson Jr., one of his own former colleagues—another escapee from the Johnson administration—is openly mocking Rostow's refusal to look reality in the face. In a satire in the *Atlantic*, Thomson imagines the national security adviser detecting the upside even in humiliating defeat. The Rostow character declares that "The fall of Saigon to the Viet Cong" means the enemy is "confronted with a challenge of unprecedented proportions for which it was totally unprepared."[52] As more and more senior figures slip away from the administration in despair, Rostow has become increasingly important to the president. *Report from Iron Mountain* could hardly have landed on a more appropriate desk.

On top of the tip-off from the director of emergency planning, the White House has also had "tense queries from within the Government about the origins" of the *Report*.[53] Rostow's office gets hold of the galleys. He loops in one of his best men, who sets to work conducting an inquiry into whether it really is "the suppressed report of a government-sponsored study group."[54] Meanwhile, someone combs the "files and libraries of the Executive Office of the president"[55] to see if any such document is lurking there, like a left-behind land mine. They know such groups have been formed before.

While he waits for the findings, Rostow keeps the president well supplied with encouraging reports on the progress of the war. These come in from the vice president, who visits Vietnam for a couple of days and sees nothing but "confidence, spirit and determination."[56] From the U.S. ambassador in Saigon, boasting of a successful election. From a retired general's tour of the country, which, however delusional, is written up in *Look* magazine. From Defense Intelligence Agency reports of the enemy's "low morale" and "personnel problems."[57] Rostow tells the president that the United States is winning on the ground but is at risk of losing support at home, because the glad tidings aren't getting through to the public. The main front, he suggests, is now public opinion. Through this lens, the march on the Pentagon the previous weekend doesn't look like young people refusing to fight in a pointless war. They must have been misled. Rostow draws the president's attention to supportive quotes about the march in the foreign press: a Swiss paper helpfully opines that the protesters are the problem: "Those who, from their cloud-land of illusion or demagogy, exhort America to withdraw, are delaying peace."[58]

But there is a ghost at the crackpot feast; a traitor inside the tent. Robert McNamara, the secretary of defense, is the architect of the war: the cool-eyed systems analyst who for years was every bit as gung ho as Rostow. But over many months, he has been gradually, painfully coming to realize that it's not the anti-war movement that is lost in a cloudland of illusion but the administration itself. In response to Rostow's clamor for the unrestricted bombing of North Vietnam, to the point of triggering famine, McNamara sends the president a memo condemning the bombing as pointless and pressing for disengagement.

That same day, November 1, the *New York Times* carries the first advertisement for the *Report*. One of the paper's reporters, John Leo, calls the Dial Press to check that the book is genuine. He is advised to check the authenticity of the footnotes, which duly stand up. The London *Evening Standard*'s Washington correspondent points out that, a year earlier, seven university professors published "an astonishing but scarcely noticed report" for the U.S. State Department, "criticizing President Johnson's disarmament proposals as unworkable and contrary to the interests of American foreign policy." This is the report which said "that a disarmed world, far from promoting peace, could have a destabilizing effect on world politics and that to abolish national military forces would make foreign policies unenforceable and is therefore tantamount to abolishing nationhood." *Iron Mountain*, the English journalist observes, "is a much more extreme and cynical document but the resemblances are basic."[59]

Finally, Rostow's staffer reports back. There are "relatively few tip-offs that the document is bogus," but he judges it to be a "rather cleverly done parody."[60] The Executive Branch, writes one reporter, "breathed more easily."[61] That evening, two hours after sending Johnson a memo about why McNamara is wrong about the bombing, Rostow is able to reassure the president that "It turns out on investigation . . . that the Dial Press book is a Hoax."[62]

But this points up two crucial things. First, amid the crises of the actual war, this strange report on the undesirability of peace seems to have troubled the president. And second, it has taken five days to decide it's fake. No wonder *U.S. News & World Report* calls it "A Book that Shook the White House."[63]

. . . And then more sources quietly tell journalists that it remains perfectly possible *Report from Iron Mountain* is genuine, and could have been sponsored by the White House, a congressional committee, or a federal agency.[64] The president of the Dial Press affirms that it is authentic. Harold Hayes of *Esquire* tells the *Times* he trusts this assurance. And so journalists are forced to hedge: John Leo can report only that while some spy a hoax, others take it seriously. His story is eye-catching enough to make the front page of the *New York Times*.

Among those quoted by Leo who seem ready to accept that the *Report* may be real is Arthur Waskow, resident fellow at the Institute for Policy Studies in Washington. This is the alternative think tank set up in 1963 by young refugees from the Kennedy administration; it has won a hearing in the "corridors of power" for its radical but real-world policymaking.[65] As a peace activist, Waskow disagrees with the *Report*'s contention that "the end of war would wrench and destroy the nation-state system," but admits that "this is the best case I've ever read on the other side." The *Report* cites a "privately circulated" paper of his, "Toward the Unarmed Forces of the United States," which "only about 60 people in Washington ever saw." He concludes that "if the report is authentic it would probably have come from the Bureau of the Budget or the Central Intelligence Agency." And if it's a hoax? It "must involve somebody high up."[66]

"If it's authentic, it's an enormous roaring scandal," Leo quotes an academic sociologist as saying. "If it's caricature, it's a brilliant job." Because, he says, "There are people who really think like that."[67] As the *Times* describes it, the argument of the *Report* is that the abolition of war would have such a severe impact on America that it would have to take extreme steps to absorb it: inventing an alien threat, reviving slavery, poisoning the atmosphere. *This is how some people in power think?* What are the Don Drapers of the world, scanning the *Times* on their commuter trains into Grand Central, to make of *that*?

*Times* readers are able to pick up a copy of the new *Esquire* from a newsstand the following day and try to work it out for themselves. Opposite a beautifully photographed ad for Seagram's V.O. Canadian Whisky, there it is. "This report is 28,000 words in length and so depressing that you may not be able to take it," runs the lede. "But if you persist, Merry Christmas anyway, and on earth war, ill-will toward men."[68] On November 8, Leonard Lewin appears on TV, on WNDT, saying he hopes the *Report* will cause a "more candid discussion of the possibilities of the elimination of war."[69]

That Sunday night, on WNET, the *Report* is televised, in an edition of a two-hour experimental show called *Public Broadcast Laboratory*, which worries away at the question of whether power can be trusted. The *Iron Mountain* segment is preceded by a tetchy studio exchange about whether the "mirage-makers" of the ad industry are corrupting politics. Readings from the book reverberate over footage of mushroom clouds, missile launches, flag ceremonies, East African warriors, and an old Vietnamese woman keening over a dead child. The voice-over points out that, in line with the *Report*'s thesis about the uses of war, "The assembly line grew out of firearm needs in the Civil War." And then who should appear to discuss the book but Herman Kahn himself. He declares himself unconvinced; he agrees that "a majority of Americans believe that war makes the economy prosperous," but argues the *Report* goes well beyond that:

> the interesting thing about this book is the number of people who are willing to believe that serious people in the government think this way. These are people who are presumably anxious to feel the worst of their government. Somehow there's something very, very wrong there. . . . [A] book like this would never have been taken seriously two years ago. This has to do with the CIA, with Vietnam, with the race riots, with poverty issues. . . .[70]

He admits, though, that if it's "overwritten satire," it's clearly getting something right, given how many people have accepted it. Only after Kahn has finished does the voice-over admit that the show's producers think the book is fiction—a delayed reveal for which they will come in for criticism. But the voice-over maintains that, "hoax or not, there is agreement that the book is penetrating and poses critical questions."[71] This strange sequence is followed by a long, agonized debate among congressmen about the Gulf of Tonkin resolution and the legality of the war in Vietnam, before the anchor closes the show with a bleak observation: "Never in our history has there been such an avalanche of information, so little believed or believable."[72]

On November 15 come more official denials. Lagging behind the White House by a couple weeks, the Defense Department has finally finished investigating whether "there was any study group that had been established after 1963 that might have fit the description in *Report from Iron Mountain* or that might have written such a report"[73]—and has concluded that there was not. The man announcing this is the deputy assistant secretary of defense, Richard Fryklund, an admirer of Herman Kahn[74] and the author of a 1962 study called *100 Million Lives: Maximum Survival in a Nuclear War*—another of those calm, Kahn-style analyses of how best to manage the apocalypse. A second admirer of Kahn's thinking,[75] the Harvard academic Professor Henry Kissinger, is busy trying to broker peace with North Vietnam—with the blessing of the State Department, which he will later run. He takes time out to dismiss the *Report* as the doings of an idiot.[76] The State Department announces that the Arms Control and Disarmament Agency has conducted a similar investigation and has come to the same conclusion: the report is not authentic. A deputy assistant secretary of state accuses Lewin of making it all up and tricking Dial into publishing it.[77]

But in the wake of the Warren Commission and the Gulf of Tonkin, official denials aren't what they used to be. Richard Baron, publisher of Dial Press, shoots back that "the Defense Department and the CIA made a lot of denials on matters a few months ago, and the officials found they had to reverse themselves."[78] "Let people believe what they want," Leonard Lewin tells the *New York Times Book Review*, "as long as they think about the content of the book . . . the "value-free" approach of the Defense intellectuals."[79]

And perhaps the *Report* has got under the Pentagon's skin in a way a march could not. Behind the "facade" of official optimism, "private pessimism" is already spreading, not least among civilian staffers who are being challenged about the war by their families.[80] One Pentagon source, who works "at the highest levels in strategic planning," whispers that he has colleagues who agree with the *Report* that the Vietnam war helps keep America stable. Another says it is so akin to past documents that there is no reason to think it isn't authentic. A State Department source tells *Newsweek* that the

*Report* is initially all too convincing. If nothing else, the fuss is prompting people to admit some eye-watering things.

The Johnson administration has reportedly cabled its embassies, telling them to stress the book has no link to American policy.[81] The problem is that, as the legendary CBS news anchor Walter Cronkite points out, it reads as though it does.[82] The president is "said to have 'hit the roof'—and then ordered that the report be bottled up for all time."[83]

And then comes another disorienting intervention, from one of the intellectual pillars of the age. The witty patrician John Kenneth Galbraith, six foot eight in his socks, is a star among Harvard academics, and the kind of economist who writes books people actually read. He has also been ambassador to India—appointed by Kennedy, who was once one of his students. In "Book World," a supplement published in both the *Washington Post* and the *Chicago Tribune*, Galbraith playfully reviews the *Report* under a pseudonym—though everyone knows it is him. Writing as "Professor McLandress," he claims he was asked to participate in the Study Group, and had to decline, but that he was consulted. He says its conclusions are "thoroughly sound"—but the public should have been "psychologically conditioned" before they were permitted to learn its contents.[84]

---

If the officials are right and it *is* a hoax, who is responsible? Some in Washington fear it's a deliberate smear. Others worry that, whoever wrote it, it hands a propaganda gift to the Soviets.[85] In the *National Review*, James Burnham, a veteran conservative cold warrior, speculates that it might be a "psywar ploy."[86]

A hunt begins aimed at unmasking the mysterious professor who was Lewin's chief source. The list of suspects is revealingly long. The search casts America's intellectuals in a strange sidelight: illuminating their relationships with power and what they believe it is capable of. All caught for a moment in the low winter sun.

One possibility is that it is someone who is just sending up the whole idea, like Richard Rovere, the *New Yorker*'s man in Washington. He is currently reporting on how the White House press secretary has been branding inconvenient facts "misinformation."[87] And he once wrote a much-celebrated satirical essay for *Esquire*, mocking the earnest search for the mysterious "American Establishment."[88]

But this is a book of more than one hundred pages, heavy with footnotes. It seems more likely to be the work of an anti-war academic. Some wonder if it is Kenneth Boulding, a British-born economist, originally from Liverpool, who coedited one of those early 1960s studies of the economic impact of disarmament—and who is also a Quaker peace activist who organized the first anti–Vietnam War "teach-in" at the University of Michigan. Or Irving Horowitz, a sociologist who has edited collections of C. Wright Mills's work.

A more striking suggestion is that it is one of those public figures who marched on the Pentagon: a pioneering scholar of linguistics named Noam Chomsky. He has recently shot to public attention with an eviscerating polemic for the *New York Review of Books* called "The Responsibility of Intellectuals." Scholars and writers in Western democracies, he argues, could choose to "seek the truth lying hidden behind the veil of distortion and misrepresentation, ideology, and class interest through which the events of current history are presented to us."[89] But instead, men like Rostow, Kissinger, and Kahn have been co-opted by power. Chomsky decries the Cold War intellectuals and their facade of rationality, tough-mindedness, and pseudoscience. He condemns "the cult of the expert" as "fraudulent." He calls out the deceptive language which hides atrocities behind cant about the "defense of freedom."[90] This is a world view as certain, in its way, as Rostow's, but here, it's the dissenters who seek and speak the truth. Perhaps, then, he is unlikely to have fabricated a hoax.

Others point their suspicions in the opposite direction, suggesting that Professor "John Doe" is one of those figures Chomsky condemns: the kinds of people who seem actually to believe the *Report*'s thesis that war is integral to America's well-being. After all, as Arthur Waskow told the *Times*, "If it's a hoax, it must involve somebody high up." At least one person suspects Rostow himself; *Time* magazine calls him "humorously" to ask if it's true.[91] More seriously, eyes turn naturally to Herman Kahn, whose "unthinkable" mix of cold logic and lurid scenarios the *Report* resembles. He is, after all, currently employed at the Pentagon as a consultant, applying that logic to Vietnam.[92] The *Evening Standard*'s Washington correspondent tells his readers back in London that Kahn is "widely suspected of knowing more about this book than he will admit."[93] In the *Times*, Kahn denounces it as "nutty . . . either a practical joke or something sinister," insisting, "We had nothing to do with it."[94] But after his TV appearance claiming the *Report* was unconvincing, it was noted that Kahn "didn't offer any convincing refutations."[95]

Or, if the *Report* is satire, it might make more sense that the author is *both* a seasoned ex-insider *and* a critic of the U.S. military machine. Some suspect speechwriter Richard Goodwin, one of the disillusioned members of the Kennedy and Johnson administrations who has resigned over Vietnam. He has aligned himself with Robert Kennedy, who Johnson was convinced was "the guiding spirit of some immense conspiracy" to drive him from power.[96] And Goodwin has reportedly been writing scathing, anonymous satires of the president for the *New Yorker*. Earlier in the year, in the course of an article criticizing the centralization of power, he wrote:

> We still mock our Presidents, sometimes brutally, but not because they are futile, comic, or unimportant. The springs of today's satire are fear and rage rather than condescension. For the target is immense.[97]

But perhaps, after all, it is John Kenneth Galbraith, who has openly urged at least one journalist to buy *Report from Iron Mountain* "as soon as possible."[98] Not only does Galbraith write satires in *Esquire*; having grown disillusioned with the Johnson administration, he has turned his patrician wit against the lies and delusions thrown up by the war. His most recent book, *The New Industrial State*, is an analysis of the way power has accrued to what he calls the "Technostructure," which sounds not unlike the military-industrial complex. The separation between the Pentagon and its supposedly private-sector contractors is now "imaginary," he points out, even if this "notion is rather fiercely resisted."[99] At the same time, in a short book called *How to Get Out of Vietnam*, he contends that the war effort is driven by a "conspiratorial vision": America is trying to fight a global communist plot which "turned out not to exist." Galbraith agrees with Chomsky that the "Administration's case was grounded . . . on a false image." He just thinks it's less an evil deception by an omnipotent power elite, more an embarrassing case of self-delusion, which is making them look "ridiculous," to the point where people just don't believe them anymore.[100] What better target for satire than the ridiculous delusions of the powerful? No wonder Galbraith is the media's chief suspect—especially given his heavy hint, in his "Book World" review, that he was involved in the *Report*.

And so he was. But he just provided advice on economics. Eventually, Raymond Heard—the young, South African–born journalist from the *Montreal Star* who'd reported on the Pentagon march—spots evidence that the man behind the *Report* is a far less grand figure. Not only is this person a professional satirist; he has just written a "scathing" review of a new book by Herman Kahn. Heard points out that the reviewer describes Kahn's thesis like this: "war may be a necessary and even desirable feature of a stable world order, and should thus be more efficiently and affirmatively planned on a long-term basis."[101] That reviewer is Leonard Lewin. Though Lewin still refuses to admit it, he was the real author of *Report from Iron Mountain* all along.

There was no professor, no intimidating phone call from Washington, no three-year project. As any reporter could have checked with a quick trip to the clippings library,[102] the Iron Mountain shelter did not even open until January 1966. That is around the time Lewin started writing, but more than two years after the "Special Study Group" supposedly first met there. As the paper that broke the story, the *New York Times*, eventually writes: "It is, of course, a hoax—but what a hoax!—a parody so elaborate and ingenious and, in fact, so substantively original, acute, interesting and horrifying, that it will receive serious attention regardless of its origin."[103] (Even then, another writer chips in a week later in the same paper to keep the mischief running: "It is a part of the grim joke of his book that [Lewin] may only think that he has invented his study group. Such a group may in truth even now be working."[104]

But why did Lewin do this? Did he hoodwink Dial into publishing it, as the State Department charged? Did he pull the whole thing off alone, or were there others behind it? And, either way, why did anyone—not least in the heart of power—believe even for a second that any real government report would advocate deliberate pollution, eugenics, "blood games," and the revival of slavery?

# 3

# THE CONSPIRATORS

It was not only the Johnson administration that had a thing for make-believe. Had you wandered eastward along Bleecker Street in Greenwich Village one day in January 1966, past the Village Gate where the comedian Dick Gregory was appearing on weekends, then headed north to the corner of Washington Square Park, you would have come upon what looked like a warehouse—but was actually a new, experimental theater. It was home to a wildly successful new musical: *Man of La Mancha*, a sixties spin on *Don Quixote*. The story of a man lost in delusions and enthusiastically acting them out had apparently caught the moment. Robert Kennedy went to watch the show three times, and saw in it something of his own crusade against "real monsters."[1]

If you'd continued across the square, you might have passed the kind of people C. Wright Mills had complained were ruining the Village: Madison Avenue advertising executives "who are not—but who wish to appear to be—intellectuals and artists."[2] Or perhaps you'd have seen some teens pretending to be Beats. This is where, if you were young and trying hard, you came to parade your look. A Bob Dylan–style top hat. Enormous Audrey Hepburn shades. Or a costume from the country's combative past: oblong Benjamin Franklin glasses, a thrift-store relic from the Civil War, or a navy pea jacket from a shop that advertised "Groovy Government Garments!"[3]

And had you kept going through the Washington Square Arch, ignoring the statues of the revolutionary turned president, and headed up Fifth Avenue, you would likely have walked right past the old gray stone building on the corner of West 14th Street—number 80. But if, on a whim, you'd turned into the lobby and taken the elevator up to Suite 702, you might have spied a curious sight. Because it was up here that *Report from Iron Mountain* was born. There was never a conspiratorial "Special Study Group" meeting in grand secrecy in the forbidden vaults of Iron Mountain. The only conspiracy was the one cooked up right here, in this cheap and cheerful office.

This was the not very sinister lair of a satire magazine called *Monocle*. As you entered, the anteroom opened out into a big space like a loft, chopped into cubicles. Off to the left, there was a messy office; inside, Victor Navasky, the magazine's thirty-three-year-old editor, was sitting at a big table with his two chief henchmen, looking through the newspapers. As ever, they were hunting for ideas. And Victor was about to spot one that would run for over half a century, right up to today.

———

Navasky had created *Monocle* with fellow grad students at Yale Law School in 1957, as a first step in avoiding the fate of his father, who had wanted to be a writer but got stuck in *his* father's garment business. Victor was a veteran of Greenwich Village's Little Red School House, where they sang the left-wing songs of Pete Seeger and Woody Guthrie; of the Quaker college Swarthmore, and of two years' service in the army, where Seeger, Guthrie, and the Quakers were of little help. He'd gone to Yale on the GI Bill, but obviously didn't want to be a lawyer. Instead, he invented a satire magazine, before satire was fashionable.

The name came from the proverb about how, in the land of the blind, the one-eyed man is king. *Monocle*'s goal was to puncture pretensions and "question the official line"[4]; and right from the start, it put the boot in, skewering the ludicrousness of America's building a "clean" Bomb: "Those whom we incinerate will be dispatched and purified in a single operation."[5] He recruited art students to design it and others to fold the pages: an early sign of Navasky's knack for bringing people together to turn his schemes into reality.

People like one of the two men sitting around the table with him that morning in 1966: Richard Lingeman, executive editor, and one of *Monocle*'s main writers. He'd escaped from the Midwest to college, then served three years as a special agent in the army's Counterintelligence Corps in Japan. After that, law school was boring. Being sought out by Victor to craft parodies spurred him to drop out and write. "It was a time," he remembers, "when you could take chances."[6]

By 1959, *Monocle*'s circulation had risen to three thousand, and they decided to try to make a go of it in New York. There they recruited the third man at the table: Marvin Kitman, a comic writer for a racing paper, who heard about them while researching a piece about . . . monocles. He became their "news managing editor," but really their political stuntman. He liked goofy capers, like trying to phone Mao Zedong collect from Leonia, New Jersey, or running for president.

The timing of their move to Manhattan turned out to be perfect. In the early 1960s, a wave of satire drenched American culture. Confident young men and women, who'd grown up in the most prosperous and powerful place on earth, looked around at all the timid old angsts and hang-ups, the euphemisms and pretenses, the hierarchies and taboos—and couldn't stop laughing. Mike Nichols and Elaine May played gossiping office workers by the water cooler, discussing how the government had messed up on the racial integration of schools—but was at least tackling the fakery on a TV quiz show. "It's a moral issue!" May's character exclaims. "And to me that's so much more interesting than a real issue!"[7] Marvin Kitman found himself on a TV panel show with the cartoonist Jules Feiffer, who delighted in sending up the gap between public piety and what people really thought.

Then there were the pioneers of modern, satirical stand-up. Mort Sahl drew on his disillusionment with militarism, insisting he "dug" nuclear bomb tests in Nevada: "I figure they're good for business . . . I'm not planning a large family anyway."[8] Lenny Bruce was arrested in San Francisco for obscenity, for saying onstage that "come is a verb" and anyone who found that upsetting to hear probably couldn't. Dick Gregory sent up the ludicrousness of racism. He related how he'd moved to a white part of Chicago, where his new neighbor, assuming he must be a cleaner, asked him what he got for shoveling snow outside his front door. "Oh," Gregory replies, "I get to sleep with that woman inside."[9] From England, where satire was booming too, there came the topical TV satire show *That Was the Week That Was*, for which Richard Lingeman wrote a sketch. And *Beyond the Fringe*, whose star Peter Cook visited the *Monocle* office and became an "editorial associate." There was talk of the magazine merging with its British equivalent, *Private Eye*.

Having Kennedy as president fired *Monocle*'s imagination. Bumbling old Eisenhower "satirized himself,"[10] Navasky wrote later, but JFK was worth the work. They sent up his family's dynastic grandiosity, his too-good-to-be-true marriage, his "pressmanship," his role in the Bay of Pigs—even his undoubted heroics in the war, and the way his father had exploited them to set Jack on the road to the White House. Drawing on his time in east Asia, Richard Lingeman wrote a "translation" of an article about a made-up book, *Destiny's Deckhand: The Autobiography of a Seaman on the Japanese Destroyer That Rammed Kennedy's PT-109*.[11] One historian suggests *Monocle*'s politics frequently echoed the "independent radicalism kept alive during the fifties by I. F. Stone and C. Wright Mills." Dan Wakefield, a Mills protégé, wrote an article for the magazine mocking Kennedy's cautious centrism as the "Thunder in the Middle."[12] When Kennedy failed to live up to his promise to ban discrimination in housing "with the stroke of a pen," they exhorted people to send bottles of ink to the White House until Kennedy's press secretary finally called them and asked them to stop, as it was messing up the mail room.

Lampooning topical issues was tricky in a magazine that only came out four times a year, so in 1962 they launched the weekly *Outsider's Newsletter*. This turned Herman Kahn into the star of a cartoon strip, in which Kennedy sends "Super-Kahn—the only superhero under contract to the United States government"—on top secret missions.[13] When the New York papers went on strike, Navasky's team hacked out parodies—*The New York Pest, The Harold Tribune, The Dally Noose*—that sent up big league writers so successfully that a *Monocle* writer was hired by the one of papers they were mocking. This was the wildly successful Nora Ephron, who was thus launched on her way to *Esquire*, and from there to Hollywood glory.

Intriguingly, when *Monocle* ruthlessly mocked power, it was not out of a sense of revolutionary destructiveness or resentful disempowerment. These people had been quite close to power in some ways and could have had more of it if they'd wanted. While *Mad* magazine's fakery-skewering satire was guzzled by giggling teens, *Monocle*'s audience was its creators' peers: young graduates rising fast in government, law, and publishing: "the people who would be running things."[14] The *Monocle* gang devoted a whole issue to sending up the CIA, but they were mostly Yale men all the same—just like some of the agency's leading lights and Kennedy's "best and brightest." They did not pay Kennedy and his team so much attention out of hatred. The dean of Yale Law School in Navasky's time was one Eugene Rostow—Walt's big brother. He looked benevolently on his students' satirical efforts, and later helped Navasky get a job writing speeches for a liberal Democratic governor, G. Mennen "Soapy" Williams of Michigan, who was brought into the Kennedy administration soon afterward. Soapy introduced Victor to another ex–Yale Law alumnus, a man named Adam Yarmolinsky, one of Kennedy's whiz-kid Pentagon modernizers. Yarmolinsky was not much liked by the left, and was denounced with a weird, embarrassing fury by General Edwin Walker; Navasky, by contrast, recruited him to write for *Monocle* "undercover." And he was not the only one: reportedly, *Monocle* took copy from other "White House and Pentagon staff men who wish[ed] to unburden their spirits."[15] *Monocle*'s distributor in Massachusetts, meanwhile, was the future state governor and presidential candidate Michael Dukakis.

There could hardly have been a better embodiment of the upbeat, confident, satirical young New York of 1962 and 1963. Greenwich Village was a minute away, literary New York was thriving all around, there was Shelley's coffee bar up the street for takeout. And then there were the parties. Anne Strongin was a secretary, bored with dating Wall Street types. She remembers Victor inviting her to a *Monocle* party and finding a huge cartoon of Jesus in the anteroom, with the caption: "He was a great teacher, but he didn't publish."[16] These were the people she wanted to hang out with, she decided; she and Victor were married from 1966 until his death in 2023. Other people met life partners at these parties, too, helped along by Chinese food, junk wine, and "coexistence cocktails."

One of the writers, Eleanor Foa Dienstag, says the *Monocle* office wasn't the kind of place where you could take things at face value or expect a straight answer: everything was the means to a joke. And so when she came out of her cubicle one day, and Marvin Kitman told her that the president had just been shot, she said "You know, Marvin, that's really not so funny." He insisted it was true—his wife was on the phone with the news—but at first "no one believed him."[17] Only later did people start crying.

In the days afterward, Navasky recorded how people were walking around in a sleepless "three-day daze," dealing with the realization that "it can happen here." Finally, the *Monocle* team got "around to the avoided question—where is the place for satire in this new scheme of things?" Their CIA special issue had just gone to the printers, featuring a Lingeman headline about the president's timidity on civil rights: "Kennedy Missing." People asked him: "What, did you know or what?" That was one way "satire gets fouled up [by] reality."[18] They had to issue an apology.

In this less happy-go-lucky new mode, their satirical eye turned on the right and its opposition to civil rights. Marvin Kitman ran for the Republican nomination for president, mockingly outdoing the conservatism of the right's new champion Barry Goldwater by running on Abraham Lincoln's policies from a full century earlier. At a dollar-a-plate fundraiser at the Waldorf Self-Service Cafeteria, he offered to deploy the CIA's expertise at overthrowing governments against the racist governors in the South. But by the end of 1964, they had run out of funding and were running up debts.

This was not helped by their advertising manager who refused to inflate the magazine's circulation numbers by half, as was the standard lie, so people assumed they were selling fewer copies than they were. To make money, they started working as book packagers, hiring researchers to compile what they dubbed "un-books," such as an anthology of famous funny telegrams called *Barbed Wires* and an *Illustrated Gift Edition of the Communist Manifesto*. More seriously, they oversaw the creation of a book on the university free speech movement called *Revolution at Berkeley*.

As Navasky, Lingeman, and Kitman sat in their office that day in January 1966, they'd just sent out their newest book to leading politicians, accompanied by sarcastic letters. The book was called *Vietnam Speak-Out*. Unlike most of their un-books, this one was credited as the work of *Monocle*— it was billed as the latest edition of the magazine, and it was darker than ever. It consisted of a decade's-worth of quotations from French, American, and South Vietnamese leaders, incessantly proclaiming that victory over the communists in Vietnam was just around the corner, accompanied by cartoons of the dead taunting the politicians' hubris. One has Robert McNamara sunnily declaring, in January 1963, that "The war in Vietnam is going well and will succeed,"[19] next to a cartoon of him being straddled by a skeleton.

So when Navasky spotted an article about Wall Street's attitude to the Vietnam War, it caught his eye. It reported that the brokers had been ruffled by a "peace scare." In response to news that the Vietnam War might be wound down, a flurry of selling had sent stock prices into a slump.

This chimed with all those angst-ridden attacks on the permanent war economy and the military-industrial complex. Almost a decade earlier, in *The Causes of World War Three*, C. Wright Mills had written:

Since the end of World War II many in elite circles have felt that economic prosperity in the U.S. is immediately under-pinned by the war economy and that desperate economic—and so political—problems might well arise should there be disarmament and genuine peace.

Conciliatory gestures by the Russians are followed by stock-market selling. When there is fear that negotiations may occur, let alone that a treaty structure for the world be arranged, stocks, by their jitters, reflect what is called a "peace scare."[20]

Likewise, one of those early 1960s articles about the difficulties of a transition to peace had observed that any "student of the stock market can tell you what happens on the rumor that peace is breaking out."[21]

Nonetheless, Navasky was shocked: At the time, he naïvely believed "that the prospect of peace would be as welcome on Wall Street as it was"[22] to him. The financial industry's anxious reaction struck him and his colleagues as a moral absurdity worthy of the great satirists, like H. L. Mencken and Mark Twain. Or even the eighteenth-century Irish writer Jonathan Swift, author of "A Modest Proposal for Preventing the Children of Poor People from being a Burden to Their Parents, or Country, and for Making Them Beneficial to the Public." Swift had published this essay anonymously, as though it were genuine. It suggested that those parents sell their children to the wealthy as food.

Kicking their "peace scare" idea around, Navasky, Lingeman, and Kitman thought: What if we made up a story about how the government had commissioned a group of experts to scope out the transition away from the war economy—and how the group concluded that without war the American economy would come apart? And how the implications were so grim Washington had to bury it? They "decided to publish the story of the suppression of this report."[23] The main purpose was to "focus attention on the reliance of the U.S. economy on war or the threat of war."[24] But perhaps there was something else, too. By this time, "it was common for the government to lie," remembers Lingeman. So "maybe this was a way of hitting back."[25]

Either way, now they needed someone to write it.

Leonard Lewin really was worrying away about the difficulties of the writing life when someone got in touch about a strange project. Not a mysterious professor, but the *Monocle* conspirators.[26] Lewin had written for them before. He clearly knew more than most about American satire: he'd recently edited a *Treasury of American Political Humor* in which he was very complimentary about *Monocle*. Plus, Navasky knew that Lewin "cared passionately about issues of war and peace."[27]

At first, though, Lewin was not at all keen to take on the "hoax book"[28] Later, he remembered: "I liked the premise for the book, and decided that, to make the premise of the book more compelling and believable, I would actually write an allegedly high-level government "think tank" report which addressed the issue of whether peace was desirable for the good of the country's national interest."[29] When he finally signed up, he added a whole new dimension to the hoax, expanding it beyond a send-up of the idea that the economy needed war. He also wanted to satirize the way those in power *thought*: the think tank mentality that claimed to be purely objective. In Lewin's view, their claim to take "a value-free approach to social problems" was ludicrous but "appallingly dangerous," because it was "accepted in very high places."[30] But at first, on top of his existing commitments, this looked like a hell of a lot of work.

Anne Navasky remembers how, where Victor would make jokes about politics, "Leonard was more seriously angry."[31] And for that, he may have had good cause. He was pushing fifty: a decade and a half older than the happy-go-lucky *Monocle* editors. Perhaps this is one reason the hoax was so effective. Those youthful Yalies had the chutzpah to launch it in the first place, but it also needed the committed political rage of a less lucky generation.

Like Navasky's father, Lewin had been determined to escape the family business and succeed as a writer. Unlike Navasky senior, he finally managed it, but it took him a long time, and more than one attempt. Lewin's father, Morris, was "an entrepreneur, and a hustler":[32] a Ukrainian Jewish sugar chemist, born Mikhail Lewin, who arrived in New York alone, aged twenty, in 1910. He started out as a "sugar tramp," working in refineries from the

Great Plains to the Caribbean. He had dealings with a high-end fraudster; flew across the Andes in leather suit, helmet, and goggles; hired a small army to help him break the Guggenheims' iodine cartel. Improbably, the fruit of those and other audacious efforts allowed Leonard to grow up in a wealthy home—until he was thirteen, when his father lost his money in the Wall Street crash of 1929. Leonard was so smart he went to Harvard early; by the time he graduated in 1936, with an AB cum laude in psychology, Morris was in the process of building a new enterprise. This was eventually incorporated two years later, in Indianapolis, as Liquid Sugars. After twenty-six years of striving—during the course of which Leonard's younger brother had fallen ill and died—Morris expected his surviving son to join him in his business.

When Leonard refused and said he wanted to be a writer, Morris "cut him off financially."[33] To make a living, Leonard ran a bicycle shop and even read novels for film companies. He was a committed supporter of the labor movement and, for a time, a member of the Communist Party. He tried to go and fight for the socialist republic in the Spanish Civil War, only to be thwarted by an ulcer. He became an organizer in the United Electrical Workers Union, driving from branch meeting to branch meeting through a Connecticut winter, screening movies for members.

By the mid-1940s, he was married to Iris, a fellow union organizer, and had two children. He quit working for the labor movement and started writing for the radio, but it was impossible to make ends meet. In 1948, after twelve years, he gave in and went to work for his father. Indianapolis was conformist, paranoid about communism, religious and self-righteous—and segregated. Leonard and Iris sometimes socialized across the divide, and hosted jazz musicians, but this was not their kind of city. When one of his parents insulted Iris, he broke from his father again and tried to scrape a living as a traveling salesman. A friend offered him a job, but with McCarthyism at its height, Leonard turned it down for fear that he might harm his friend's business by association. He eventually reconciled with his father and retreated once again to Liquid Sugars. Only when Morris died, in 1958, could Leonard finally escape. In 1960, separated from Iris, having sold his father's business, he relocated to New York, to take his last shot at becoming a writer.

And he did it. One breakthrough piece was a satire for the *New Yorker* on the Cuban missile crisis and the journalists who boosted the heroic Kennedy narrative. But even that was hard-won: as the crisis intensified, he'd been sufficiently scared by the threat of nuclear war to call his son, Mike, at Harvard and tell him he wanted to take the family to the relative safety of Mexico. (Mike refused.) Little wonder, after all this, that Lewin was willing to craft a satire of American power.

———————

Navasky may have hired an ideal writer, but what sensible publisher was going to risk trashing their reputation by playing along with a hoax government report? He approached a company *Monocle* had previously worked with on a packaged book. The Dial Press was based in a modernist glass cascade on Third Avenue. It was a subsidiary of a big publishing corporation but was pointedly independent.

To Navasky's delighted surprise, both Dial's editor in chief, Edgar Doctorow, and its publisher, Richard Baron, agreed to the whole wheeze straight off, before Lewin had written a word. In the contract, the project's working title is "Peace Hoax Book." As with those un-books *Monocle* had created through its book packaging operation, the magazine's name would not appear on the final product—and, of course, for the hoax to work, Lewin would not be credited as the real writer of the fake government report. Baron and Doctorow even offered to put the book on their nonfiction list, and to "forget" to tell their sales team it was a hoax. Dial had a reputation for being "willing to try things other publishers weren't."[34] Even so, why would they agree to such a scheme?

For Richard Baron, whom we last met calling the CIA and the Pentagon liars, publishing *Report from Iron Mountain* can hardly have seemed very terrifying. At ten years old, this born Manhattanite was talking the doorman into letting him drive a car back and forth outside his parents' building. In the army, even before he reached Europe, he'd had to clear a $1,300 debt in Alabama's gambling hotspot, Phenix City, by working as a shill—something he "thoroughly enjoyed."[35] He'd fought in Italy and France, and had endured bullet wounds, seeing his men killed, and his own capture, solitary confinement, and brief interrogation by the SS, then prison camp hunger, and the near-fatal failure of his bid to escape. He once took James Baldwin to a club so exclusive that even the waiters were all white. Looking back, Doctorow called Baron the "perfect publisher for the 1960s," because he was "totally fearless and backed us in every crazy thing we wanted to do."[36]

Doctorow himself clearly had a yen for this kind of thing. As a teenage journalism student in the 1940s, he'd wowed his teacher by turning in a harrowing interview with a German-Jewish doorman at Carnegie Hall—only to have to admit that he'd made it up. (Or so he said. Navasky thought *the whole story* was made up—though school friends of Doctorow confirm that it really happened.[37]) In the 1970s, as the world-famous novelist E. L. Doctorow, he would weave fiction from historical figures to create novels like *Ragtime*. Would any other editor have been quite so willing to play games with the "non-" in "nonfiction"? On January 28, 1966, the same day Lewin recorded that he'd said yes to Victor, he noted that Dial's editor in chief was "very sharp."[38]

If that cheered him up, it didn't last long. The cold feet came back; the structure of the book drove him crazy. There were regular meetings with Navasky, Lingeman, and Kitman at *Monocle*, as well as with Doctorow, where, Lingeman remembers, they "talked it over and kicked it around, and we contributed ideas."[39] *Monocle*'s interns were deployed "to track down original sources."[40] But Julie Lewin's image of her father during the writing process is of a man clasping his head in despair. He decided to seek advice, and hopefully find a new format along the way, or give up. He started making calls.

Thanks in part to Victor's bursting Rolodex, Lewin encountered some of the late 1960s' sharpest critics of American power and its delusions. One

April Monday, he was off to Washington for a "busy day" of meetings, including one with Arthur Waskow, from that alternative think tank, the Institute for Policy Studies, whose paper Lewin would go on to quote in the *Report*. In November 1967, when the story broke, Waskow would tell the *New York Times* that the paper concerned was one that "only about 60 people in Washington ever saw."[41]

Waskow was closer to the New Left than either Lewin or Navasky; he'd never believed Kennedy was a progressive. He'd been skeptical about Mills's *Power Elite* until he went to work for an idealistic congressman who'd witnessed the devastation of Hiroshima and went into politics to ensure it never happened again. Waskow watched how even *he* was successfully pressured, and decided Mills was right. By the time of Lewin's visit, he'd developed a detailed critique of defense intellectuals, in a book called *The Limits of Defense*, which argued that for each of the armed services, "the weaponry was controlling the strategy, not the other way around." As for Herman Kahn, Waskow regarded his thinking as not just "nuts, in the sense it was detached from reality," but evil, and he told Kahn so, to his face.[42]

Now ninety years old and still politically active as director of the Shalom Center in Philadelphia, Rabbi Waskow has no memory of Lewin's visit, but doesn't dispute that they met.[43] The paper of Waskow's that Lewin drew from, "Toward the Unarmed Forces of the United States," argued that the "war system" had to be seen as obsolete, not morally but strategically. It set out to "isolate the specific functions the war system now plays: functions that would have to be played by substitute institutions if the world were to be demilitarized."[44] That is, it starts from the same question as *Report from Iron Mountain* but gives a nonsatirical answer. Looking back, Waskow finds the way Lewin used quotations from his paper rather puzzling, but thinks *Iron Mountain* mostly makes "satirical sense" as a way "to show that the people running the government thought peace was impossible."[45] Lewin found his meeting with Waskow a "very useful session."[46]

Next, Navasky brought him to a building on Vanderbilt Avenue, across the street from Grand Central Terminal. The Yale Club was an ornate, twenty-two-story, male-only bastion of the establishment. Somewhere among the columns and fireplaces, between the Main Lounge, the Grill Room, the roof terrace, the library, the barber shop, and the Grand Ballroom, they were there to hear from an adman his friends called "Ping."

Wilbur H. "Ping" Ferry had been a schoolteacher to John F. Kennedy, had a ludicrous aristocratic nickname, and worked in public relations; Defense Secretary Robert McNamara had once asked him to be his information officer.[47] But as Navasky laid out in a profile for the *Atlantic*, Ferry was also a peacenik—he eventually left the Democrats over Vietnam—as well as a leading player in a radical California think tank, and an unusually user-friendly philanthropist. Arthur Waskow remembers how, "if you wrote him a letter saying you had a project in mind, and it would cost the following amount, you would get a letter back within a week, saying either yes—and a check!—or no."[48]

Ferry was also, like Lewin, a satirist. He would advocate the abolition of the stock exchange and the televising of executions with a straight face, then watch as his furious opponents tied themselves in knots. He pointed up the underlying logic of deterrence by suggesting that the leaders of the USA and the USSR agree that before they fired any nuclear weapons, they personally "murder fifty children."[49] Around the time of Lewin's first encounter with him, Ferry wrote a paper attacking the political "apparatus," and the way that "we need an enemy—not just any old enemy, but one who is sinister, conspiring, terroristic, atheistic, power-hungry, monolithic, anti-human and un-human,"[50] which he contended the U.S. media had helped to "fabricate."[51]

When Ferry's friend John Kenneth Galbraith joked in his pseudonymous review of *Report from Iron Mountain* that he'd been asked to contribute, it was almost true. As a contact of Navasky's, Galbraith seems to have been in touch with the *Monocle* team direct, rather than with Lewin. He was equally at home playing insider and outsider: perfectly placed to help give the *Report* credibility. He had not only taught Kennedy, as Ferry had; he'd run price controls for the Roosevelt administration. Yet he was also a sardonic critic.

His 1958 book *The Affluent Society* had delivered an influential, bestselling critique of how postwar America had been bent out of shape by advertising. His sharp satires for *Esquire* had punctured the pomposity of the famous. And lately, he'd turned his fire on Johnson's war. The journalist Raymond Heard attended Galbraith's standing-room-only lectures, peppered with one-liners, and was struck by the contrast with another soon-to-be-famous Harvard professor. Henry Kissinger's classes were "frightening . . . ruthless, factual and totally without humor."[52]

The economic argument of *Report from Iron Mountain* might have come straight from the book Galbraith was completing. As mentioned in Chapter 2, *The New Industrial State* criticized the cozy bond between the Pentagon and its huge military contractors, invoking Eisenhower's attack on the military-industrial complex. Galbraith even argued that U.S. foreign policy was "based on an imagery that derives in part from the needs of the industrial system."[53] He saw arms spending merely as part of the overall need for "a large public sector" in "the stabilization of aggregate demand." But, he argued, this reached "its highest state of development in conjunction with modern military procurement."[54] This was because "weapons competition" had "been the area where the largest amount of money to support planning was available with the fewest questions asked."[55]

Through the summer Lewin continued to struggle with the book, eventually rewriting the whole thing in a new format—just the report and the introductory material that set up the story of the call from Washington, the professor, and the Special Study Group. Meanwhile, he had another kind of draft to wrestle with: his son, Mike, was trying to free himself from the state's demand that he "go and try and kill strangers."[56] Mike applied to be a conscientious objector. Lewin found him a lawyer: his friend Leonard Boudin, a renowned left-wing civil liberties attorney who'd once represented members of the Fair Play for Cuba Committee. Lewin took his son to meet Boudin, as Mike remembers, "to try to keep me from going to Vietnam or to Canada or to jail."[57]

At last, Lewin sent a version of the hoax manuscript to Doctorow,

Navasky, and the others. He finally seemed upbeat, confiding to his journal in late October that it had been like "no other job I've done."[58] While he prepared to rewrite, he attended an American Management Association seminar about behavioral research, which gave him a "glimpse of the future."[59] One of the speakers was from General Electric; it reminded Lewin of Kurt Vonnegut's dystopian novel *Player Piano*, which drew on the author's time at GE to sketch a near-future America ruled by technocrats. Lewin felt that what he heard at the seminar confirmed how he was taking current trends to their logical conclusions in *Iron Mountain*.

Throughout the writing process, Lewin would go "on and on" to his daughter, Julie, about how, whatever the think tanks claimed, there was "no such thing as amoral thinking."[60] That, as much as anything, seems to have driven him on, through all the difficulties of the writing. In April 1967, he finished the new version. A few days later, he went to a conference at a college in the Bronx, "Education for Peace." And there he heard a speech by, of all people, Herman Kahn—who told his audience that the "saturation bombing of Viet Nam is exclusively an 'instrumental' question, not a moral one."[61] The question now was whether Lewin's prodigious efforts to satirize this mentality would have the slightest impact.

———

Finally, the book was announced, the White House flew into a tizzy, and the media went ballistic. Anne Navasky "didn't know anybody who would be on the front page of the *New York Times*"; now she discovered that she'd just married someone whose cunning plan had accomplished something even more delicious. Victor had landed his hoax story on page one, while he himself stayed out of sight. Anne had kept the secret from the beginning. Even so, when her brother, who was away in Brazil with the Peace Corps, emerged from the rainforest and read of the book in *Time*, he wrote to say that he suspected Victor's hand at work behind the story. She remembers Victor himself saying he knew people in the Johnson administration who were "terrified to say anything about it, because they didn't know—maybe the Kennedy administration *had* done that."[62]

An astonished Leonard Lewin watched as his creation shot straight onto the *New York Times* top ten bestseller list. The shops ran out of copies. He recorded how an anti-war professor at City College was convinced *Iron Mountain* was real, no matter that a colleague told her it really wasn't—that the writer had links with *Monocle*. A third professor confided that he'd assigned it to students, most of whom thought the author must be Galbraith, because of his review in "Book World." The professor thought so, too. A friend called to recount a story from a bookstore at Cornell University in upstate New York. A student, hunting for a copy, had been directed to a display table, not realizing it had sold out again. The student was "frantic," saying he had to have it "by Friday!" The saleswoman told him it was a hoax: "Terrible thing for [a] man to do." The student shot back: "but doesn't it say important things?"[63]

Lewin was whisked off on a publicity tour, including a visit to England. He "really loved" doing this, his son, Michael, remembers—despite having to pretend that he didn't write the incendiary report in his surprise bestseller, or at least having to dodge the question. At one point he came back from a series of radio interviews, proudly declaring that, technically at least, he had "never lied."[64] A recording of one of these survives, from a public station in New York called WRVR. When the host asks Lewin about challenges to the authorship of the *Report*, he replies:

I am no longer offended by them. I've obviously been hearing them for several months. I'll say the following. I think the whole question of whodunit? is really not terribly important, except if you read the introduction of the book carefully . . . you will realize that if the book is authentic, and is exactly what it says it is, I cannot conceivably prove it, unless a member of the Special Study Group is willing to step forward. On the other hand, the people who are so certain that it is a hoax or a satire and who have been so quoted—like Mr. Rostow, for example, of the National Security Council—cannot prove the contrary either.

So I would rather skip this part of the discussion. I will say in general, though, although it is unprovable at this point either way, that the *Report* at any rate is fundamentally authentic—and I think most reviewers, even those who have assumed it to be a hoax, have agreed to this. It is authentic in what it represents.[65]

The host readily agreed, remarking later in the interview that "I don't accept the fact that this is a real report, but it doesn't really matter." He thought it showed "the depth to which the society has sunk that something like this is published . . . without being rejected offhand as being the product of someone's imagination." It was, he told listeners, "the one book which seems to me to sum up the age in which we live more than anything else I could possibly recommend."[66]

For Lewin's daughter, Julie, who lived near Columbia University, "It was great." She recalls that her father "was a real celebrity in certain circles."[67] *Report from Iron Mountain* seems to have had a particular impact on the younger generation, for a fairly obvious reason. In his piece on the *Report* and its implications, Raymond Heard highlighted its line that war was a "generational stabilizer" which "enables the physically deteriorating older generation to maintain control of the younger, destroying it if necessary."[68] This, Heard remembers, was "very much" the feeling at the time. *Iron Mountain* confirmed the views of younger people—that the war in Vietnam was being fought for the military-industrial complex.[69] When it came out, Heard wrote that the *Report* raised "awesome moral questions which no society had the guts to face until now"—regardless of whether it was genuine.[70]

At Stanford University, an English student named Jeremy Baker picked up what Lewin was driving at. In a long article for the *Stanford Daily Magazine*, he argued that the *Report* revealed the fraudulence of systems analysis' claims to be value-free. But, as he remembers today, the view from Stanford was very different from the radical militancy across the bay in Berkeley. Stanford was focused on designing the future; what *Iron Mountain* exposed was that it was the older generation's hopeless incompetence at using new systems that was sending so many young men to pointless deaths. Once in charge of those systems, the younger generation would do far better. Reading his article now, Baker says the "general air of superiority" made him "cringe."[71] Nonetheless, his article grasped the hubris that Lewin was trying to expose. It pointedly quotes a fantasy speech written for President Johnson by an English writer, in which Johnson would admit that "There is no such thing as control over Southeast Asia"; that he could not even "transform the slums within a five-mile radius of the White House."[72]

The generational divide over *Monocle*'s hoax and its implications is captured neatly in a documentary shot in the place where, in a way, it had its origins: Yale. In early December, the governor of California spent a few days at the university as a Chubb Fellow. Between the blue walls of the billiard room at St. Anthony Hall literary society, Ronald Reagan was grilled by students about Vietnam and the military-industrial complex, while two other students played billiards right behind him. When one of his interlocutors suggested the defense companies are "making money off the war," Reagan said "by and large the American industrial complex stands to do far better in the peacetime economy than they do in war." A second asked, to nervous laughter, "Have you read the *Report from Iron Mountain on the Possibility and Desirability of Peace?*" Reagan said he had not. Starting to sound like Kennedy, he pointed out that there was a long-standing myth "of the munition makers who are out pulling strings to create a war." The student backed off somewhat—"I wouldn't say that."

But no sooner had Reagan lanced one myth than he pumped up another one, insisting that reports he'd been hearing from Vietnam had a new "confidence and an air of 'we're doing alright.'"[73]

---

*Report from Iron Mountain* was hardly the only satirical attack on Johnson and the war machine. Once you looked, they were everywhere. Since the larky hilarity of the early sixties, satire had become harder and darker as the war got worse. Satirists were less bothered about being funny, more about having an effect. This was no longer the world of Nichols and May or *Beyond the Fringe*. Dick Gregory was running to be mayor of Chicago, and not just as a put-on reminiscent of Marvin Kitman's running for president. Gregory took to fasting for peace, and poured his time and money into the civil rights struggle; he was beaten, shot at, jailed "for parading without a permit."[74] Mort Sahl, meanwhile, was quoting the anti-Vietnam slogan "War Is a Basic Industry—Invest Your Son."[75] The playwright-cartoonist Jules Feiffer was increasingly driven to attack what he saw as politicians' lies, madness, and self-delusion by "logically extending a premise to its totally insane conclusion, thus forcing onto an audience . . . unwelcome awareness."[76] The breakthrough that made all this possible had come in 1964, with the movie *Dr. Strangelove* and its groundbreaking depiction of the men controlling America's nuclear weapons as variously incompetent, evil, and crazy. At first, its cowriter and director Stanley Kubrick had discarded story ideas on the basis that people would simply laugh at them—until he realized that those "were the things which were most truthful."[77] As one critic later noted, after *Strangelove*, "no office or ideal of the U.S. establishment would ever again be considered off-limits to satire."[78]

This was a revival of a long, aggressively democratic tradition in America, as Lewin knew better than most. Right from the start of the *Iron Mountain* project, Navasky had in mind the model of Mark Twain. One of the samples of Twain's work that Lewin included in his *Treasury of American Political Humor* shows why. "To the Person Sitting in Darkness" is a ferocious attack, published in 1901, on American imperialism in east Asia, and on the grasping, canting, self-righteous missionaries who fronted for it. Twain imagines the confusion of the supposedly benighted Asian of the title, trying to reconcile America's claims to virtue with its bloodthirsty, treacherous behavior. It skewered a moment when the United States's power was suddenly expanding and the country was having to decide what to do with it. Which of course is what had been happening again, far more spectacularly, in the wake of the Second World War.

*Dr. Strangelove* had managed to match Twain; others were trying to have an impact, too. In February 1963, an academic journal published an unusual article by a scholar in Hawaii. "On Serving Your Fellow Man" was a reasoned argument for accepting that postnuclear shelters would inevitably run short of food, and that planning for "orderly cannibalism" in advance was essential. Advertisers should start promoting human flesh right away. *Not* to take such steps risked "convincing the Soviets that we really do not intend to use our nuclear capability," which was "positively to invite attack."[79] This echoed Herman Kahn's arguments for building such shelters with unnerving precision. The following year, a magazine called *Fact* asked psychiatrists to offer their professional judgment on whether the Republican candidate Barry Goldwater was psychologically fit for the presidency.

Young theater companies experimented with ways to break through audiences' complacency, with varying success. While he was writing *Iron Mountain*, Lewin went to see shows like *Viet Rock*, a musical that ended with the actors going out into the audience and "confronting and touching individuals." According to the playscript's introduction, "This final gesture throws the problems of the war, its cruelty, inanity, horror, and political shortsightedness directly at the audience."[80] Or it may simply have been embarrassing. The most successful of these experiments in activist theater was a parody of Shakespeare's *Macbeth* called *MacBird!* This was a New Leftish take on Johnson, Vietnam, and the Kennedy assassination. The play was so controversial that it had to be staged at the Village Gate, normally a music and comedy venue, because nowhere else would take it. The witches were a Black Muslim, a beatnik, and an Old Leftist worker; the ingredients they tossed into their cauldron included "gore of gook" and "sizzling skin of napalmed child."[81]

Yet Richard Goodwin, who'd fled the Johnson administration and had himself been satirizing it in the *New Yorker*, was struck by the "contrasting attitudes toward power in *MacBird!*, and in the Shakespearean plays of which it is a pastiche." *MacBird!* was resigned to a "deepening disgust with political life itself."[82] Which, Goodwin felt, was all too prevalent a feeling in America in 1967.

————

*Report from Iron Mountain* was not just a satire. It was also a hoax. Here, too, it was tugging on a long American tradition. A strand of that tradition was the kind of hoax text that exposes something about how those who swallow it think. Alongside Twain, Navasky had had in mind the provocations perpetrated by the Baltimore journalist and satirist H. L. Mencken. In particular, a piece Mencken wrote in 1917, in which he insisted that the bathtub had only been introduced into the United States in the mid-nineteenth century, in the teeth of fierce opposition. Mencken was despairingly surprised that so many people took this seriously, despite his repeated emphasis that he'd made it all up. That same year, the Russian Revolution erupted, and soon afterward word reached America that the Bolsheviks were nationalizing women: making them the property of the state and declaring them sexually available to men under certain regulations. U.S. politicians and newspapers trumpeted the terrifying news. But this unlikely scare story began in part as an anti-regime skit in a Moscow newspaper.

While Lewin was crafting *Iron Mountain*, an obscene example of the form was perpetrated by a magazine called the *Realist*, which specialized in this kind of thing. When the magazine's editorial team heard that Jackie Kennedy had insisted on the removal of sections of William Manchester's book *The Death of a President*, they saw their chance. In May 1967, they printed what they claimed was one of the censored sections. It purports to describe how, on the presidential plane returning to Washington after the assassination, Lyndon Johnson did something unrepeatable to the bullet hole in Kennedy's throat. According to the magazine's editor, people were convinced by this, "if only for a moment." He claimed "the imagery was so shocking, it broke through the notion that the war in Vietnam was being conducted by sane men."[83]

Maybe. At least, like *Iron Mountain*, such hoaxes weren't intended to *permanently* deceive—unlike another tradition: the hoax as propaganda. In December 1863, for example, a pamphlet appeared that was entitled *Miscegenation: The Theory of the Blending of the Races, Applied to American*

*White and Negro*. This was supposedly an honest argument for the benefits of race mixing. In fact, it was concocted to smear Lincoln's administration by purporting to prove that it supported the idea. Lincoln won the election, but the ugly term "miscegenation," which had been invented for the pamphlet, entered the language. During the California gubernatorial election in 1934, the chiefs of the MGM film studio were so horrified at the idea that the Democrats' socialist candidate might win that they apparently had producers concoct fake interviews, which were intercut with real ones and presented as "California Election News."

While *Report from Iron Mountain* was, in part, an anti–Vietnam War book with concealed origins, a pro–Vietnam War book that presented fiction as fact had actually appeared years before. In 1956, a youthfully idealistic U.S. Navy doctor, Thomas A. Dooley, published a runaway bestseller called *Deliver Us from Evil*. This was the stirring story of Dooley's drive to rescue innocent Vietnamese Catholics who were fleeing the depredations of monstrous communist guerrillas—winning hearts, minds, and the Cold War with kindness. The problem was that Dooley's lurid stories were fiction. The book's editor later insisted that its mythmaking was fair: after all, it had "the essence of truth."[84] Where *Iron Mountain* concealed its true identity, for a time, to give readers a satirical jolt, the Dooley enterprise sought to fool people permanently.

Just as his own hoax was being launched on the world, Lewin was reading about one of the most famous modern cases: Orson Welles's October 1938 radio dramatization of H. G. Wells's *The War of the Worlds*, presented in the style of a news report of a Martian invasion of New Jersey. Lewin noted how Welles had deliberately dragged out the early part of the show before springing his surprise—Martian attack. Welles had no real intention of convincing the public the aliens were coming; nevertheless, the production quickly became famous as a "hoax" because it supposedly caused mass panic along the Eastern Seaboard. But as the cultural theorist Charles Acland has pointed out, this is something of a myth. The audience research survey on which the "mass panic" story is largely founded "did not allow for the possibility that listeners might have been aware that they were listening to a play and yet were frightened at the same time."[85] In other words, the researchers assumed that their fellow Americans could not tell the difference between fact and fiction. The question for Lewin now was whether *Iron Mountain*—which really *was* a hoax—could lure people across that line.

---

Pulling this off was more of a close-run thing than it looked. John Leo of the *New York Times* came close to outing Lewin; the conspirators debated whether to feed him red herrings, telling him it was Galbraith, or Rostow, or Secretary of State Dean Rusk. The *Times* wasn't happy about having been taken in by a publicity stunt. Leo ran into Navasky at a party and snapped that he wouldn't "be a shill for your friend's book" anymore.[86] Meanwhile, Howard Junker, the young journalist at *Newsweek* who wrote the article talking about how the *Report* had triggered "megatons of speculation," remembers that his boss told him, "This is a hoax, but just try to take it seriously. Because it's getting a lot of attention and somebody has to do it."[87]

When Johnny Carson's *Tonight Show* wanted someone to come and be interviewed about the book, *Esquire* editor Harold Hayes suggested sending a man in a mask, presumably to masquerade as Lewin's mysterious professor. But then Hayes threatened to sue Dial and Lewin's literary agency, William Morris, for $150,000, the equivalent of more than $1.3 million today. Why? Had Dial hoaxed him, too? Had he unwittingly paid them handsomely for a twenty-thousand-word spoof? A pair of contracts that survive in Hayes's papers holds a clue. These were sent by Lewin's ferocious young agent, Lois Wallace. They were based on a meeting she'd attended on July 27, 1967, with Hayes, Baron, Doctorow, and Navasky.

This meeting—particularly the fact that Navasky was present—suggests that Hayes was in on the hoax. So why was he threatening to sue? The contracts reveal that for first publication rights on *Iron Mountain*, *Esquire* would pay $3,500 (just over $30,000 today); its condensed version would appear in the Christmas issue, which would hit newsstands on November 9. The book would then come out three weeks later, and Dial would ask bookstores not to put it on sale ahead of the official publication date—but if Dial made that request, some bookstores simply ignored it.[88] At some point, these were sent to Hayes with a note from one of his staff: "Here's Leonard Lewin's contract in the event you would like to contemplate it for a bit. . . ."[89]

So it seems more likely that the dispute that provoked the threat of a suit was over the fact that the book had found its way into the shops too early, allowing consumers to simply buy the book rather than head to their local newsstand to pick up a copy of *Esquire*. If the magazine's exclusivity had been compromised, Hayes perhaps had a legitimate grievance. Either way, it appears he was in on the hoax and happy to serve it up to his readers. Perhaps *Esquire*'s faithful were meant to realize that it was all part of the magazine's knowing, side-eye style. After all, this was the magazine that was known for factual writing that was written like fiction; here was a fiction written like fact.

Either way, the row triggered frantic phone calls; Lewin was desperate for Baron and Doctorow to settle their differences with Hayes. Lois Wallace, furious, threatened to sue his publisher. But with the *Times* threatening to break the story of the *Esquire* lawsuit, Baron and Doctorow seemed to think it was good publicity.

Amid the hullabaloo, Navasky was demanding they stage a press conference to hold off a story in *Time*, and Lewin was fielding no-nonsense phone calls from Warren Boroson, formerly of *Fact* magazine but now editor of a high-minded anti-war journal called *Trans-action*. Its guiding intellectual spirit was that Mills enthusiast, Irving Louis Horowitz. He was convinced the *Report* was real—despite the fact some suspected him of writing it—and he wanted to devote a forthcoming edition of the magazine to it. But Boroson was a tough muckraking journalist who'd recently weathered a lawsuit brought by Senator Goldwater over that article asking psychiatrists if they thought he was nuts. So Boroson was having none of it. He kept calling Lewin, demanding to know if the *Report* was real, saying "Come on, now" over and over. Rather than a genuine report, he thought it was "C. Wright Mills stuff, but better written."[90] Boroson managed to stop Horowitz from making a fool of himself.

It would be utterly impossible today, but none of this found its way into the public domain. The journalist who interviewed Kahn after the television visualization of the *Report* confided to Lewin that he personally thought it was a hoax. But the show presented it to the public, except for a couple of brief comments, as though it was real. Finally, journalists began to work out that it was likely that Lewin had concocted the Study Group and its findings, but they still didn't know the full story.

On December 1, after a month of this speculation and media pressure, the conspirators headed to West 55th Street to celebrate pulling off their hoax. The threat of the *Esquire* suit still hung over them, but they'd generated enough belief in the *Report* for the uncertainty to stir up a frenzy of debate. Lewin, Navasky, Doctorow, and Baron gathered for a "very jolly" lunch at one of Manhattan's bastions of French haute cuisine, La Côte Basque— the setting for a crucial part of Truman Capote's unfinished last novel, a disastrously self-destructive mélange of fact and fiction. The hoaxers talked about the fourth print run (the book had officially been out for barely a day), and the possibility of a Pulitzer Prize. Lewin's diary for these weeks has none of his old glumness. Instead, he was working on a movie treatment, and delightedly recording all the reports friends sent him of the high demand for his creation. Better yet, Doctorow was offering him new projects.

---

*Trans-action* magazine did eventually devote most of an edition to the *Report*, recruiting a platoon of social scientists to debate its themes and how well it tackled them, and to wrestle with the notion that it might be a satire. Strikingly, several argued that in the end it didn't matter whether the *Report* was genuine or fake, because it was making an important point.

On a visit to London to launch *Iron Mountain* in the UK, Lewin suggested its impact was a direct consequence of government deceit, explaining that ordinary Americans "are fed up with lies, endless lies: they feel the need for discussion, something to grab hold of."[91] He still wouldn't divulge the real author of the Study Group's conclusions. But one of the other conspirators, John Kenneth Galbraith, was in England too, and finally admitted his involvement, saying he didn't want to take a good joke too far. He confessed to the *Times* of London that he was "a member of the conspiracy."[92]

In the years that followed, Lewin's book was translated into fifteen languages—and academic seminars and journals continued to debate it. There are people who remember its being assigned as required reading for students. In Richard Lingeman's view, *Report from Iron Mountain* was like Swift's "A Modest Proposal," both in the brilliance of its satire and its impact.[93] But why had it had such an impact on Americans, and why, in later years, would it provoke ever-growing curiosity, even obsession? It was not just because of Vietnam. To answer that question, we need to find our way back to Iron Mountain itself, as it was in 1966.

# 4

# IRON MOUNTAIN

The Amtrak service from Penn Station north into Westchester County and beyond is not exactly a bullet train, but it takes the traveler into the past at surprising speed. For much of the journey, the line follows the east bank of the Hudson River. Even before the railroad came, this was the trade route to the Great Lakes, and to Canada, and the scenery still looks much as it did then: the cliffs across the wide water, the gentle hills beyond, the endless trees.

During the Revolutionary War, controlling this terrain became a crucial objective. A couple of miles past Croton-on-Hudson, you might catch a glimpse, on the far bank, of Stony Point. Here, George Washington orchestrated a surprise attack by night, to force British troops to retreat toward New York. Further north, across the river from Rhinecliff station, lies Kingston, where the British forced local militias to flee, then set the town on fire. Just before the train arrives at Hudson, around 110 miles north of New York City in Columbia County, it passes the spot where those same soldiers torched the mansion of a landowner for siding with the patriots.

Driving out of town, through wooded valleys, past solitary clapboard houses, the blue-black mountains in the distance, what's most striking is how quiet it all is. Peace has lasted here for a long time. Signs invite passing motorists to pick their own apples and pumpkins; the landscape around here is an agricultural patchwork. This is what the United States of America was meant to be: a republic of small farmers.

After about half an hour, on the right side of County Route 10, there is an orchard sloping down the hill, behind a wire fence. Opposite, off on the left, there's a narrow side road, which snakes past a sign saying "RESTRICTED AREA—WARNING—KEEP OUT,"[1] and then disappears into the trees. Satellite photographs show that, out of sight of the highway, the road runs up to a small white building. It appears to have been built right into the landscape.

———————

Iron Mountain is as old as the United States. From the eighteenth century, the site was an iron mine; during the Civil War, its ore was used for cannonballs. In the 1930s and 1940s, it was a mushroom farm. But during the Korean War, under the shadow of the Bomb, its owner saw an opportunity and began the long process of transforming it into first a vault, then something more extraordinary. In 1966, no doubt keen to show off his creation, he allowed journalists to visit. The *Wall Street Journal* ran the story on the front page. Its reporter was able to reveal that, somewhere near Hudson, "a mammoth corporate bunker lies hidden in the hollowed-out core of Iron Mountain—protected from blast, heat, and radiation by countless tons of rock, soil, and iron ore. A 28-ton steel door in the mountainside swings open. . . ."[2]

In its segment on *Report from Iron Mountain*, *Public Broadcast Laboratory* showed eerie footage from inside the bunker. The camera retreats backward down an empty white passageway, past a series of black doors, leaving the outside world farther and farther behind. For most of its seven hundred customers, these corridors just housed a document store, but for a few they led to luxurious corporate hideouts, ready in case, one day, the great fear of the age exploded into reality. As the *Journal* noted, "New York, 115 miles to the south, could be incinerated but Iron Mountain offers protection against all but a near-direct hit by a multi-megaton weapon."[3]

The bunker of the Standard Oil Company of New Jersey was reached via an elevator that was built into the rock at 45 degrees; deep beneath the surface, its three floors of facilities were ready to accommodate ninety executives and their loved ones. The visitor wandered "through offices, kitchens, dormitories, communications facilities";[4] there were medical services, a generator, a well. In one room, a nuclear family could relax on a "red-and-gold couch" and listen to music,[5] or if the mood took them, there was a recreation room for watching movies—though presumably not *Dr. Strangelove*. At some point, the bunker acquired a wall-size map displaying the company's global reach and, in the dining room, some chandeliers.[6] The reporter from the *Boston Globe* thought the entrance to Shell Oil's complex resembled "that of a night club. Overhead one can see the bare rock, and on one side there is a planting of exotic but artificial shrubs, illuminated with red and green spotlights."[7] Inside, there were "yellow desks with stylish wooden tops"[8] in a lemon-colored operations room. And "chintz curtains on windows that are not there."[9] The third bunker belonged to a bank, Manufacturers Hanover Trust, which had recently run a highly successful exercise there, testing its capacity to reconstruct part of the business after a notional nuclear attack.

All three nodes of the power elite—business, government, military— had underground nuclear bunkers like this: a literal deep state in waiting. This was surely one reason Lewin chose Iron Mountain as the location for his satire. Navasky's original idea of a fake report was prompted by Vietnam, but Lewin wanted to broaden the target area to encompass the whole Cold War mentality, which this place captured perfectly.

The *Wall Street Journal* report on the Iron Mountain bunkers, published just as Lewin was mulling the hoax assignment, revealed that most of the top five hundred U.S. corporations had an alternative headquarters. The American Telephone and Telegraph Company (AT&T), for instance, maintained a brace of bunkers, one on each side of the Hudson. "Key personnel" reportedly carried "wallet-sized maps and alert plans showing escape routes" to help them get there from a stricken New York City.[10]

The military leadership, meanwhile, would retreat to what *Life* magazine called the "alternative Pentagon":[11] the caverns of the Raven Rock Mountain Complex in Pennsylvania. The Strategic Air Command would try to win the third world war from its huge complex under Offutt Air Force Base near Omaha, Nebraska. And as Lewin agreed to accept the project the New York *Daily News* was reporting that North American Air Defense Command had just opened its new nerve center in Colorado: "a grid of tunnels burrowed into Cheyenne Mountain—more startling than the props for the movie 'Dr. Strangelove.'"[12]

The locations that would shelter political leaders were a more closely guarded secret: Congress's hideout in West Virginia wasn't revealed until 1992. But in May 1966, a journalist visiting the Blue Ridge Mountains in Virginia picked up rumors that an old weather station had been transformed into "a huge underground redoubt, one of several of its kind in the Appalachians to which a part of the government would repair in the event of a nuclear attack."[13]

This was all very impressive, but there was an elephant in the bunker. In his mock review of *Iron Mountain*, Galbraith claimed that he "knew the place well," because it was where he'd helped a bank decide which of its executives would be protected in the event of a nuclear strike. He was jabbing at a sore point among the staff of these companies. Who among them did their bosses think was worth saving from the bombs?

————

Iron Mountain embodied the change that drove America mad—the change Lewin set out to skewer. The republic of small farmers had emerged from the Second World War as a huge, omnipotent superpower: an iron mountain, casting its shadow far across the earth. America was no longer rebelling against the mightiest nation in the world. It *was* the mightiest nation in the world. But what did that mean for ordinary Americans?

It is striking how many reviewers compared *Report from Iron Mountain* to George Orwell's *Nineteen Eighty-Four*.[14] The news anchor Walter

Cronkite, for instance, opened a segment on CBS Radio by invoking Orwell's novel about an "all-powerful state" that declared that "War is Peace." He even suggested Lewin's work might "take its place" alongside *Nineteen Eighty-Four*.[15] This comparison might seem rather off the mark. Surely Orwell's primary target was Stalin's Soviet Union, whereas Lewin's was Johnson's America? But look closer, and the similarities are right there.

Both books are deeply worried about centralized, militarized state power, and the ways in which it uses permanent war to maintain economic stability and political control. Both books worry that this will be normalized by gutting words of their meanings and by manipulating the population through stoking terror of the "enemy." Both fear for the fate of the little guy in the face of the big state. This calls to mind C. Wright Mills's fears in *The Power Elite* and *The Causes of World War Three*. None of this is a coincidence. Orwell was writing fiction, whereas Mills was writing nonfiction—and Lewin was writing fiction masquerading as nonfiction. Nonetheless, all three were responding to the same basic nightmare: the concentration of power in the hands of America's warfare state, as revealed by the dropping of the atomic bomb in August 1945.

Within three months of the U.S. Army Air Force's destruction of Hiroshima and Nagasaki, Orwell published an essay that set out how he feared this development could upend democracy. It was called "You and the Atom Bomb." He argued that "when the dominant weapon is cheap and simple, the common people have a chance. . . . The great age of democracy and national self-determination was the age of the musket and the rifle." The "combination of qualities" of the flintlock musket, he wrote, "made possible the success of the American and French revolutions."[16]

In the shadow of the mushroom cloud, Orwell feared that "ages in which the dominant weapon is expensive or difficult to make will tend to be ages of despotism." With the advent of the Bomb, everything might be about to change: "we have before us the prospect of two or three monstrous superstates, each possessed of a weapon by which millions of people can be wiped out in a few seconds, dividing the world between them." Instead of fighting "bigger and bloodier wars," they may agree not to use it, which will mean that "power is concentrated in still fewer hands and that the outlook for subject peoples and oppressed classes is still more hopeless."[17]

Lewin was thinking along similar lines. In one radio interview, he said he was tired of the euphemistic term "Defense Department"—he preferred "War Department"—which was a very Orwell-esque observation. He argued that this deceitful use of language sprang from that shift in weapons technology Orwell had identified:

> The biggest euphemisms of all, I think, are predicated on modern technology in the sense that the most appalling kinds of murder are committed by perfectly decent people who just push buttons. In the old-fashioned days of war there was this much to be said for the cruel professional killer who killed at the end of a bayonet—he had to have the courage required by the full knowledge of what he was doing because he could see it.[18]

In *The Power Elite*, Mills expressed much the same feeling, pointing out that in the Civil War, a general "did not earn the respect of his men by logistical planning in the Pentagon; he earned it by better shooting, harder riding, faster improvisation when in trouble.[19]

Even by 1945, that was long gone. In "You and the Atom Bomb," Orwell drew on *The Managerial Revolution*, a controversial 1941 book by an American writer named James Burnham, to argue that the future would be ruled by a new class of technocrats. He also took from Burnham the idea that these new elites would carve the world into super-states: that "the surface of the earth is being parceled off into three great empires . . . each ruled, under one disguise or another, by a self-elected oligarchy." Each will be "at once unconquerable and in a permanent state of 'cold war' with its neighbors."[20] This became the world of *Nineteen Eighty-Four*, in which the tiny elites ruling Oceania, Eurasia, and Eastasia agree not to use atom bombs, but instead maintain permanent low-level war to keep themselves perpetually in dictatorial control.

*Report from Iron Mountain* hints at the relevance of the novel to Johnson's America, where nearly half a million young men had been forced into the military by the state. In the section floating slavery as a way of controlling society's potential enemies, the *Report* suggests that "the fantasies projected in . . . *1984* have seemed less and less implausible over the years since [its] publication."[21]

Meanwhile, James Burnham, that pioneering cold warrior whose cynical geopolitics were satirized in *Nineteen Eighty-Four*, was still very much alive in 1967—and read *Report from Iron Mountain* with some enthusiasm. True, in his piece about it in the *National Review*, he wondered whether it might be a "psywar ploy"—or indeed a hoax. Nonetheless, he concluded that "on its merits, *Report from Iron Mountain* is certainly worth reading. . . . You can read it in an hour, but you'll be thinking about it a good deal longer."[22] Unlike most reviewers, he wasn't noticeably horrified by the premise that war is the basic engine of society. But then again, he did write a weekly column in the *National Review* called The Third World War. And in the late 1940s he'd advocated dropping atom bombs on the Soviets before they had a chance to develop their own. The *Report* was an attack on exactly the kind of performatively hard-nosed, amoral, come-what-may analysis Burnham had long made his own, but he appears not to have noticed. In his diary, Lewin wrote: "*National Review* interesting—places 'conservatives' where we said they were. Nihilist."[23]

The *Report* had other roots in the hopes and fears that emerged in America in the wake of the Second World War. One of the arguments it makes for the undesirability of peace is that the "elimination of war implies the inevitable elimination of national sovereignty and the traditional nation-state."[24] The implication is that we would end up in a one-world state. To some, the creation of the United Nations in San Francisco in 1945 promised to begin the realization of a dream—a benign world government overseeing a peaceful planet. United Nations enthusiasts included not only "many of the early anti-nuclear activists"[25] but people like the young John F. Kennedy, the then-liberal Ronald Reagan, and Orson Welles, who in the months after the war poured much of his boundless energy into advocating for the UN and world peace. To others, however, like General Edwin Walker and the John Birch Society, all these liberal one-world dreams stirred old conspiracist nightmares of global domination.

———————

As Iron Mountain's own past suggests, the *Report*'s fear of centralized, militaristic power sounded echoes deep in American history—much deeper than the 1940s. The United States was founded in the 1770s, when the colonies' small farmers joined George Washington's revolutionary army to overthrow the increasingly coercive British Empire. In May 1774, the British Parliament voted to impose a series of "Intolerable Acts" on the colonies, and put a rebellious Massachusetts under the rule of a royally appointed governor. As a British general set about trying to suppress colonial dissent, the Virginian radical Thomas Jefferson wrote that British actions "prove a deliberate, systematical plan of reducing us to slavery,"[26] despite the fact he owned enslaved people himself. Other revolutionary leaders were talking in similar terms. Two years later, in the Declaration of Independence, Jefferson wrote that the colonists had suffered "repeated injuries and usurpations" at the hands of the British. This was evidence of a plot by King George III, to establish "an absolute Tyranny over these States." As the literary scholar Edwin Gittleman wrote, by the end of the Declaration, King George stands accused of "conspiracy, harassment, obstruction of justice, theft, arson, kidnapping, murder, and high treason."[27] But as some American historians have long argued, "George III was not the would-be tyrant of tradition."[28] Power lay with Parliament, not the monarch, and Parliament's desperate attempts to assert authority over the colonists, however oppressive, were not a scheme for permanent despotism or slavery. The claim that George was plotting to impose "absolute Tyranny" on America was crucial to justifying the revolution, but it had something in common with conspiracy theory.

This thinking was not unique to America. As the historian Bernard

Bailyn has charted, the colonists' fears had deep roots in British political nightmares of standing armies and arbitrary power. More immediately, they were influenced by British pamphleteers' attacks on the corruption and co-erciveness of the London government. (And once the American Revolution began, some of its opponents in Britain were convinced it was being stirred up by "secret emissaries" sent by the French.)[29]

Nonetheless, Americans' fear of tyranny did not disappear with the de-parture of the British. It was refocused on what powers should be granted to the new federal government. And, as Mills put it, the Constitution was "con-structed in fear of a powerful military establishment."[30] America's founding wariness of would-be tyrants and their schemes has lasted ever since, ready to react to signs of a new concentration of power, whether in the hands of government, business, or the military. During the Civil War, President Lin-coln declared that enslaved Americans were free. His assassin was so angry at what had been done to the proslavery states, and talk of giving formerly en-slaved people the vote, that he shot Lincoln while shouting about tyrants. As part of postwar Reconstruction, the Fourteenth Amendment transformed the Constitution by guaranteeing the rights of those newly emancipated citizens; to gain readmittance to the Union, the ex-Confederate states were forced to ratify it. Yet the notion that the federal government was a tyranny remained relatively fringe; conspiracy theorists tended to target immigrants, Catholics, and secret societies. For decades after the Civil War, frightening new concentrations of power were much more visible in the economy.

In the 1860s, Iron Mountain was home to a small, private business, exca-vating iron for cannonballs. By the 1960s, it was one of the places where the elite would, if necessary, wait out the destruction of ordinary people—and the company with the biggest bunker embodied what had changed. In 1870 Standard Oil had been forged by John D. Rockefeller, who ruthlessly over-powered and absorbed his competitors until he'd built one of the first truly gigantic corporations. He could do this because, with the coming of the rail-road, America's local economies were being corralled into one vast national network. This offered staggering prizes to those who were ruthless and clever enough to exploit the huge, high-stakes new economy to pick off their competitors and seize monopolies of vital resources. Rockefeller's fellow robber baron Andrew Carnegie built his gigantic steel company by similar methods. (In 1966, like Standard Oil, U.S. Steel executives had a bunker waiting: a ninety-acre facility built in "an abandoned limestone mine north of Pittsburgh."[31])

Rockefeller's America was no country for little men and women: "an enormous variety of family businesses" were appropriated or driven to the wall, as banks and big business boomed.[32] The republic of small farmers—and independent storekeepers, artisans, and tradesmen—became a kingdom of often exploitative wage labor. The booming economy was hungry for migrant workers, too. As industry and the economy expanded, the cities—and their slums—ballooned. People began to worry that the whole way America was meant to work was threatened by a handful of monopolistic tycoons, powerful enough to have outsize influence on the state. As the historian Steve Fraser writes, "new corporate and bureaucratic organizations" now "dwarfed, in their reach and complexity, the puny undertakings of the government or its army."[33] American democracy was suffocating under what the future Supreme Court justice Louis Brandeis called the "curse of bigness." That curse provoked a populist reaction that united voices on left and right. Some of these critics were progressive and focused on busting trusts and winning workers' rights; others muttered darkly about Eastern elites, and the malign influence of the British, or the Jews.

So that ultraexclusive Standard Oil bunker was dramatic evidence of the way the division between elites and ordinary people was intensified by an additional factor: world war. In 1917, for the first time since the Founding, the federal government conscripted its young men to fight in a European war. Now government concentrated its power, as the robber barons had. The central state grew. The Committee on Public Information sent thousands of speakers propagandizing across the country. Anti-war dissenters found themselves menaced by what would become the Federal Bureau of Investigation under the 1917 Espionage Act and the 1918 Sedition Act, which made criticizing the government illegal. New theories sprang up about who was behind this hardening of the state, and even the most far-fetched notions found plenty of adherents.

This, too, is audible in the reactions to *Report from Iron Mountain*. For example, in how Ronald Reagan, when challenged by that student at Yale, countered that there was a persistent myth "of the munition makers who are out pulling strings to create a war." Reagan was old enough to recall how, in the years after the First World War, that idea had caught hold.

President Woodrow Wilson had promised that American boys were being sent to fight in Europe only because they were building a new world of prosperity and peace. By the 1930s, with Depression at home and the threat of another war in Europe, this sounded like a sick joke. A series of books appeared with titles like *Iron, Blood and Profits* and *Merchants of Death*, alleging that the munitions makers and bankers had not only profited from the war but had actually conspired to provoke it.

A pacifist named Dorothy Detzer, who had watched her brother die from the mustard gas he had breathed in on the Western Front, began to campaign for an official investigation. She was on the left, but attracted support from right-wingers like the American Legion and Henry Ford. By September 1934, a Senate committee investigation was hard at work. It was chaired by the Republican senator Gerald Nye of North Dakota, a state that harbored "a popular fear of banks and eastern 'interests.'"[34] The members and the committee staff held a spectrum of views, from socialist to conservative, but all wanted to challenge those vested interests.

But then Senator Nye crossed a line and accused the late president Wilson himself of taking the United States to war on a lie, despite not finding proof of that, or of the guilt of the merchants of death. His investigation flopped, yet the idea that government might do such things stuck. Even when war broke out in 1939, there were those who suggested a plot was afoot once more. Some, like the aviator Charles Lindbergh, baselessly blamed a Jewish conspiracy. A journalist named John T. Flynn, who'd worked with Nye's committee, argued that President Roosevelt had had warning the Japanese were going to bomb Pearl Harbor, but let the attack go ahead to provide a pretext for war.

Flynn insisted the president had done this because he wanted to make militarism "the great glamorous public-works project of the nation."[35]

Not surprisingly, this accusation, along with the lack of evidence, discredited the theories about the "merchants of death." Eisenhower's speechwriters mentioned the idea in one of their early conversations about the military-industrial complex address, only to explicitly reject it. Three years later, in 1964, Richard Hofstadter identified it as a classic instance of the paranoid style in American politics.

Yet, on the left, as America sank into the Vietnam quagmire and citizens wanted to know why the hopes of the early 1960s had soured, the idea came back. Eisenhower's notion of the military-industrial complex began to take on a much more sinister, totalized meaning. One of those critics in *Trans-action* wrote of *Report from Iron Mountain* that its peace-scare premise was "a modern variant and updating of the old Nye investigation of munitions-makers," and was more persuasive than the original theory, because the arms industry had "become the great military-industrial complex that President Eisenhower warned us about," on which much of the economy depended. "Peace, in fact, does threaten it, and many of our own perquisites along with it."[36]

So was *Iron Mountain*, in effect, a conspiracy theory—that the Johnson administration was deliberately prolonging the war in Vietnam to help defense companies make money? No. Lewin was attacking the "permanent war economy," and extended the logic of Kahn, Rostow, et al. to expose its absurdity. Just as Swift's "A Modest Proposal" was not an attempt to prove that the rich *actually* ate babies, *Report from Iron Mountain* was not conspiracy theory but satire.

Not everyone, however, drew a clear line between the two.

———

At the moment when *Report from Iron Mountain* appeared, Kennedy assassination conspiracy theories seemed to be shadowing it everywhere. The edition of "Book World" that ran John Kenneth Galbraith's review of *Iron Mountain* also included a critical assessment of *Accessories After the Fact* by Sylvia Meagher, an amateur assassination investigator. The Christmas *Esquire*, containing that *Iron Mountain* extract, also carried a short story called "Application to Elysium," about Oswald trying to gain admittance to heaven. And in the edition of the *New York Times* that carried the initial advertisement for the book, there was a notice for a play called *The Trial of Lee Harvey Oswald*, which had had its first preview that night in a Broadway theater. It was accompanied by a quote from Jim Garrison, the district attorney of New Orleans, who was investigating the assassination afresh, convinced that he was about to expose a vast conspiracy. "The question is whether Lee Harvey Oswald killed the President alone and unaided," Garrison declared. "If the evidence doesn't support that conclusion—and it doesn't—a thousand honorable men sitting shoulder to shoulder along the banks of the Potomac won't change the facts."[37] (The *New York Times* declared the play a dubious enterprise, and it closed after nine performances.)

By the start of 1968, the neoconservative writer Irving Kristol had had enough. In a piece in *Fortune* magazine, he complained that an "extraordinary number of people these days will accept as true practically anything that is to the discredit of the US Government or any of its agencies." His two main examples were theories about the murder of Kennedy and *Iron Mountain*, neither of which he could believe so many serious people found convincing. He thought "such shadowy and sinister terms as 'establishment,' 'power structure,' and 'power elite'" were fostering this sort of world view, and asked: "Are we becoming a nation in which all obvious truths are suspect and only political fantasies are credible?"[38]

Satire and conspiracy theory might look like opposites—one skeptical, one credulous—but in the treacherous information environment of the late 1960s, they seemed to keep overlapping, not least on the New Left. While *Ramparts* did not in the end run an extract from *Iron Mountain*, it did have fun running a review of a made-up book called *Time of Assassins* by an invented author, "Ulov GK Le Boeuf." Yet the magazine also ran a long piece laying out Garrison's conspiracy theories. As the historian Peter Richardson observes, *Ramparts* was at once prone to swallowing such theories and capable of recognizing that "these tales frequently shaded into delusion or baseless distrust of the government."[39] Likewise, an advertisement for the *Realist* magazine offered subscribers highlights from its "5 most truthful" issues. Under the heading "Conspiracy Theory," these included a piece on "The role of the CIA and the police in the murder of Malcolm X"—which might just possibly have been serious—and one that asked "Who killed Adlai Stevenson?," which surely wasn't.[40]

On a much bigger stage, two of the most brilliant comedians of the satire boom had also become Kennedy conspiracists. Mort Sahl actually joined Garrison's investigation and became so obsessed by the assassination and the wrongs of the Warren Commission that he all but blew up his career. He took to telling people that the Kennedy's murder was "a license to kill everybody."[41] Dick Gregory became similarly immersed. In 1968, he ran for president, for the far-left Peace and Freedom Party. In some states, his running mate was a curious figure named Mark Lane—a lawyer and former Democratic state congressman in New York—who had found fame through his bestseller *Rush to Judgment*, the book that had taken Kennedy conspiracy theory mainstream.

Why did this overlap keep happening? Satirists and conspiracists each seek to criticize power by starting from some real evidence and extending it to a "logical" conclusion. And both like to look you in the eye and say, "But what if that's baloney and the real story is *this*?" But only one says it with a smile. It was perfectly possible to satirize power without conspiracy theory, as Lewin had shown. The premise of the *Macbeth* parody, *MacBird!*, implied that Johnson killed the saintly JFK. But the play itself was deeply skeptical about the Kennedys, attacking their image-making machine and sinister ambition. *Fact* magazine mocked the Kennedy theories by reminding readers that people had said the same about the deaths of many other famous Americans, from Lincoln onward.

As the last few years have shown, conspiracy theory can all too easily end up bolstering the worst people in politics. So understanding the difference between how satire and conspiracy theory each seek to criticize power is crucial. Jim Garrison was trying to make sense of similar issues to those Lewin was addressing in *Report from Iron Mountain*, in the same febrile moment: How much power did the military-industrial complex have? And what was it prepared to do with it? And, much later, these two men's work would become entangled. So we need to make sense of what Garrison was thinking and how it differed from Lewin's perspective.

In an interview with *Playboy* magazine, published a few weeks before *Iron Mountain*, Garrison blamed Kennedy's murder on anti-Castro Cubans, and the ultraright, and ex-CIA agents—at first, but by the end he was talking about the military-industrial complex and the influence of the Pentagon, and warning of a coming national security–fascist state. The image of malign, omnipotent power was the monster at the core of his shifting theories.

This was not based on nothing. Garrison had been present at the liberation of the Dachau concentration camp and had seen the bulldozers making "pyramids of human bodies." He became a fan of the libertarian novelist Ayn Rand, and even before the assassination had said "As an individual, I am not going to be pushed around by all the power in the state."[42] (As Kathryn Olmsted has pointed out, that did not stop him from using his powers as DA to persecute New Orleans homosexuals.) He worried that America was turning fascist, telling the man from *Playboy*:

> it's based on power and on the inability to put human goals and human conscience above the dictates of the state. Its origins can be traced in the tremendous war machine we've built since 1945, the "military-industrial complex" that Eisenhower vainly warned us about, which now dominates every aspect of our life.

Garrison feared that, along with other pressures on American life, "the awesome power of the CIA and the defense establishment" were "destined to seal the fate of the America I knew as a child and bring us into a new Orwellian world where the citizen exists for the state and where raw power justifies any and every immoral act."[43]

By February 1968, Garrison was telling Dutch television that Kennedy's assassination was "a CIA plot," carried out because the agency's allies in "the military-industrial complex" had "a vested interest in maintaining the cold war," and because Kennedy had ordered a "reduction of troops in Vietnam."[44] The "military-industrial complex" had become an expression of the paranoid style. As the White House speechwriters had prepared the farewell address in which Eisenhower had popularized this idea, they'd rejected the "merchants of death" theory. But Garrison and others embraced it, turning the military-industrial complex into an all-powerful, invisible cabal. Garrison may have been a fan of Ayn Rand, but in the context of Vietnam, his vision appealed to the far left.

Yet as we saw earlier, Kennedy himself had dismissed the very idea that was blamed for his death. In 1961, he said the notion that "War could be attributed to munitions makers or international bankers" was a case of his far-right critics' tendency to seek "a simple solution, an appealing slogan or a convenient scapegoat" for unwelcome events. In the same speech, he defended himself against their accusations that he was soft on communism by pointing out just how much his administration was spending on armaments.[45] As for his plans on America's role in Vietnam, had he lived to deliver his speech in Dallas, he was going to insist that "we dare not weary of the task."

As Hofstadter had put it the night before Kennedy was killed, "if for every error and every act of incompetence one can substitute an act of treason, we can infer how many points of fascinating interpretation are open to the paranoid imagination." This led to "heroic strivings for evidence to prove that the unbelievable is the only thing that can be believed." People talked of cover-ups and the "accumulation of detailed evidence so extensive and so palpable" that it seemed to put their convictions "beyond any reasonable doubt."[46] An early conspiracy researcher, Edward Jay Epstein, saw a parallel between Garrison's behavior and Joseph McCarthy's talent for "exploitation of inchoate fears" and "organizing a popular flight from reality"[47]—exactly what Kennedy had criticized.

---

Even as Garrison was insisting that the military-industrial complex was omnipotent, it was revealing itself to be anything but. In those 1966 reports on the corporate bunkers, there is no resentment that the elites planned to flee to safety, leaving most of their staff to burn. Instead, people thought they were deluding themselves. As one piece put it:

> The corporate mind is a curious phenomenon. To large numbers of our leading business executives, a nuclear war does not represent the end of everything, but merely a dislocation of business. It has come to light that most of the top US corporations are setting alternate headquarters in caves and quarries all across the country, hoping to carry on business-nearly-as-usual soon after the first bomb drops.[48]

As for the idea that a firm could reconstruct its business after an attack, provided it had the right paperwork, the writer remarked: "All they'll need is customers."[49] And even that rested on some other large assumptions. As the *Wall Street Journal* observed: "all-out nuclear attacks on US cities would make transportation a nightmare"[50]—a line which must have jerked its readers' complaints about New York City traffic congestion into a fresh perspective. After all those descriptions of luxury facilities, the reporter admitted that "companies with alternate headquarters concede that many of their key personnel may not be able to find their way out of the confusion—if they survived the initial attack." One executive observed that, "If the bombs come, there won't be anything left to administer."[51]

Crackpot realism was becoming harder to ignore. At the same time, the Johnson administration's optimism about Vietnam was about to come under intolerable pressure. The real problem was not that a tiny elite was running the world but that it thought it could.

---

At some point toward the end of the 1960s, a high, piercing wail began to sound through American politics, a kind of keening for all of the loss, and it did not stop for years. Perhaps it never has. The sound of shock and fear and failure, of structures creaking and tearing and coming apart, of the death of all those confident postwar hopes. You can hear it in the opening of the Rolling Stones' "Gimme Shelter," in voices in old news clips raised in can't-take-it-anymore rage, in that photo of a young woman kneeling open-mouthed by her shot-dead friend on the blacktop of an Ohio university. No doubt different people heard it first at different times, but one such moment came on the afternoon of January 29, 1968, in Washington, which was early morning in Vietnam. Suddenly, all those boasts that the war was being won met Tet.

The National Liberation Front chose Tet, the Vietnamese lunar New Year holiday, to launch a wave of surprise attacks across South Vietnam: on towns, cities, American bases, and even the U.S. embassy. The TV news was soon showing footage of bodies in the compound. The Tet Offensive was rapidly defeated militarily, but it was aimed at American hearts and minds, and support for the war never recovered. In vain, Walt Rostow exhorted President Johnson to seize his chance to make a warrior speech, and "slay the credibility dragon with one blow."[52] Could he really not hear the irony? Robert McNamara, who'd arrived in office with such faith in the power of computing and systems analysis, departed, weeping in despair. Johnson chose not to escalate the bombing further. With his presidency in ruins, he decided not to run for reelection.

*Report from Iron Mountain* had arrived to satirize Johnson's mighty war machine at the height of its hubris, just before it crashed into its nemesis. With the shock of the Tet Offensive, the administration's claims were exposed not just as lies but delusions. And yet a strange thing happened. The image of the omnipotent military-industrial complex, and of the power elite and its authoritarian control, only became more vivid. This was the start of a phenomenon that has continued ever since: a tenacious fear of what we now call the "deep state," which has grown even as the overall power and reach of the real postwar U.S. state has faltered and fallen back.

This seems to have been driven by a strange combination of factors. First, the lingering memory of the postwar state's undoubted power. Second, the way that, as it lost control toward the end of the 1960s, it became more desperately draconian. In March 1968, the *Atlantic* turned over its entire edition to a sixty-four-page piece by Dan Wakefield, protégé of C. Wright Mills. "Supernation at Peace and War" was based on a four-month tour of the United States; it was later expanded into a book. Wakefield began by noting that America was seen by "most historians and experts as the most powerful nation of its planet and perhaps in the entire history of its planet," something which many regarded with "satisfaction and awe," by others, with "uneasiness, and even great fear."[53] But that, either way, it was not only at war in Vietnam but with itself. Both of these wars were driven by the Johnson administration's loss of control, yet both produced images of immense state power, visible and invisible.

The invisible version was there in the talk about the military-industrial complex. Senator Eugene McCarthy, who challenged Johnson for the Democratic nomination, declared that the war machine had "become almost a kind of republic within the republic."[54] The anarchist writer Paul Goodman, a veteran of the Pentagon march, thought the anti-war movement assumed "that there has been a usurpation by a hidden government."[55]

By 1968, the visible version of state power was hard to miss. In March, *Esquire* ran a piece by Garry Wills, also based on a tour of the nation, called "The Second Civil War." This set out how riot control had become a thriving business. America, Wills reported in alarm, was now "an alien, armed place."

That April, Martin Luther King was assassinated. In June, Robert Kennedy, who had joined the race to replace Johnson, was killed, too, extinguishing liberal hopes that he could end the war and heal the nation's wounds. The fear both of chaos and of malign invisible forces sharply intensified.

This drove some on the left to fight back against a state that seemed to have the kind of sweeping power implied in *Iron Mountain*. In August, as Democratic Party delegates gathered in Chicago to pick their presidential candidate, anti-war protesters arrived in strength; Mayor Richard Daley banned protests; and the city became that alien, armed place Wills had warned about: an all-too-visible vision of authoritarianism. Demonstrators chanted "Two, four, six, eight, organize to smash the state!"[56] TV viewers saw seventeen minutes of uncut footage of cops and National Guardsmen on the rampage, beating even children and the elderly with clubs and rifle butts, and "dragg[ing] women through the streets."[57] As the historian Mark Kurlansky suggests, activists like the revolutionary prankster Abbie Hoffman were keen to expose the brutality of the state—and won a media victory as memorable as Tet. Even inside the convention hall, the Colorado delegation complained of "the police state of terror," and a Democratic senator denounced "Gestapo tactics,"[58] which prompted Mayor Daley to scream anti-Semitic abuse. That was caught on camera, too.

The New Left pioneer Tom Hayden was one of the leaders of the Chicago protests. He realized that "The power elite, which C. Wright Mills had portrayed as invincible, was under siege on all sides. The Tet offensive, student uprisings, Lyndon Johnson's resignation, and the killings of Martin Luther King and Robert Kennedy led to a meltdown of the system's core."[59] But this led him to worry not that the system was too weak but that it might be plotting to reassert absolute control:

> I felt that our movement's long debate over the nature of American power, started by C. Wright Mills and continued at Port Huron, might be resolved in this election year. Was there a stable power elite above even the president? . . . Would the elite suspend the democratic process

in favor of repression if their interests were too deeply threatened? Or could democracy—not just democracy at the ballot box but democracy in the streets—be an effective antidote to the conspiracies of the state?[60]

In November, Richard Nixon was elected president, without any sinister suspension of the democratic process—and the chaotic mix of repression and elite meltdown continued. In December 1969 in Chicago, Fred Hampton, a twenty-one-year-old Black Panther leader, was shot to death by police as he slept. Five months later, as the anti-war protests escalated, the Ohio National Guard shot and killed four unarmed students on the campus of Kent State University. In the aftermath, the mayor of New York wasn't alone in fearing that "The country is virtually on the edge of a spiritual, and perhaps even physical, breakdown. For the first time in a century we are not sure there is a future for America."[61]

———————

Throughout this time, Leonard Lewin had never publicly admitted that he'd written *Report from Iron Mountain*—with the exception, of course, of the introductory material. But in 1972, he finally decided to come clean, in an article in the *New York Times*. He'd been spurred to do this, he said, because government documents were emerging that were as unhinged as anything he'd invented. The so-called Pentagon Papers, a secret official history of America's calamity in Vietnam, which had been leaked by a young military analyst named Daniel Ellsberg, had begun appearing in the press the previous year. These revealed the extent to which the Johnson administration had systematically lied to Congress about its successive expansions of the war. As had the Eisenhower and Kennedy administrations before it. Lewin also pointed to a Pentagon study—revealed soon after *Iron Mountain*—on "how to take over Latin America."[62] As he told a radio interviewer at the time, this was set up "to work out contingency plans to maintain what was called

U.S. hegemony."[63] The Pentagon thought its conclusions might be misinterpreted, and it was suppressed. And then there was a Special Action Group established by Henry Kissinger, Nixon's replacement for Walt Rostow. This team was reportedly planning "how to help Pakistan against India while pretending to be neutral." Some of these documents, Lewin wrote "read like parodies of *Iron Mountain*, rather than the reverse."[64] At *Esquire*, Harold Hayes had had a similar feeling that satire was being overwhelmed by reality.

There was something else Lewin felt he should explain: why he'd sustained the uncertainty about whether the *Report* was real. It had been crucial, he wrote, to its satirical job of making people see how mad things had become:

> What I intended was simply to pose the issues of war and peace in a *provocative* way. To deal with the essential absurdity of the fact that the war system, however much deplored, is nevertheless accepted as part of the necessary order of things. To caricature the bankruptcy of the thinktank mentality by pursuing its style of scientistic thinking to its logical ends. And perhaps, with luck, to extend the scope of public discussion of "peace planning" beyond its usual stodgy limits.[65]

He added that "if the 'argument' of the *Report* had not been hyped up by its ambiguous authenticity—is it, just possibly, for real?—its serious implications wouldn't have been discussed either. At all."[66] He revealed that he'd taken care to include a fail-safe "to help me prove, if I ever have to, that the work is fictitious":[67] among the book's many genuine footnotes, he'd included two fake ones.

Lewin had just published a new work of satire. *Triage* was a novel about an organization which fixes social problems—overcrowded hospitals, drug addiction, underfunded welfare homes—by secretly killing people. Eventually the outfit wins presidential blessing to organize the deaths of those deemed unproductive or costly to society, on the grounds that it's the only way to avert overpopulation and social chaos. It acts under the direction of a Special Commission on National Priorities: another secret committee of hard-nosed realists, taking "the longer view of the general welfare."[68] Like *Iron Mountain*, it is a series of exercises in extending the logic of a political standpoint to its horrific conclusion. (As in Mills, the public are already "at the mercy of vast unseen social processes"—so they are too unsure to detect a plot.[69] During the Covid pandemic, as we'll see, many people came to suspect something like Lewin's satirical vision in *Triage* was happening for real.) For added realism, Lewin constructed the book largely in the form of newspaper articles and overheard dialogue. He once described it to his son, Michael, "as not a novel, but a 'faction'—that is a fact-based fiction."[70] This time, however, he added a note, emphasizing that "All persons and events described" were "imaginary."[71]

––––––

*Iron Mountain*'s editor, E. L. Doctorow, had written a new novel, too, and it made his name. *The Book of Daniel* was inspired partly by the killings at Kent State, partly by the treatment of Julius and Ethel Rosenberg. Daniel is the child of communist parents, unfairly executed in the 1950s for helping Stalin's Soviet Union get hold of atom bomb secrets.[72]

Like *Report from Iron Mountain*, the novel, as narrated by Daniel, is highly critical of the influence of militarism on American society. He argues that the official U.S. attitude after wars has been that "enemies must continue to be found."[73] In this account, the Cold War was a deliberate decision: refusing to share atomic bomb know-how with the Soviets ensured the arms race. The war system is protected by the "objective" official narrative in sanitized schoolbook history, by deliberately scaring "hell out of the American people,"[74] as a Cold War senator once put it, and by state force and privilege dressed up as law. This system is particularly obvious in the novel's dystopic vision of the California landscape, where the military-industrial complex is "highly visible,"[75] and a mysterious dark green helicopter buzzes continually overhead.

Daniel realizes that the Old Left's attempt to resist the overmighty state through earnest analysis is hopeless. Through Daniel, Doctorow takes a New Left approach instead, working to disrupt the structures of the official narrative. Though it is clearly a novel, the book draws heavily on the facts of the Rosenberg case and incorporates real events, such as the march on the Pentagon. And there were two other details Doctorow plucked across the line separating fact and fiction. Daniel's address, 601 West 115th Street, was where Lewin's son, Michael, lived, when he was writing his first book, which was initially edited by Doctorow. And Daniel's surname is Lewin.

———

*Report from Iron Mountain* had suggested the American economy had achieved a state of permanent plenty, with military spending needed as both stimulant and stabilizer. And it was true that all those contracts were good for some of the United States's regions and industries; the war also reduced unemployment, which helped boost wages. But the furor stirred up by the *Report* was barely over when the conditions that inspired it began to fall apart. By the end of the 1960s, the idea that the war was good for business was looking decidedly shaky. All else aside, it was fueling inflation. As for Lewin's joke that the Great Society was too *cheap* to absorb the economy's surplus, that was good satire, but even President Johnson saw the colossal spending soaked up by the war in Vietnam as a drain on his war on poverty.

The whole optimistic postwar model of high government spending was dependent on the long postwar boom, which finally burst into 1970s stagflation—just as the supposedly all-powerful American war machine was humiliated by a Vietnamese peasant army. The draft was ended, never to return; as a percentage of GDP, military spending slumped from its Vietnam-era peak. Domestic spending came under far greater pressure. The disaster of Vietnam challenged the whole postwar utopian vision that smart young men and their computers could predict, manage, and control society for the benefit of all. Politics in the 1970s was not about grand dreams of new frontiers or great societies; it was about crises of energy and confidence, and the threat of Japanese manufacturing. The hubris of the late 1960s looked like a good problem to have.

In 1980, *Report from Iron Mountain* fell out of print. In the years that followed, Lewin tried to interest publishers in reprinting it. Ping Ferry sought to help. A letter drafted by Lewin in 1987 to one major publishing house, written with Ferry's encouragement, argued that the book had remained on reading lists until it was no longer available, and that the rise of the peace movement in response to new fears of nuclear war made it relevant once more. Ferry reported that John Kenneth Galbraith was ready to write a fresh introduction. But it was all to no avail. To publishers, Lewin's attention-grabbing stunt seemed like a relic from another time.

And then the world turned upside down.

# 5

# THE LOBBY

By 1990, Leonard Lewin had retired to the quiet of the Connecticut countryside, to a small house on what had once been a farm. Big windows looked out on the trees. He was seventy-four years old—born just before America entered the First World War, now watching the Cold War come to an end. These days he kept company with a New York magazine editor, but he lived alone. He traveled quite frequently, not least to England where his son, Michael, now himself established as a novelist, lived with his family. His daughter, Julie, a campaigner for the rights and protection of animals, lived much nearer. That old world of *Monocle* satires, Riverside Drive, toasting a *New York Times* bestseller at La Côte Basque: all that was far in the past.

Then that fall, he got some news. *Report from Iron Mountain* had been republished. By right-wing extremists. Who thought it was real.

In the course of September, two of Lewin's acquaintances contacted him quite separately, to let him know that his book was being advertised for sale in a weekly magazine called the *Spotlight*. He got hold of the last four editions. Sure enough, in each there was an ad for *Report from Iron Mountain*.

This wasn't a normal weekly. The front page of the September 17 edition warned that the country's leaders were plotting "mass arrests" and "'preventive detention'"[1] of dissidents in makeshift concentration camps, to be activated as soon as the United States went to war in the Gulf. Over the page there was a denunciation of the *Washington Post* as "pro-Soviet." And here was his book being offered for sale, by an organization of which he'd never heard: Liberty Library. What the hell had happened?

———

The *Spotlight* claimed to have a hundred thousand subscribers. As that edition made clear, it was published by an organization called Liberty Lobby, which had a mailing list, in the 1980s, of four hundred thousand. It was headquartered in a smart town house on Capitol Hill, just behind the Library of Congress. It was thought to have a budget that ran into the millions. As of 1984, more than one hundred radio stations broadcast its shows. Yet these were true extremists. On January 6, 2021, the far right invaded the Capitol building, but long before, they'd had offices two blocks away.

Liberty Lobby was the sworn enemy of centralized, centrist power, in the manner of General Edwin Walker. "Establishment" was one of its curse words; it set its face against the mainstream press. It had a hair-trigger fear of imminent tyranny that it spied lurking everywhere from the Federal Emergency Management Agency to judicial encroachments on the right to bear arms. It was very suspicious of bankers and their secret meetings, especially if their surname was Rockefeller. In Walker's day, the far right had fretted about the Council on Foreign Relations; they still did in the 1990s, but now newer elite bodies had also fallen under their suspicious eye. The Trilateral Commission, for example, was a private internationalist body co-founded by the banker David Rockefeller. It was the subject of much legitimate criticism for its rather high-handed attitude to the chaotic democratic politics of the 1970s, but the *Spotlight* went far further than that. One book it advertised called the Trilateralists "the world shadow government," alleging that it planned to "merge the US and USSR."[2] Another alleged world shadow government (why were there so many?) was the Bilderberg Group that periodically gathered leading figures in politics, business, and academia to talk. When the *Spotlight* managed to get hold of the guest list for one such conference, it ran it as a "Who's Who of Global Elitists."[3] For some reason, the paper was particularly excited to report that not only Henry Kissinger had been invited but so had the former British foreign secretary, Lord Carrington.

Though not always upfront about it, the paper also had a record of promoting the lie that six million Jewish people weren't murdered by the Nazis—even branding *The Diary of Anne Frank* a hoax. The September 17, 1990, edition had a sympathetic story about the supposed persecution of a leading Holocaust denier for his "research into the alleged gas chambers at Auschwitz, Birkenau, and Majdanek."[4] In one of the editions Lewin got hold of, there was an advertisement for tapes of a Lobby convention. The speakers featured included Eustace Mullins, a prominent neofascist who was there to denounce the "tyranny" of the Federal Reserve.[5]

Bizarrely, another of the speakers at this extreme-right gathering was the comedian-campaigner Dick Gregory, whose stand-up routines Lewin had enjoyed watching in the late 1960s. Gregory had once been a true satirical genius, but his conspiracism had long since led him down some very strange paths. What would he have made of those ads for *Report from Iron Mountain* popping up in the *Spotlight*? If a curious incident a decade or so earlier is anything to go by, the ad placements would have made perfect sense to him. For a brief period, Julie Lewin had a relationship with one of Gregory's colleagues in conspiracy research—a left-wing activist named Ralph Schoenman. The two men often shared their discoveries. One day, Gregory called—and Julie realized he was telling Schoenman about *Report from Iron Mountain*. Schoenman mentioned that Leonard Lewin's daughter, Julie, was sitting right next to him. As the conversation continued, Julie remembers saying, "Ralph, he knows it's a hoax, right? He knows my father wrote the whole thing?" Schoenman duly mentioned this, too. But Gregory wouldn't believe it. He insisted that the only reason Lewin said he was the real author was "because the CIA threatened his life."[6]

———————

The ideology on offer in the *Spotlight* had its roots in the kind of isolationism and paranoia that followed the First World War: the mood that produced those conspiracy theories about the "merchants of death," the Federal Reserve, and Pearl Harbor. These were the kind of right-wingers who revered the American nation, its Constitution, and its borders and loathed and detested bankers, free trade, paper currency, the East Coast foreign policy elite, and Jewish people. Yet Liberty Lobby was convinced that its "populist, America-first philosophy" was "truly the wave of the future."[7]

In the September 10 edition, there was a review of *Iron Mountain*, headlined "Perpetual War Engineered." Here, Lewin could read how his book had been reframed to fit into the Lobby's fevered world view. According to the review, the Establishment's line was "War is a good business—invest your son": an echo of that old Mort Sahl line from the 1960s. If you disagreed with that horrifying notion, the *Report* was "highly recommended"[8] as a way to understand how wars kept happening.

The review also revealed the Lobby's attitude to truth. They clearly believed Lewin's hoax was an authentic product of government. The review set aside any concerns that *Report from Iron Mountain* might be a satire, on the grounds that "the fact that so many of its observations and predictions have come true validates its basic premises."[9] No doubt Lewin was surprised to learn that he'd predicted Gorbachev's reforms and the disarming of the Soviet Union.

Using the number in the ads, Lewin called Liberty Library. He introduced himself, asked them to confirm they were selling his book, and requested a copy. The person who answered said they'd have to check. When Liberty Library called back next day, Lewin made clear that he hadn't given permission for the *Report* to be republished. So who had? The woman on the other end of the phone said she didn't know, but gave him a number for the organization from which they'd sourced the book: the Institute for Historical Review.

The respectable-sounding name was a hoax. This wasn't a scholarly institution. It was one of America's primary promoters of Holocaust denial. Its first director had been a member of the National Front, the British neo-fascist party of the 1970s. A few years before Lewin got the shocking news about the far right's appropriation of his book, a real scholar—the American historian Deborah Lipstadt—had begun to study the rise of Holocaust denialism, not least as it was appearing on university campuses. She eventually set out her findings in a book, published in 1993, called *Denying the Holocaust: The Growing Assault on Truth and Memory*. She argued that, from its founding, the IHR had "camouflaged its actual goal by engaging in activities that typify a scholarly institution."[10] Its publications were "enveloped in the aura of research." Strip that away, Lipstadt wrote, and "they would be dismissed out of hand for what they truly are: fanatical expressions of neo-Nazism."[11]

As *Report from Iron Mountain* had shown, footnotes in themselves are no guarantee that the document they adorn can be trusted. Yet here were people who pulled that trick not to help make a satire hit home but to "plant seeds of doubt" that would come to fruition in the future, when no more survivors of the death camps remained alive. Over thirty years ago, Lipstadt was already finding that "certain computer networks have been flooded with their materials."[12]

The IHR insisted it wanted to destroy myths, but in reality it promoted them. By claiming history had been distorted, it distorted history. Preemptively reversing the truth like this is a well-established technique: falsely accuse your opponent of lying before they can truthfully accuse you.

But there was something else at work here, too, which helps explain the decision to republish *Iron Mountain*: Holocaust denial also incorporates narratives about war and power.

As Lipstadt notes, deniers argue that "war is evil," and is only ever a struggle for power.[13] Up to a point, this is reasonable enough, but it implies that claims to moral superiority can be dismissed as no more than the boasts of the victors. That might make sense of the First World War, but it does not make sense of the Second. The deniers' narrative about war works to set up their insistence that real power is absolute and malign, and is conducted in secret, obscured by lies. It's only one more step to the idea that that secretive all-powerful warmongering elite is Jewish. Next, the critical concept of the "official narrative" is sucked into the conspiracy theory. As Lipstadt writes, "According to the IHR, exposing the truth about the Holocaust also exposes the secret group that controls much of America's military and foreign policy."[14] This conflates the abhorrent practice of Holocaust denial with the essential task of questioning the powerful.

At some point in what followed, Lewin or his lawyers obtained a copy of the IHR's newsletter for January 1990. This exhorted readers to buy audio- and videotapes of the Institute's Tenth International Revisionist Conference: "Watch or hear these history-making men deliver the hidden facts, the stunning revelations, and the powerful insights which have the Establishment's myth-mongers and whitewashers on the run!"[15] The institute was making a similar case just over a year later: "if there were a general knowledge of *real* history, instead of the propaganda-as-history incessantly peddled by the government and media, our leaders would not have been able to inveigle us into an interventionist 'New World Order.'"[16] There was talk of "big interests" and "carefully guarded secrets."[17]

It's not hard to see why the IHR and their conspiracy-minded brethren at the *Spotlight* seized on *Report from Iron Mountain* and its "revelations" of a cabal using permanent war to hold on to power. In their keenness to see *Iron Mountain* as genuine, they'd fallen for a satirical use of their own trick. This exposed their inability to deal with evidence. Not that this was particularly cheering for Leonard Lewin as he prepared to try to stop them.

When the book arrived, it appeared to be a photocopy of the original— the Dial Press's third printing—wrapped in a new, yellow-on-black cover. On the back, Lewin found promotional copy headed "Secret Protocols . . . or Brilliant Satire?" Lewin's claim to have written the whole thing, it said, was more likely "just another move in a deception game being played with exceptional cunning." The copy said the book offered:

a recognizable facsimile of how the brainstrust of the Bilderbergers, the Trilateralists, the Insiders, the Establishment—call it what you will—operate to insure that war remains a functioning business, a going concern, in which you can continue to invest not merely your sons, your brothers, your husbands, your lovers, but in this nuclear age all of humankind—unless we, all of us, call an end to this madness![18]

*Report from Iron Mountain* and its satirical vision of nefarious power had captured the imagination of real conspiracy theorists. Lewin's brilliance in confecting the *Report* had come back to haunt him.

The copy on the back of this edition of the book jumbled together the idea that it was "essentially true" with the idea that it was actually genuine. It insinuated that those calling it a satire were doing so out of defensive self-interest, whereas the plucky heretics who thought it was real could see the truth. And strikingly, the promotional description claimed that this latter group encompassed the left as well as the right:

> While perceptive critics from the far Right and Left hailed the book for its insight and forthrightness, such Establishment, interventionist, "megadeath" intellectuals as Henry Kissinger and Herman Kahn damned *Report from Iron Mountain* passionately. "Bad satire," they called it, even as many of America's leading intellects and top-level government policy makers took *Report from Iron Mountain* for unvarnished fact.[19]

Lewin was "horrified" that a reader might get the impression that he "approved the inclusion of such language in my book,"[20] or that he supported the views of people who muttered darkly about Bilderbergers and Trilateralists. Or, worse, that he'd written that description of the book himself. He still didn't know who'd given permission for this, so he asked the publisher that had bought Dial to investigate. Meanwhile, the *Report* was still being advertised in the *Spotlight*.

Finally, he heard back: no one at the publisher, however mistakenly, had authorized republication. So he hired an attorney, and they tried to figure out how to respond. It was "a very unpleasant task that absolutely needed to be done," Julie Lewin remembers. "It was extremely alarming and it had to be stopped. And it was up to him."[21] This process of setting things right wasn't made any easier when Leonard's lawyer, who was only forty-nine, died in her sleep. There was also the impediment that among those treading on Lewin's copyright were individuals who believed *Iron Mountain* to be an official government report, hence in the public domain and free to be published without anyone's permission.

But why was any of this happening in the first place? Whoever had taken it upon themselves to pirate his book hadn't replaced the original copyright page with one of their own. This made what they had done that much more blatant, but it also meant Lewin didn't know who the book's pirates were. Until, in February 1991, one of the men who tipped him off in the first place, a former book editor named Bram Cavin, sent him two new leads. The first was a series of letters from a retired military officer he'd once published, one Colonel L. Fletcher Prouty. These letters revealed that Prouty had given an unmarked copy of the book to a man from the Institute for Historical Review. (It was this copy that was then pulled apart, photocopied, and rebound with a new cover to produce the pirated edition.) The second lead was a catalogue, from a California company called Noontide Press (not to be confused with Noonday Press). On the cover was an eerie photograph of a chiseled stone head, harshly lit: a man with blank eyes staring pitilessly ahead, resolute in deep shadow. The catalogue was advertising Lewin's book in a section alongside such books as *Say No! to the New World Order* and *The Protocols of the Elders of Zion*, the notorious forgery from 1903, which purports to reveal a Jewish conspiracy to subjugate the world. Other sections included "National Socialism," "Holocaust Revisionism," and "Healthy Living." Lewin set about hiring new lawyers.

––––––––––

At around the same time, Iraq's dictator Saddam Hussein had ordered his troops to invade Kuwait. And so, for the first time since the Gulf of Tonkin

Resolution in 1964, Congress had voted—narrowly—to authorize offensive military action. This began with air strikes on Kuwait and Iraq on January 17, 1991. As a huge U.S.-led coalition land force prepared to invade, there was much fear that this was the start of another Vietnam.

The *Spotlight* played on this to recite its standard story about power. It claimed that it always opposed intervention, at least until it began, "as well as every attempt to impose American 'values' on foreign countries through CIA-orchestrated 'dirty tricks' and other foreign policy tools so beloved by the Establishment."[22] It warned that the cost of going to war to force Saddam out of Kuwait—in money, economic damage, and terror attacks—would be devastating. And the Bush administration was not even giving a straight answer about why this had to happen.

The *Spotlight* knew what was really afoot: like all wars, it was to enforce "the dictates of the international elite, the bankers and Big Money interests across the globe." More specifically, "to destroy an enemy of Israel, to perpetuate the Trilateral monopoly on Mideast oil, to further move America toward a world government . . . and to distract attention from the corruption of the crooks in the federal government."[23] And while they were at it, the state would execute a power grab, restricting and interfering. The Bill of Rights would be "set aside"; critics were "likely to be thrown into concentration camps."[24] One editorial cried: "Support Our Troops. Get Us Out of the Middle East."[25]

This was a direct echo of an anti-Vietnam slogan from the 1960s, and the Vietnam War and the torrent of government lies that went with it had clearly made this kind of conspiracist case easier to make. But it's revealing that this line of argument was used to hawk more copies of tapes from that Holocaust denial conference: "As our young men and women prepare to shed their blood in the Arabian sands for a cause their president cannot (or dare not) make clear, an understanding of the hidden causes and devastating consequences of modern war is more vital than ever."[26]

Liberty Library was keen to seize the moment, too, and put together a new *Spotlight* ad, which appeared in February's latter three editions. It was headed "America at War" and showed a degraded photograph of a desolate landscape, vaguely suggestive of the Western Front. The ad offered a pair of books that discussed "the impact of war on our society." The first was a polemic from 1935 by retired marine corps brigadier general Smedley D. Butler, which drew on the criticism of the industrialists' profits to declare that *War Is a Racket*. The second was *Report from Iron Mountain*.

---

On February 25, the *Spotlight* was running these ads while confidently predicting the likely reintroduction of conscription—three days before the Gulf War ended in victory. That same day, Lewin's new attorneys fired off cease-and-desist letters: one to the Lobby-owned Liberty Library, one to Noontide Press, one to the Institute for Historical Review. But who would emerge from this thicket of organizations to respond? An ex-military officer perhaps? Or a smart young far-right zealot, fresh from law school?

The first attorney to come forward was representing Liberty Lobby. This was none other than Mark Lane, the pioneering Kennedy conspiracy theorist who'd made his name as a star of the sixties left.

Lane had been on a very strange political journey—one that reveals much about why the far right had embraced *Report from Iron Mountain*. We last encountered him in 1968, basking in the runaway success of *Rush to Judgment*, his attack on the Warren Report, and running for president for the far-left Peace and Freedom Party with Dick Gregory. He went on to work with the group Vietnam Veterans Against the War, writing a book titled *Conversations with Americans* that drew on former soldiers' stories of atrocities. Whereas VVAW checked the testimonies they gathered, Lane did not, and some of those he spoke to turned out to have been lying. Lane's approach was investigated and exposed by Neil Sheehan, a journalist and a leading critic of the war, who condemned it as amounting to "a new McCarthyism, this time from the left," in which any "accusation, any innuendo, any rumor, is repeated and published as truth."[27]

In 1973, Lane cowrote a novel called *Executive Action* about the murder of President Kennedy. The plot suggested that the assassination was all the work of the standard shadowy cabal of businessmen, politicos, and spies—plus a man from the RAND Corporation. Kennedy's supposed determination to withdraw from Vietnam was just one of a whole menu of reasons making it vital to the power elite that he be eliminated. (One of the plotters in Lane's 1970s novel, an anti-Semitic oil tycoon, was a member of Liberty Lobby—his future ally.)

The following year, *Executive Action* was made into a movie; one liberal reviewer thought the film was such a mélange of improbabilities that it would send "C. Wright Mills spin[ning] in his grave"[28] at the perversion of his original conception of the power elite. The movie was at least prefaced with a get-out clause saying that, while it was based on research, it merely offered a possible scenario.

From there, Lane ventured deeper and deeper into the disputed territory between fact and fiction. In the late 1970s, he was investigating the assassination of Martin Luther King. As with the JFK killing, Lane thought he detected a government plot. He wrote a book about it—with Dick Gregory—and then a radio docudrama. His investigation needed money, so he funded one conspiracy theory by promoting another, on behalf of a very sinister figure indeed.

The Reverend Jim Jones was the leader of a left-wing religious cult in San Francisco that called itself Peoples Temple. It had relocated to South America to escape the supposed creeping fascism of the United States, but could not shake off accusations of abuse and coercion. So Lane accepted the cult's money to claim that Jones was innocent. Posing as an impartial investigator, he declared that there was a "massive conspiracy to destroy Peoples Temple . . . initiated by the intelligence organizations of the United States."[29] At one point, as Jones's biographer Tim Reiterman observed, this involved trying to extract information from a dubious private detective by pretending to be making a film about Peoples Temple. A fake meeting about a fake fiction about a fake conspiracy.

In 1978, Lane was forced to confront the reality of the dark places to which seeing conspiracies everywhere can lead. That November, he was in Jonestown, the cult's makeshift settlement in the Guyanese jungle. A congressman was coming to investigate its activities; Lane acted as the increasingly paranoid cult's spokesman. Jim Jones was convinced—so he said—that his people were in imminent danger from the kind of sinister, CIA-like forces Lane was always talking about. As the cult leader harangued his followers about the need for desperate measures, two of his armed henchmen told Lane, "We're gonna commit revolutionary suicide" and "We'll die to expose this racist and fascist society."[30] Terrified, Lane fled for his life through the jungle, as hundreds of Jones's followers swallowed cyanide, and the congressman was shot to death. Lane made it back to America . . . but he was soon blaming the government for the horrors perpetrated by his paymaster. He remained lost in the jungle of his own imaginings.

Finally, his pursuit of the phantoms and shadows of the JFK assassination helped to draw him from the progressive left toward the far right. In 1980, this former Democratic state congressman who'd campaigned against the Vietnam War agreed to represent Liberty Lobby in a defamation case. The case concerned an article in the *Spotlight* alleging that E. Howard Hunt, one of the men implicated in the Watergate bugging scandal, had also been involved in killing President Kennedy.[31] (Lane eventually won the case, on the basis that the article was not malicious; naturally he took this to indicate that the jury backed his Kennedy theories.) From there, Lane became the associate editor of *Zionist Watch*, an outlet for conspiracy theories about Israel supposedly controlling American foreign policy, based in the same building as Liberty Lobby and the *Spotlight*. The Holocaust deniers of the Institute for Historical Review tried to induce donations from supporters by offering a videotape of Lane making the research director of the Jewish Anti-Defamation League "squirm."[32]

This, then, was the person who first came forward to answer the lawyers' charge that Lewin's work was being republished and sold without permission.

In his letter of response, Lane tried to defend the Noontide Press's unauthorized publication of *Report from Iron Mountain* with four arguments.

First, the book was copyrighted to Dial Press, not Lewin. Second, as Lewin had initially contacted the Liberty Lobby six months earlier without objecting to the republication, that constituted him giving "tacit approval." Lewin, Lane wrote, was "hardly in a position to seek to profit by his attempted entrapment of my client."[33]

Third, the book must either be a government document, as originally claimed in 1967, or an act of fraud. As ever, Lane was very open to the idea that nefarious government agencies were the real villains. And fourth, he argued that the Lobby's Liberty Library had not itself published the book but had merely bought it from "various distributors and publishers."[34]

Perhaps Lane thought this was a strong case. Eight days later, Lewin's lawyer, Laura Handman, wrote back, and took it apart. Unlike Lane, she cited specific legislation, knocking down his assertions one by one.

Lewin's copyright was clear from the U.S. Copyright Office registry; had Lane's client bothered to check, they could have established that quite easily. Handman helpfully enclosed a copy of the relevant page. Lewin's call six months earlier, she added, quite obviously did not constitute approval, and talking about entrapment was "offensive and baseless."[35] The six-month delay had happened because his first lawyer died.

In response to Lane's suggestion that the book was either a government publication or a fraud, she wrote: "I direct your attention to the back cover of the edition your client distributed, which points out the satiric origins of the book. Mr. Lewin long ago revealed to the public his own authorship of the entire work."[36] For the avoidance of doubt, Handman enclosed Lewin's article from 1972, in which he said just that.

But it was her filleting of Lane's claim that the Lobby's Liberty Library had not itself published the *Report* that was most telling. The assertion that the book had merely been bought from distributors was "disingenuous at best."[37] She pointed Lane to a judgment in a case from 1988 in which he'd represented the Lobby. In this old file, Lewin's lawyer had spotted something:

behind the pseudoscholarly institute, the esoteric publisher, the weekly magazine, and the Washington town house, there was a single, sinister figure: a man called Willis Carto.

There was "evidence in this record," wrote the judge, "that Mr. Carto specifically designed the Liberty Lobby/Legion/Noontide/IHR network so as to divorce Liberty Lobby's name from those of its less reputable affiliates. . . . It is Mr. Carto's right to pour his political activities into whatever corporate shell he desires. What he may not do is silence those who see through the form to the reality."[38]

Here was a judge doing what conspiracy theorists regard as their mission: exposing the hidden connections between organizations and the shadowy mastermind lurking behind front organizations. But in this case, it was actually true. Carto also operated through an entity called the Legion for the Survival of Freedom, once chaired by General Edwin Walker, that now encompassed Carto's California-based creations, Noontide and the IHR. If all it took to demolish a conspiracy theory was argument and evidence, the legal exposure of Carto's various fronts would have been devastatingly effective.

Carto did all he could to stay behind the scenes, creating a battery of publications and corporations but downplaying his own influence: avoiding interviews, writing under pseudonyms, and keeping his name off his publications' mastheads. His base was in Southern California; he was said to control his various organizations from a "plush penthouse apartment,"[39] but made a point of conducting his business using mail drops and pay phones. In 1992, the researcher Chip Berlet would describe Carto and his front organizations as "the major engine behind right-wing conspiracism in the United States."[40]

Here was the man who bore ultimate responsibility for the purloining of *Report from Iron Mountain*. The true nature of his political project sheds useful light on why Lewin and his lawyers were now locked in battle with this murky political underworld. Carto's secretive mission also has something to tell us about how American politics got itself into its current state.

Carto was born in 1926 in Fort Wayne, Indiana. By the late 1950s, after transitioning from college to the army to a stint as a bill collector in San Francisco, he'd found his way into the burgeoning right-wing ecosystem that was developing in reaction against the postwar consensus. He set up Liberty Lobby in the late 1950s, blending the economic populism and nativist resentments of the interwar period with conspiracy theories. It saw patriotic "real" Americans working hard and creating wealth "while fighting against 'parasites' at the top and bottom of society who pick their pockets."[41] In this, Liberty Lobby had something in common with the John Birch Society, a resemblance made even more interesting by the fact that the Birchers' leader found Carto's anti-Semitism "too extreme."[42] By 1967, Carto's Liberty Lobby was well established in its town house on Capitol Hill; his biographer George Michael reports that it was sending representatives to testify before Congress "on average about 12–15 times per year."[43] It rode out revelations in February of that year that he'd written letters praising Hitler and attacking "international Jews."[44]

Toward the end of the year, as *Report from Iron Mountain* was sending flurries of excitement across Washington, Liberty Lobby was publishing its own attack on the Pentagon mentality. *Robert Strange McNamara: The True Story of Dr. Strangebob:* took aim at the faith that the defense secretary and his "arrogant 'whiz-kids'"[45] had placed in computers, management techniques, and "cost analysis studies."[46] It charged that this approach failed to make sense of the reality of war, and that McNamara had wriggled out of the consequences by bamboozling President Johnson and Congress with fibs and flip charts. Meanwhile, America had ended up "bogged down in a seemingly endless war,"[47] never properly declared, with hundreds of thousands of young Americans being sent to die in what was meant to be the South Vietnamese people's fight. The book denounced "armament profiteers,"[48] alleging that, without proper competition, big military contracts had been entered into with "politically powerful but inefficient corporations."[49] It attacked a cynical attitude that saw deaths in war as an "investment,"[50] and decried the manipulative "image-building" of "skilled psycho-politicians."[51] It even suggested that McNamara and his coterie saw themselves as "gods,"[52] controlling the population through nuclear terror.

If this sounds similar to left-wing attacks, it's probably not a coincidence. As the historian Frank Mintz noted, Carto and his allies were aware "of the conspiracist tendency in left-wing radicalism" and were keen to appeal to those who thought that way. One of his newspapers talked of "building a bridge to the left." Carto himself "addressed a congenial forum on the need for both left and right to fight the nefarious "super capitalists" who controlled the Federal Reserve System."[53] Indeed, one of the phrases on the pirate copy's promotional description to which Lewin objected was "megadeath intellectuals": a term used in the early 1960s by some on the New Left. This might explain why Carto believed a left-wing satire was real. It appeared to confirm his own organization's theories about the malign thought processes of the power elite.

Yet this was only half the picture. *The True Story of Dr. Strangebob* was a deeply confused piece of work. It objected to the war in Vietnam, but it also claimed that McNamara was trying *not* to win it, because he was a leftist pacifist who wanted to disarm the United States and integrate the military by force. The book defended General Walker's propagandizing to his troops. It parroted military chiefs' demands for more military spending, on the basis of hysterical rumors of Soviet space weapons. And, as ever, it blamed a Jew: it cast Adam Yarmolinsky, that Yale-grad Pentagon official recruited by Victor Navasky to write for *Monocle* undercover and so loathed by General Walker, as a "sinister character,"[54] the "shadowy figure"[55] who'd supposedly maneuvered McNamara into his job and had carried on manipulating ever since.

Beneath this contradictory line on war, there lay a much clearer story about power. Carto believed that American foreign policy, and financial policy, were controlled by a "high elite" with mostly "Jewish names."[56]

However, he did not think the problem was that power was concentrated in the hands of a small, shadowy group of men. The problem was it wasn't concentrated in the hands of *his* small, shadowy group of men. The Anti-Defamation League alleged that in 1970 Liberty Lobby held a secret fundraiser for a project called "Operation Survival" that reportedly aimed "to finance a right-wing dictatorship."[57] The following year, the conservative *National Review* judged that his philosophy was one of "pure power,"[58] and reported that in the 1950s Carto had "established, and promoted secretly, the Joint Council for Repatriation—a send-'em-back-to-Africa movement."[59] He believed, wrote Deborah Lipstadt, "in the need for an absolutist government that would protect the 'racial heritage' of the United States."[60] He derived his political beliefs from the writings of a paranoid Hitler worshipper named Francis Parker Yockey, who'd been discharged from the U.S. Army in 1943 suffering from "marked delusions of persecution."[61] Yockey wanted to see the restoration of the "authority and dignity of the Absolute State," which he regretted had been overcome by democracy, with its "irresponsible, private, rule of anonymous groups, classes, and individuals, whose interests the parliaments serve."[62]

Carto's minions promoted *Report from Iron Mountain* as a revelation of the evil plots of the establishment. One of those was the reintroduction of eugenics, which Lewin included to satirize the think tankers' high-handed attitude toward ordinary people. But Carto thought that eugenics was a good idea, provided he and his ilk were in charge. In 1967, Noontide Press published a book titled *Sex Versus Civilization*, which argued that state governments ought to impose limits on the number of children "dumber" couples could have, "based on the couple's IQs, character, and school work. Once a couple reached their quota, they would be sterilized."[63] So much for lobbying for liberty. Perhaps it's not surprising Carto didn't hold meetings in his office. Reportedly, it contained four bronze busts of Hitler.

Carto's plan for achieving power involved not only reaching out to left-wing conspiracists, and aping the old populist attacks on bankers and big business, but uniting as much of the right as he could. He created many front organizations, all under his control; from the mid-1960s on, these were variously designed to appeal to nationalists, eugenicists, paramilitary groups, and supporters of the segregationist George Wallace, who ran for president in 1968.

Carto even set up a group called United Republicans for America, to try to take over the Republican Party. The kind of racist, far-right politics espoused by Carto were associated in many people's minds with the horrors of the Holocaust, which made it harder to attract supporters. He created the Institute for Historical Review in 1978, in part to try to address this, by spreading the baseless claim that the Nazis had been unfairly accused of genocide. In 1984, he created the Populist Party and threw his organizational weight behind the 1988 presidential candidacy of David Duke, a former grand wizard of the Ku Klux Klan. And for a time, this particular move seemed to be having some effect. Duke's run for president went nowhere, but the following year, Liberty Lobby's support helped him run for the Louisiana House of Representatives as a Republican. He won, and went on to back legislation to pay those on welfare to be "temporarily sterilized."[64] In 1990, he won the Republican nomination for one of Louisiana's seats in the U.S. Senate and captured 44 percent of the vote with his appeal to "young white males with poor job prospects."[65] He denounced "government by big business, international finance, and organized minorities"—and the supposed "Zionist" control of the media.[66]

Duke's worrying run of success soon ended. Liberty Lobby may have been convinced that its brand of "America First" populism—anti-immigration, anti-free trade, anti-foreign wars—was the wave of the future, but Carto was too obviously fascist. There were other, more mainstream voices, however, who articulated similar positions, minus the outright fascism. In October of 1987 the Christian TV evangelist Pat Robertson announced his candidacy for the Republican nomination for president. And that same year a forty-one-year-old New York businessman began dropping hints in interviews about running, and placed a full-page ad in the New York Times, the Boston Globe, and the Washington Post. This salvo demanded faster disarmament talks with the Soviets and cuts in aid to Saudi Arabia, Japan, and other wealthy U.S. allies: "Let's help our farmers," wrote Donald Trump. "Let's not let our great country be laughed at anymore."[67] In the end, however, he told a rally he wasn't seeking the Republican nomination.

Not yet, anyway.

---

After Mark Lane, the second figure to emerge in response to the letters from Lewin's lawyer was a man named Tom Marcellus, the director of Noontide Press, who wrote from the conservative redoubt of Orange County: the man to whom Colonel Prouty had sent the unmarked copy of *Iron Mountain* for copying. Marcellus wondered "if Mr. Lewin and/or the US government is interested in suppressing distribution of the book and, if so, why."[68] Dark forces, he seemed to suggest, were at work.

It took years of legal wrangling before the case was resolved. In July 1992, having tried, unsuccessfully, to stop the book from being sold and find agreement, Lewin's attorney filed suit in federal court. The defendants demanded a jury trial, but this was rejected. Eventually, Willis Carto and Mark Lane accepted that, however much *Report from Iron Mountain* may have confirmed their biases, it had simply been made up by Lewin. At Noontide, Marcellus had stopped selling the book, suspicious though he had seemed to be about Lewin's objections.

In December 1993, Lewin set out in an affidavit that what had happened to his book was not just a matter of copyright infringement:

> The idea that the public would believe that my Work was associated with any of these entities was, and is, severely disturbing to me, not only because I am Jewish, but because I find such views repugnant. I would rather my Work not be published at all than have it published, distributed, advertised and sold by organizations or individuals ascribing to such views or associated in the minds of the public with such views.[69]

To bring this to an end, it was necessary to go back to the beginning. Victor Navasky, whose original idea the *Report* had been, had long since moved on from his days at *Monocle*; since 1978, he'd been editor of the independent-minded left-wing weekly *The Nation*. Now, though, he was called on revisit the old days, to corroborate Lewin's account of the *Report*'s origins.

And when Lewin's lawyer made her pitch to the judge for a summary judgment, the plentiful evidence she was able to present included those articles from 1967 that declared the *Report* a hoax and speculated that Lewin had written it.

Having heard oral arguments, the judge ordered that Lewin's complaint was granted: he was awarded damages of $100,000, plus his legal costs. Carto's many fronts were permanently banned from selling any more copies of *Iron Mountain*. Liberty Library had sold 368 of its ill-gotten stock, but still had 184; the Legion for the Survival of Freedom had a lot more. The very existence of these yellow-on-black pirated editions of *Iron Mountain*, with the repugnant promotional copy on the back, had been plaguing Lewin for more than three years. Now he ended up with around a thousand of them, piled up in his house.

————

So this seems a simple tale—gullible far-right conspiracy theorists got the wrong end of the stick and swallowed a demonstrable hoax. But hold on. Who were the acquaintances who tipped Lewin off that the *Spotlight* was advertising his book? And how did they come to know about it in the first place? The answers to those questions open up a whole other dimension to the story.

Further investigation reveals that one of those who tipped Lewin off was a man named Lud Arons. Like Lewin, he was very much on the left; unlike Lewin, he was a conspiracy theorist. He is an elusive figure, his name barely appearing in the press, but he was somewhat known for a series of audio-tapes, made in the late 1980s, called *Why Bad Things Happen to Good People, and Why Good Things Happen to Bad People*. These productions open with Arons setting out how the system that faces the individual seems hopelessly massive and powerful, impossible to take on. But that, he argues, is *what they want you to think*. The tapes offered to liberate the listener from the disempowering mind control of the establishment media. Arons seems to have had a highly attuned sense of the threat of power turning fascist, and to have viewed *Report from Iron Mountain* through this lens. He even took it upon himself to send a copy of *Iron Mountain* to Bantam Books, lauding Lewin as "remarkably prescient."[70]

Around this time, Arons was in touch with one of the doyens of JFK conspiracy theory—a man who'd authored many books about it, published and unpublished. In the 1940s, Harold Weisberg had worked in the intelligence services; in the 1950s, he'd been a victim of McCarthyism. Arons's correspondence with him was triggered by their shared outrage at a piece in *The Nation* that disputed a cardinal tenet of the conspiracists: that Kennedy had been intent on withdrawing from Vietnam. Arons was, if anything, even angrier about this than Weisberg, denouncing it in a letter to Navasky as a "Goebbelsian lie."[71] When Iran threatened the life of the novelist Salman Rushdie for his book *The Satanic Verses*, and leading writers, including E. L. Doctorow, voiced their support, Arons was livid. Where had they been when several writers about the Kennedy case had been murdered? It was left to Weisberg, himself steeped in conspiracy theory, to try to reassure Arons that the people concerned really hadn't been killed. They'd just died.

Bram Cavin, the other contact who tipped off Lewin, was a more mainstream figure. He and Lewin likely got to know each other at Collier Books in the early 1960s. Lewin worked there writing cover copy, among other tasks, while he was getting started as a writer. Cavin was there as a radical, nonconformist editor. He persuaded a young African American named Claude Brown to write *Manchild in the Promised Land*: a novel about the rigors of growing up in gangs and reformatories in postwar Harlem.

In the context of the Kennedy assassination, and the Vietnam War, and its endless blizzard of official lying, Cavin seems to have developed a very wary view of how power worked in America. In the early 1970s, he edited a book by Fletcher Prouty, that old colonel who sent *Iron Mountain* to the far right. It was called *The Secret Team: The CIA and Its Allies in Control of the United States and the World*. Cavin's journalist son, Tony, recalls that Prouty was the kind of person his father found fascinating because "he understood how things work,"[72] but from a critical standpoint. Cavin went on to work on an investigative study of DuPont, one of America's biggest chemical firms. This featured a chapter called "Merchants of Death," which went as far as saying that the company—at that time, a leading maker of munitions—had pressed for the United States to enter the First World War, but did *not* allege a full-blown conspiracy. Even so, legal battles ensued; it appears the dispute cost Cavin his job.

But why was a left-winger still in touch with Prouty twenty years later, when the old colonel was buddying up with the extreme right? Tony Cavin believes that, had his father "been at all aware of it, he would have been absolutely horrified":

> The people who ran the newsstand . . . when I was a kid, when we lived in Pleasantville, New York, had the numbers from the camps on their arms. And [my father] explained to me that this meant that they were survivors. I mean, he was Jewish, culturally, and he did not try and hide that fact—he was not religious, but he certainly was aware. So I think if he'd been aware that there was a Holocaust denier involved, he would have been quite upset by it.[73]

Enthusiasm for Lewin's *Report* had slid from the East Coast left to the extreme right. But this move through the looking glass wasn't simply bad luck. The two sides were utterly opposed in their political goals, and yet, like Mills and Walker before them, they also shared a deep suspicion of the centralized power elite that had grown up during the Cold War. Lewin's vision of an ultracynical military-industrial complex that would stop at nothing to protect its interests was one that made sense to fascists, too. The crucial difference was whether you remembered that the *Report* was satirical fiction, exaggerated to the point of horrifying absurdity. For all his suspicions of power, Cavin clearly had that in mind; that's surely one reason he alerted Lewin.

Prouty's interpretation of the *Report*, however, was rather different.

Lewin had simply been anxious to get his problem resolved, and treated Prouty's letters as a source of information on who was illegally reproducing his book. But a closer look shows why it was that Colonel Prouty had been driven to help extremists pirate *Report from Iron Mountain*, causing Lewin three years of expensive stress.

It also reveals that Prouty's influence went way beyond one obscure publisher. He helped to shape many Americans' dark vision of those in power, in ways that still deeply affect politics today. And he built his case on *Report from Iron Mountain*.

# 6

# MISTER X AND THE HIGH CABAL

In those letters to his old editor, Colonel Leroy Fletcher Prouty often comes across as a harmless old fellow, enjoying his retirement hobbies—railroads, word processors—at home in an ancient Virginia town that had been absorbed into Washington's sprawl. But his obsession with *Report from Iron Mountain* had consequences for many more people than Leonard Lewin: it shaped the most influential conspiracy theory movie ever made. And the more that emerges about Colonel Prouty, the more curious he seems.

He and Lewin were almost exactly the same age. After long service in the military, including as a pilot in the Second World War, Prouty was assigned in 1955 to the air force's Directorate of Plans, tasked with creating "an office for the military support of the CIA's clandestine operations."[1] He was awarded the Legion of Merit, in part for his "outstanding ability to formulate and implement plans and operations on a global scale."[2] He was, he wrote, in "continuous, day-to-day contact with the highest echelon of CIA officials . . . constantly aware of the CIA's operations, from the mundane and routine to the most significant and sensitive."[3] And this continued when, in 1960, he moved to the Pentagon, as the air force's senior representative in the Office of Special Operations. This unit, based in the Office of the Secretary of Defense, looked after the Pentagon's "contacts with the CIA, Department of State, and White House on intelligence matters" as well as being "responsible for the activities of the NSA."[4] The decisions about CIA covert operations were taken by something called the "Special Group";[5] when the agency wanted air force support for their ops, they had to come through Prouty.

In January 1961, with the inauguration of John F. Kennedy, Robert McNamara arrived with his brisk young whiz kids. By the fall, the new defense secretary had scrapped the OSO, and Prouty's work on special operations was moved to the office of the Joint Chiefs of Staff. He was now overseeing the CIA's requests to the Pentagon for military help, from the air force and beyond. By July 1963, he was "Chief, Special Operations Division."[6] His work had put Prouty close to the heart of power, just as the Pentagon was coming under increasing suspicion both from the likes of C. Wright Mills on the left and from General Walker and his supporters on the right. By November 1963, Prouty had arranged to retire early—and then, just before he left, President Kennedy was murdered. As Prouty settled into a second career, in banking, the men he'd worked with went on to mastermind the Vietnam War.

Over time, Prouty grew more and more suspicious of his old colleagues and what they'd been up to. In one of his letters to Bram Cavin, he talks about "that poorly explained 30-year slice of our history since September 1945."[7] His strange post-Pentagon odyssey seems to have been driven by a need to understand how his country had been transformed by the Second World War and the secret state of which he'd been a part.

In 1973, he published the book that Bram Cavin had edited, *The Secret Team: The CIA and Its Allies in Control of the United States and the World.* He asserted that a permanent power elite ran U.S. foreign policy: an analysis that steered close to conspiracy theory. He suggested, for example, that the Vietnam War wasn't the consequence of delusion and hubris but the culmination of "twenty-five years of driving, devoted work by Secret Team members."[8] He noted that the "national defense industries" strongly backed the war, from which they had "benefited tremendously."[9] In a later edition, he related a story told by an eminent British lawyer in which, one night during the Second World War, in the basement of the Admiralty, Winston Churchill had been heard to reveal the existence of a mysterious "high cabal" who have "made us what we are." "Who could know better," Prouty asks, "that there exists, beyond doubt, an international High Cabal?"[10]

It is striking, given the claims that would later make him famous, that in 1973 Prouty only tentatively raised the idea that Kennedy was assassinated because he was intending to end United States involvement in Vietnam. He talks of evidence "to support the germ of the idea that a sinister conspiracy may have arisen."[11] The U.S. Army's journal, the *Military Review*, called Prouty's account of the supposed Secret Team "a fascinating mélange of derring-do activities, gross errors in fact, and unsupported assertions." But the reviewer also conceded that Prouty had made two good points about the CIA. First, that it was dangerous to combine intelligence gathering and covert operations in one organization. And second, that it was risky to carry out those ops "as a reaction to intelligence,"[12] not in the service of the nation's foreign policy. But from here, Prouty's thinking started to drift farther from shore.

In the mid-1970s, even as its actual fortunes soured, the idea of the omnipotent power elite soared. Hadn't it got away with killing Kennedy? And hadn't President Nixon, both a conspirator and a conspiracy theorist, used his office to spy on, burgle, and persecute his enemies, even as the Watergate scandal slowly broke him? Watergate exposed what a real conspiracy often looks like: criminally malicious in intent and disastrous, finally, for the small, tight-knit network responsible. But it also fostered the feeling that vast, nefarious forces were at work. A wave of public distrust prompted congressional inquiries that forced disclosures about the FBI's illegal attempts to destabilize the radical left, and also about illegal CIA schemes. These included MK-Ultra, an experimental brainwashing program that was, inevitably, a failure. Such revelations were a humiliation for the agencies involved—yet somehow also a confirmation of their sinister power.

One of the triggers for these inquiries was the screening, on March 6, 1975, of the home-movie footage of President Kennedy being shot, filmed by a Dallas bystander named Abraham Zapruder. The footage found its way onto ABC's late night show *Good Night America* with the help of Dick

Gregory. Looking back, the instant when the fatal bullet slammed into the president might have been seen as the point when the postwar dream of American omnipotence was exposed. It was a warning, four years before Tet, that an apparently powerless man can do a lot of damage when he catches you by surprise.

But others interpreted the Zapruder film differently, seeing in the pattern of how the bullets hit evidence that there were multiple shooters and, therefore, a conspiracy. By the mid-1970s, around four-fifths of Americans, Prouty among them, believed Oswald hadn't acted alone. A few months after the Zapruder film was screened, the colonel wrote an article for the *Playboy*-style magazine *Gallery* called "The Guns of Dallas," plunging into the minutiae of bullets and firing speeds.

Then Prouty discovered *Report from Iron Mountain* and its revelations about the secret, terrifying logic driving the power elite. In the mid-1980s, he wrote a series of nineteen articles which were published in *Freedom*, the investigative magazine of the Church of Scientology. These return again and again to the Special Study Group's conclusions: that war is the basis on which society is organized and stabilized, the underpinning of government's authority over the population, the guarantor of national sovereignty. As Prouty stressed in one article, the identities of the group's members were still secret more than twenty years later. But the document they'd produced was public, and—by applying his inside knowledge of the Kennedy Pentagon—Prouty was able to show that it revealed a momentous secret. The exact motive, as applied in real time, behind the assassination of the president.

In his tenth article, "JFK and the Thousand Days to Dallas," he notes that the process that led to the *Report* began shortly after Kennedy took office. He is very struck by the account in the *Report*'s "Background Information" of how McNamara and others close to Kennedy were "impatient" that "no really serious work had been done about planning for . . . a long-range peace,"[13] and by the fact that the *Report* was spurred by "the big changes in military spending that were being planned."[14] This, Prouty considers, is "a most portentous line."[15] He sees the appointment of the Special Study Group in August 1963 as part of the changes to military spending announced by McNamara that April.

McNamara had stressed that the administration had *boosted* military spending by ten billion dollars; it just had to be spent carefully. As part of this, he'd insisted that the navy and air force share a new fighter, the TFX, rather than having one each. (By this time, Prouty was working under the Joint Chiefs and no doubt noticed how they felt about this.) To Prouty, the implications of all this were all too clear. Alongside McNamara's speech, the creation of the Special Study Group to explore what a transition to permanent peace would involve "confirmed" the Kennedy "agenda." Once he won reelection, Prouty concluded, Kennedy was planning to instigate permanent peace:

> Nothing, absolutely nothing, could have had a greater impact on the enormous military machine of this nation. This Kennedy plan jeopardized not hundreds of millions, not even billions, but *trillions* of dollars. It shook the very foundation upon which our society has been built over the past two thousand years. As the *Report From Iron Mountain* says:

> *War itself is the basic social system. It is the system which has governed most human societies of record, as it is today. . . . The capacity of a nation to make war expresses the greatest social power it can exercise; war-making, active or contemplated, is a matter of life and death on the greatest scale subject to social control. . . . War-readiness is the dominant force in our societies. . . . It accounts for approximately a tenth of the output of the world's total economy.*[16]

Kennedy and his men, wrote Prouty, were playing "a dangerous game."[17]

This might have looked like a compelling analysis except for one thing: Prouty was basing his case on a fiction. How could he not have spotted this? The odd thing is, he *had*. He knew Lewin had confessed in 1972 to making it all up, but from the very first time he read the *Report*, Prouty felt as though he was back having lunchtime discussions with McNamara's whiz kids in the Pentagon, who "were saying the very same damn things that Lewin was saying in his *Report from Iron Mountain*."[18] Specifically, those principles about war keeping society stable, underwriting national sovereignty, and giving states the authority to rule over their people. As he told an interviewer at Washington's National Press Club, "I've heard these things said, that without war we can't run this country."[19] Lewin must have had "some very close inside contacts in the Pentagon," he mused to Cavin. The *Report* was simply "too true to life to be created."[20]

Once convinced of this, Prouty deduced that Lewin must have said his book was a novel as a cover story, to avoid having to "attribute it to people."[21] He took Lewin's 1972 confession that he'd made it up as evidence that he hadn't. Lewin must have mixed his accurate material with some fiction to give him deniability. At that event at the National Press Club, early in 1991, the interviewer believed the *Report* was real and was puzzled to hear Prouty refer to it as a novel, asking, "He made it up?" "Well," Prouty replied, "that's what he *says*. . . ."[22]

Prouty's certainty about this was based on the eerily convincing voice Lewin had found in which to parody the icy detachment of Herman Kahn and think tanks thinking the unthinkable. But did Pentagon staff really sound exactly like that? Perhaps some did; such things had been whispered to journalists when *Iron Mountain* came out. However, the man Prouty names repeatedly in this context seems a slightly unlikely example. Ed Katzenbach was the epitome of those bright young(ish) men brought into the Pentagon in 1961 alongside McNamara: an Ivy League historian and specialist on military issues who was appointed deputy assistant secretary of defense for education and manpower resources. He was certainly an anti-communist, and a realist on deterrence, but a year before he arrived at his desk near Prouty, he was arguing in public that the United States should recognize East Germany and Red China to "break the log jam"[23] on disarmament. There is none of Kahn's crackpot-realist zest for negotiating the slippery slopes of the Cold War: Katzenbach sounded more worried than gleeful.

And there was a contradiction here, too. How was it that at one and the same time, McNamara was pushing forward a Kennedy plan for world peace while his own loyal staffers were remarking airily over their sandwiches that war was vital to America's well-being? At one point, Prouty describes the staffers' talk as a matter of asking or debating questions. He was also struck by how some in the Pentagon contended that the advent of the hydrogen bomb made war impossible. So perhaps it was really more their tone and vocabulary, rather than their supposed cynical cruelty, that matched Lewin's made-up, satirical extremes. But it was enough for Prouty to make the case again and again, from the late 1980s, that Lewin's satire was actually evidence of deep state nefariousness.

And then something happened that seemed to make *Iron Mountain*'s dark speculations about peace seem more urgent than ever.

---

The Berlin Wall had been thrown up almost overnight in August 1961 amid that summer's tense nuclear standoff between the superpowers. By the end of the 1980s, the wall had long symbolized the way Cold War Europe was frozen in division, with citizens in the Soviet bloc trapped, no longer able to flee to freedom in the West. And then suddenly, in the summer of 1989, peaceful revolutions swept across Hungary and Poland and Czechoslovakia and East Germany, and the Soviets didn't send tanks to crush them—and there, atop the Wall, were ecstatic Berliners clambering westward and hacking at the hated "anti-fascist protection rampart" with pickaxes. The whole architecture of the Cold War was falling apart. That old *Iron Mountain* scenario—permanent peace—was coming true!

A galvanized Fletcher Prouty redoubled his push to bring the *Report* to America's attention. On December 14, 1989, he took to the airwaves. He was a regular guest on a show called *Radio Free America* that broadcast "every weekday coast to coast."[24] This was yet another Willis Carto outlet: the show was sponsored by Liberty Lobby and the *Spotlight*. It was part of the growing late 1980s phenomenon of talk radio that was becoming an outlet for voices from the far right, whether as callers, guests, or, as in this case, the host. Prouty's interviewer, the voice of *Radio Free America*, was a man named Tom Valentine, another Carto ally. And so, as yet another communist regime—Romania—faced collapse, Valentine invited Prouty to enlighten listeners about what was really driving the geopolitical earthquake that was rippling across Europe.

Prouty was able to reveal to *Radio Free America*'s listeners that the whole thing—the fall of the Berlin Wall, the Czechs' Velvet Revolution, the election triumph of Poland's Solidarity, all of it—was really the work of the power elite, the "big money," operating "behind the scenes."[25] Specifically, David Rockefeller and something called the US-USSR Trade and Economic Council, which had been working for open trade with the Soviets since the 1970s. To make sense of what was going on, to put it in "historical perspective,"[26] Prouty pointed to *Report from Iron Mountain*, which, he explained, was said to have "evolved from a secret study by top-level power-brokers, headed by former Defense Secretary Robert McNamara."[27]

Prouty's logic here was upside down. How did the *Report*, which showed that the power elite needed conflict, explain the *end* of the Cold War? This contradiction reveals what lay at the core of his fascination with this old document: the idea that it proved the existence of a hidden, implacable, omnipotent power elite, forever in control, and bending the world to its interests. This could be used to explain any troubling event. The fact that the *Report* talks about permanent peace—even as a *threat*—was enough to lead him to conclude that the hidden elite must be behind the end of the Cold War. The fact that this completely contradicted the idea that the elite loves war—the basis on which he used the *Report* to explain the Kennedy assassination—does not seem to have bothered him. The host Tom Valentine took from this that it was "the power structure, the so-called military-industrial complex, that needs war—not governments,"[28] and wondered aloud whether a government serving its people could do without the war economy.

Prouty was still struggling to make sense of the post-1945 world; of America's sudden, immense power; of his own former role in some of its darker deeds; and now everything had been upended yet again. He and Valentine both expressed suspicion about the way a supposed enemy like the Soviet Union had suddenly become a friend of American business—just as, at the end of the Second World War, the Soviet ally had suddenly become an enemy. This smacked, they thought, of orchestration. (When Saddam Hussein was subject to a similar policy reversal a few months later, the *Spotlight* raised much the same question.) Once again, Prouty's logic was topsy-turvy. But beneath these contradictions, Prouty had a consistent story to tell: of a hidden, implacable, omnipotent power elite, always in control, and bending the world to its interests.

This was why Tom Marcellus at Noontide Press contacted Prouty. The publisher had read the colonel's articles and now, "in view of the world situation,"[29] he was keen to reprint the *Report*. He had no need to seek Lewin's permission, given that this was a genuine U.S. government publication and, as such, in the public domain. And this was why Prouty sent him a copy from which to produce a reprint, with all the misery that caused for Lewin.

At the same time, Prouty was trying to have his articles republished as a book—which is how Lewin came to hear of what Prouty was up to. Bram Cavin suggested Prouty send his articles to Cavin's wife, Ruth, an editor with St. Martin's Press in Manhattan. Very politely, she declined. A few weeks later, however, Prouty was keen to give Cavin some news. The Institute for Historical Review had decided to reissue his long-lost first book, *The Secret Team*. (He showed no indication of realizing what else the "Institute" published.) And in the same letter, he let Cavin in on a much bigger surprise. His rejected articles, explaining how *Iron Mountain* revealed the truth about the Kennedy assassination, had caught the attention of a filmmaker in Los Angeles; a man who, in 1990, was one of the biggest directors in the world.

---

Oliver Stone had made his name in 1986 with *Platoon*, a movie that broke new ground in its close-up portrayal of the fear, confusion, and brutality of the war in Vietnam. It was based on his own experiences serving as a volunteer infantryman, twice wounded, in 1967 and 1968, for which he received a Purple Heart and a Bronze Star for Valor. He'd followed up that film with *Wall Street*; *Talk Radio*; and then, in 1989, *Born on the Fourth of July*, based on the autobiography of a paraplegic veteran who turned against the war. The project for which Stone had read some of Prouty's articles would pull the camera back to take in the big political picture. It would explain why Kennedy had been killed and, with that, the real reasons behind the war. In the early 1990s, Stone's work was not particularly focused on the new post–Cold War world, but his movie would come to symbolize Americans' fear of their own government in this new, uncertain age.

Symbolically enough, the project seems to have begun at a film festival in Cuba, in 1988, when a publisher handed Stone a copy of a book called *On the Trail of the Assassins*. This was the former New Orleans DA Jim Garrison's account of his investigation into the Kennedy assassination in the late 1960s. Garrison's prosecution of a gay New Orleans businessman named Clay Shaw had rapidly failed in court. Nonetheless, Garrison's labors had led him to conclude that the assassination had been carried out by the CIA in alliance with the military-industrial complex, to stop Kennedy from not only pulling troops out of Vietnam but ending the Cold War. After his case fell apart, Garrison set it out in a book, titled *A Heritage of Stone*, that denounced the tyrannical "power elite"[30] for covering up its assassinations with "fiction."[31] But then, in 1976, he turned to make-believe himself, with *The Star-Spangled Contract*, a novel based on his theories. In the *Los Angeles Times*, one critic wondered: "Does this man know something we don't?" Had he been forced "into fiction to tell a story he couldn't do with provable fact?"[32]

The legal case had centered on Garrison's allegation that Clay Shaw had been an "unpaid contact"[33] of the CIA and was involved in the assassination. Shaw had successfully denied both charges, but in 1979, the CIA was forced to concede that Shaw, who'd since died, *had* indeed worked for them. This proved nothing about the assassination—Shaw's role was to pass on tidbits of information from his foreign trips, which for many businessmen was a routine Cold War chore. But it was enough for Garrison. He was always ready to accuse people of working for the CIA.[34] His approach to substantiating his claims has been criticized on several grounds, including that he tried to hypnotize witnesses, that he leaned heavily on guilt by association, and even that he fabricated evidence.[35] One critic has suggested that "Wherever reality failed to suit his needs, Garrison simply changed it."[36] In light of the revelation about Shaw, Garrison felt able to revisit his investigation as nonfiction. Although perhaps not entirely—Stone thought *On the Trail of the Assassins* read like a thriller or a detective story.

Meanwhile, Garrison had been corresponding with Fletcher Prouty, who shared the former DA's belief in the malign omnipotence of the military-industrial complex, his belief that there was no such thing as coincidence, and his relaxed approach to the difference between fact and fiction. Both men traced the threat of hidden power to the way the American state had emerged transformed from the Second World War.

In short order this quiet, letter-based dialogue acquired a third voice— Oliver Stone—and so was transformed into a triangle of fearful imaginings that would soon have a huge impact. Stone was engaging with Garrison's book; perhaps it was Garrison who drew Stone's attention to Prouty's articles. Either way, on July 3, 1990, Garrison called Prouty to ask him if he'd take a call from Stone. Prouty, then seventy-three, had never heard of the director, but said yes anyway. (He eventually watched *Platoon* and quite liked it.) A young woman duly called from Stone's office in Los Angeles and arranged a meeting at a hotel in Washington.

Prouty was astonished to discover that Stone—a "fine young man,"[37] he thought—had read some of his articles and had some questions about them, with an eye on a potential feature film. They chatted for around two hours. The director asked the renegade military-industrial complex veteran about his time inside the Pentagon, particularly under Kennedy. Stone said later that "I understood his own shock and disbelief at what happened to the President and what happened in the years that followed . . . here and in Vietnam."[38] Phone calls followed, then a "get acquainted" party, which went swimmingly, and a contract with Stone's production company.[39] In October, as Prouty was convalescing after an operation, Stone took the trouble to visit him at home, and brought along the first draft of what would become his movie *JFK*. This was based in significant part on Garrison's book, but it also drew substantially on other writers' work, including Prouty's. Prouty discovered, to his amazement, that one of the crucial characters was clearly based on him.

While this surprising relationship was developing, Prouty obtained a paper on *Iron Mountain* by "KC Associates" in Seattle. This claimed to reveal the names of seven of the fifteen members of the Special Study Group. Lewin's group had, apparently, included the psychologist B. F. Skinner, the psychoanalyst Erich Fromm, the historian Carroll Quigley, three political scientists—Samuel P. Huntington, Vincent P. Rock, and Henry Kissinger—and Edward Teller, the father of the H-Bomb. These were certainly the sort of figures Lewin had been satirizing, but it seems unlikely that they actually joined this group, given that it never existed. Vincent Rock was someone Prouty had known "very well," presumably when he was at the Pentagon,[40] which he seemed to take as corroboration of the *Report*'s authenticity. Carroll Quigley, meanwhile, was a favorite name for conspiracy theorists to conjure with, all the more so when one of his former students, Bill Clinton, became president. Quigley's hefty tome *Tragedy and Hope* analyzes the roles of the American and British establishments, and of elite bankers. He was open to conspiracist thinking, though in his view, Kennedy had been killed by an "unstable political fanatic."[41] Prouty told Cavin he had "no reason to question"[42] the paper's claims about the group's membership. Indeed, they were further evidence that *Report from Iron Mountain* was *not* a novel.

A few months later, Prouty found himself taking a call from none other than Leonard Lewin: the man about whose methods he had been speculating for so long. Prouty had told Cavin he'd given a copy of the *Report* to an unnamed man; now Lewin was calling Prouty, wanting to find out who that mysterious figure was. Prouty told him it was the talk radio host Tom Valentine.* But he also seized his chance to engage Lewin in conversation. And

---

* It appears Prouty was confusing Tom Valentine with Tom Marcellus of Noontide Press.

whatever Lewin said, Prouty duly took it as yet more evidence that *Report from Iron Mountain* was genuine.

———

When Oliver Stone's *JFK* came out in December 1991, it triggered an extraordinary furor—greater even than the one triggered by *Iron Mountain* a generation earlier. It told the story as a noirish political thriller—the mysterious assassination, the official narrative, the sinister figures behind the scenes, the moral maverick determined to expose the truth. If Lee Harvey Oswald had once cast himself as the autonomous rebel, up against the system, now Jim Garrison took that role. As played by Kevin Costner, Garrison challenges the Warren Report's finding that Oswald acted alone. Garrison thinks he has evidence that—via Clay Shaw—the CIA was involved. But he needs someone with real authority to assure him he's on the right track—that there really was a conspiracy and that it involved the CIA. So he travels north to meet a mysterious former insider, known only as X. This is the character based on Fletcher Prouty. The seventeen-minute sequence that follows is the crux of the movie. Without it, Garrison's alternative narrative is little more than suspicions and ballistics.

The scene's setting is Washington, 1967: the year when *Report from Iron Mountain* sent flurries of speculation through the corridors of power. After executing an immaculately discreet rendezvous on the steps of the Lincoln Memorial, X walks Garrison east along the Mall, with the Reflecting Pool in the background behind them. (Had they carried on that way, they'd eventually have reached the town house headquarters of X's future friends at Liberty Lobby.) The published version of the screenplay says X exudes "authority, knowledge, and above all, old-fashioned honesty"[43] as he lays out the full scope of the conspiracy.

Brilliantly played by Donald Sutherland, X is the blood brother of Deep Throat, the FBI man who fed crucial hints to a *Washington Post* reporter investigating Watergate, as visualized in the 1976 movie *All the President's*

*Men*. Like Deep Throat, X talks in the dramatic fashion that the genre demands. He *is* the secret story behind the official narrative, in a dark coat and a hat.

X rattles through the means by which the president was left exposed, such as the unchecked buildings on the route and the unsealed windows in Dealey Plaza, and the total blackout of the Washington phone system. But, as he himself says, his real role is to tell Garrison who was behind the assassination, and *why*. The conspiracy, he reveals, was a collaboration between two malign forces. First, the CIA, angry at Kennedy over the Bay of Pigs and its fallout. Second, the military-industrial complex. X alleges that companies like Bell Helicopter wanted Kennedy out of the way because he was determined to end the war in Vietnam, and the Cold War, too. This is partly about profit—as X explains, "no war, no money"[44]—and a lot of money is involved. But it goes deeper than that. Sitting on a bench, with the Washington Monument and the Capitol behind him, X divulges the terrible secret behind all that has gone wrong in America:

> "The organizing principle of any society, Mr. Garrison, is for war. The authority of the state over its people resides in its war powers."[45]

This was why it was imperative to do something as extreme as assassinating the president. We even see a cabal in black and white, plotting in a smoke-filled room—"defense contractors, big oil, bankers,"[46] as X has it. We see Lyndon Johnson reversing Kennedy's decision to withdraw from Vietnam, in return for the throne. Garrison is aghast, staggered by the "size" of it all: the vastness of the post-1945 state bearing down on him, a colossal conspiracy against peace and truth. As X instructs him, "Politics is power, nothing more."[47]

As many quickly pointed out, there are a lot of problems with this scene. There are the groundless assertions—how could any security detail check all the hundreds of buildings on the motorcade route—and why would they only seal windows at one end of it? There are the factual errors—Washington's phone system was not completely down during the assassination. There is the dramatic license—Prouty and Garrison never met like this. And the logical holes—once ensconced in the White House, why didn't Johnson reverse Kennedy's Test Ban Treaty, which the hawks so loathed? Why did he *stop* covert action against Castro? What about the fact that a working group on Vietnam in the CIA itself had recently recommended that "alternative courses should be examined now," including "Begin[ning] plans to withdraw"?[48] But the problem at the heart of this scene, in a movie which claimed to reveal a great truth, was that X's thesis—Prouty's thesis—was based on a hoax. Lewin's twenty-four-year-old fiction was now powering a blockbuster, on the basis that it was fact.

But then, Prouty was free to believe what he wanted to believe. Alongside his fears of the elite's ominous power, he'd developed a tendency to place himself at the heart of great events, from the 1943 Tehran Conference, at which Roosevelt discussed strategy with Churchill and Stalin, to the Bay of Pigs. In a way, he had something in common with someone else in this story. Like Lee Harvey Oswald—with his fake identities, his quixotic crusade against malign power, his talk of being "prime minister"—Prouty seems to have had a vivid fantasy life. There they were, on either side of the looking glass: two Americans, dreaming.

---

The reaction to *JFK* was deafening. It was at once a huge hit and the target of furious accusations that a film that claimed to reveal the truth was full of fiction. Depending on where you sat, the "establishment" critics making this case either looked like dogged defenders of factual accuracy and trust in politics, or the reincarnation of the Warren Commission. As before in this story, things looked very different depending less on whether you were on the left or the right, more on how far you felt from the center of power.

In a preemptive strike based on a leaked early script, the *Washington Post*'s investigative journalist George Lardner Jr., who'd actually been present at some of the events in the film, took it apart point by point. Stone accused Lardner of being "a CIA agent-journalist,"[49] before retracting this. He'd already seemed to retreat from the claim that the film revealed the truth, saying, "This isn't history, this is moviemaking."[50] *Esquire* suggested Prouty wasn't a reliable source, rather harshly bracketing him with a man who claimed to have in his possession a letter from an ex-president congratulating the assassin. When the film was released in December 1991 another attack appeared in the pages of the *Washington Post*. The conservative columnist George Will wrote that the movie echoed those interwar theories about the "munitions makers," the "merchants of death," and the notion that they'd started the First World War to make money. The idea that "[m]uch of America's establishment conspired to kill Kennedy because he loved peace and 'they' wanted war was cartoon history."[51] By April, even the head of the Motion Picture Association of America, Jack Valenti, who had once been an aide to President Johnson, was calling the film a "hoax."[52]

Stone retaliated against the initial wave of criticism by doubling down on the "merchants of death" element of Prouty's thesis: that "the nexus of interest—military, business, political—standing to profit from the hundred-billion-dollar war" provided a motive for the assassination. Garrison, he added, was being vilified because he raised "the possibility of a nightmare unacceptable to our official historians."[53] Then, in an appearance at the National Press Club, which was televised on C-SPAN, Stone went further. Some people had accused him of inventing X, he said—but they were wrong. Here he was! With that, he revealed that X was "primarily" none other than Colonel Prouty, who was sitting to his right on the dais.[54]

Leading veterans of the New Left, like Tom Hayden and the writer Todd Gitlin, could see the problems with the film. But they'd slogged through over a decade of hard-faced right-wing Republican rule—which was not how they'd hoped the future was going to go in the 1960s—and they rallied to Stone's side. Gitlin thought the X character was "utterly incredible,"[55] yet he still objected to the flak. In the early 1990s, the U.S. media was itself entangled in "credibility scandals" over issues like the use of dramatic reconstructions in TV news shows. Stone's movie was being attacked, Gitlin argued, because it "disputes the myth that the world is as the press reports it."[56]

Likewise, Hayden argued that Stone was being attacked for shattering the media's "fairy tale notion of democracy." But Hayden also went a big step further, insisting that his generation—Stone's generation—had learned the hard way in the 1960s that democracy was "threatened by invisible elites, illegal conspiracies and faceless killers, some of them officially connected."[57] Which sounds a little like another fairy tale.

There *was* a cover-up provoking the debate over *JFK*—not an attempt to conceal a vast conspiracy to kill the president but the much more general cover-up that constituted the culture of official secrecy. The high walls of the post-1945 national security state had become a blank canvas onto which left and right alike could project all sorts of fearful imaginings. Stone's *JFK* ended with an appeal for documents on the assassination to be released. It was the most expensive Freedom of Information request ever made, and surely the most effective. Within a year, new legislation mandated that a full-scale declassification be completed by 2017. Ninety-nine percent of the documents have indeed been declassified, though as the historian Steven Gillon has noted, they contain "no shocking revelations."[58]

And what about Liberty Lobby and the *Spotlight*? The far right had generally despised Kennedy when he was alive, to the point that it had immediately fallen under suspicion when he was shot, with General Walker's "Wanted for Treason" handbills still fluttering on Dallas's windshields. But once the focus of accusations had turned on the secretive American state, the *Spotlight* was happy to exploit this to promote its view of the state's malignant power. Through 1991, while Mark Lane fought on Liberty Lobby's behalf against Leonard Lewin, the paper had been busy boosting Lane's latest book about the Kennedy assassination, *Plausible Denial* (yours for $25 from Liberty Library), which argued that the CIA was behind the assassination.

So it shouldn't be surprising that, upon *JFK*'s release, the *Spotlight* hailed the film, finding entirely plausible its tale of the murder of the president by invisible establishment warmongers. It traced the "psychotic frenzy" the film triggered in the "Establishment media"[59] to its fury that the CIA was being blamed for the assassination. This bashing of the CIA was particularly resented, it alleged, among newspapers with "media outlets with long-standing links to the American intelligence community." As an example, the *Spotlight* pointed to the fact that the erstwhile head of the *Washington Post*'s parent company was a member of both the Council on Foreign Relations and the Trilateral Commission. And was not the former head of the CIA "the grandson of international financier Gates White McGarrah, who was a member of the board of directors of the Astor Foundation, which owned *Newsweek* prior to its purchase by the *Post*"? (How this would have any effect on the magazine's editorial line was left to the reader to imagine.)

Prouty appeared on the *Spotlight* editor's radio show to apply his logic to the situation. He pointed out that in the criticisms of the film, "The same things keep popping up in all that's written." This had to be conspiracy: "It's as though someone has put out instructions on what to say. Somebody is running this whole thing."[60] He was clearly feeling bruised by the whole experience. In one of his letters to Willis Carto, Prouty suggested that the two of them ought to sue *Esquire*, which had highlighted their association, and the fact that Carto had expressed admiration for Hitler. (Prouty also suspected there'd been a government spy infiltrated into the movie studio.) Nonetheless, he was hopeful that once the public had absorbed the film, they'd "explode."[61] The *Spotlight*, he told Carto, should be ready to ride the wave.

Some on the left thought they saw what the far right was up to. The political researcher Chip Berlet warned that "Many on the Left have assumed that the conspiracism promoted in *JFK* stems from a progressive critique of elite domination and intelligence-agency abuse."[62] But conspiracy theories, he argued, had generally been the fruit of the nativist far right. He noted that "several *JFK* themes echo conspiracist claims in a John Birch Society magazine article . . . first published in September 1967," which suggested that blame for the assassination lay with Johnson and the "Establishment." Surely it was possible, Berlet suggested, to ask "hard questions" of state power and its record in the 1960s and since, "without uncritically circulating the conspiratorial scapegoating fantasies of the Far Right."[63]

This dilemma played out in Victor Navasky's weekly, *The Nation*. At the climax of the movie, Garrison delivers a dramatic speech to the court—and the audience sitting in the dark with their popcorn—making public what he has learned from Mr. X. The pugilistic columnist Alexander Cockburn denounced this as revealing a "truly fascist yearning for the 'father-leader' taken from the children-people by conspiracy."[64] Garrison's oration, he wrote:

> accurately catches the crippling nuttiness of what passes amid some sectors of the left (admittedly a pretty nebulous concept these days) as mature analysis and propaganda: that virtue in government died in Dallas, and that a "secret agenda" has perverted the national destiny.[65]

"With this demented optic," he argued, "left ultimately joins hands with right"[66]—as had also happened a few months earlier during the Gulf War. In his view, Kennedy was much less of a savior and much more of a hard-faced cold warrior than his champions were willing to admit. Stone's cowriter, Zachary Sklar, disputed Cockburn's analysis; and from there, the debate raged. Much of this centered on the degree to which Kennedy had definitely committed, in a National Security Action Memorandum—NSAM 263, signed shortly before his death—to the full withdrawal of U.S. forces from Vietnam "by the end of 1965."[67] And the degree to which Johnson had definitely reversed that in a subsequent Memorandum, NSAM 273, shortly afterward.

———

The historian Fredrik Logevall argues that the Vietnam War was avoidable and that Kennedy was unenthusiastic about America's involvement, and might, in early 1965, "have opted against a large-scale American war in Vietnam."[68] Nonetheless, he does not believe that at the time of his death, Kennedy had definite plans to withdraw. Among much other evidence, Logevall points to Kennedy's refusal to seize a "golden opportunity" to pull out that appeared in summer 1963 when the South Vietnamese government's brutal crackdown on dissent infuriated the American public. He also notes that Robert Kennedy confirmed in 1964 "that the administration had not seriously considered a withdrawal."[69]

This raises another question about the theory articulated in the movie. Why kill Kennedy in such a risky fashion? In his speech at the climax of *JFK*, Stone has Garrison suggest that "political murders" have been "disguised as heart attacks, suicides, cancers, drug overdoses." Wouldn't it have been safer for the CIA to put its black ops skills to subtler use and contrive for the sickly president—who'd nearly died several times from his various medical conditions—to have, say, a heart attack in bed? If the CIA really *had* killed Kennedy, and had been as superefficient as is alleged, they might not have spent six decades under a cloud of suspicion. After all, no one thinks Harry Truman had Franklin Roosevelt quietly done away with, but FDR's convenient death in 1945 installed the hawkish Truman as president, which was arguably crucial to the start of the CIA's beloved Cold War. Not to mention the munition-makers' three-year bonanza in Korea.

As Mr. X's monologue suggests, the reason that the JFK "mystery" has gripped America for decades is not about *how* the assassination might have been contrived, or the bizarre logic of carrying out a hit in public, but *why*. It is a story about the two issues that tormented an America still struggling to come to terms with its new self: power and truth. What information can you trust when your secretive leaders wield terrifying force? The reason *JFK* in general, and the X scene in particular, stirred such fury was because, in its attempt to fight the power and reassert the truth, the movie claimed that the historical record was secondary to what Stone called "inner truth." This was the same line Prouty had crossed in his embrace of *Report from Iron Mountain*.

Strikingly, the journalist who first broke the story of the *Report* in the *New York Times*, with a hedging headline about whether it was real or a hoax, was one of those riled up by *JFK*. By 1992, John Leo was a prominent conservative columnist. He zeroed in on Stone's line about "inner truth," and a similar one from Kevin Costner about the movie's "emotional truth," declaring that such things are "the stuff of fiction, or used to be." Leo interpreted this to mean that "it doesn't much matter whether this is literally true or not, so long as it steers the culture where we want to go"—which, he feared, was part of a broader trend. Stone was "the obvious beneficiary of all the fact-blurring TV infotainment shows," which suggested that the public "no longer makes a sharp distinction between news and entertainment or between real and fake footage." *Newsweek* had run extracts from one of the great hoaxes of the age—the Hitler Diaries—and "said it almost didn't matter whether they were real or not."[70] Meanwhile, a quarterly published by *Forbes* magazine had run a story that ex-Soviet officials were taking bids on Lenin's embalmed corpse; *USA Today* and ABC News ran the story before it became clear it was a put-on.

———

Finally, one March night in 1992, this debate came to a head, in a raucous public forum at Town Hall, a Broadway theater. Chairing the event, naturally, was Victor Navasky. The speakers onstage were Norman Mailer; screenwriter and *Monocle* alumna Nora Ephron; JFK conspiracy researcher Edward Jay Epstein; and Oliver Stone himself, who won "thunderous applause."[71] For good measure, they were joined on stage by three "questioners," among them the English writer Christopher Hitchens, a contributing editor on Navasky's *Nation*. "Our goal tonight," Navasky began, "is not to determine who killed Kennedy" but "to explore the relationship . . . of movies . . . to history, of fiction to fact; of image to truth."[72]

Mailer had been dancing back and forth across this line since *The Armies of the Night*, and he'd just published a novel about the CIA and its fantasy world, titled *Harlot's Ghost*. He duly argued that while Stone had taken "considerable liberties" with the facts, "it truly does not matter." The director had dared to venture into "the echoing halls of the largest paranoid myth of our time: the undeclared national belief that John Fitzgerald Kennedy was killed by the concentrated forces of malign power in the land."[73] Ephron, who'd encountered criticism a decade earlier for her carefully researched, fact-based film *Silkwood*, also leapt to Stone's defense. She quoted a novelist who'd argued that "there is no fiction or nonfiction as we commonly understand the distinction. There is only narrative." It fell to the JFK conspiracy researcher Edward Jay Epstein to hold the line between fact and fiction. Graham Greene's novel *The Quiet American*, he argued, came "much closer to the truth than most of the nonfiction books on Vietnam"; he was not making a value judgment. Nevertheless, he said: "I believe there is a difference between nonfiction and fiction."

Much of the rest of the evening went in the direction you might expect. Stone said the Zapruder film showed the lone gunman theory was impossible. Christopher Hitchens scorned the notion that America in 1963 was remotely "innocent." Norman Mailer had a furious argument with a member of the audience.

But one of Stone's responses to an audience question stood out. The director was challenged by a man, who said he was from "an organization called New Jewish Agenda," about Stone's decision to work with Fletcher Prouty, given the colonel's links to Liberty Lobby: an organization, the questioner objected, "that peddles the theory that the Holocaust is a Jewish hoax." How could Stone have done such a thing? The director shot back:

I've checked with the ADL, he never made any single one anti-Semitic comment and he joined the Liberty Lobby late in life. I am concerned with his actions from—actually from 1940 on, to 1963. That is what concerns me. And his credibility, I think, is unquestionable. He is a strong right-winger, he was at the time, he was involved in Black Ops, and he knows a lot about these coups. You do not find, let's say, college professors in this business. People with the necessarily politically correct views. This man was an operative, and he turned against the CIA and his former position. And I think he's very brave to have done that. . . .[74]

Edward Jay Epstein had interviewed Prouty and expressed serious doubts about his reliability as a witness, though he admitted he hadn't known about the link to Liberty Lobby. Soon afterward, in a piece called "Oliver Stone's Fictional Reality," Epstein developed his argument that *JFK* had crossed the line. Through Prouty, *Report from Iron Mountain* had become "the connective logic of Oliver Stone's film."[75] The director had:

demonstrated yet again how easily pierced is the thin membrane that separates the mainstream media from the festering pools of fantasies on its peripheries. What he allowed to ooze into *JFK* from these fringes, with the help of his technical advisers like Colonel Prouty, is the tormenting concept that "secret teams" and "high cabals" fabricated entire historic events to fool them—a concept that incorporates in its schema even the Iron Mountain Hoax.[76]

Nevertheless, for Prouty, his theory's starring role in *JFK* was long-yearned-for vindication. His much-rejected book, based on his 1985 to 1987 *Freedom* articles, now easily found a publisher. *JFK: The CIA, Vietnam and the Plot to Assassinate John F. Kennedy* appeared in 1992—and was packed with references to the "power elite," the "high cabal," and *Report from Iron Mountain*. Prouty argued that "No major event during this period was the result of chance. Each was craftily and systematically planned by a power elite."[77]

And what about that mysterious "high cabal" to which Prouty said no less a figure than Winston Churchill had referred—a term Stone adopted, too? A brief investigation reveals that it is an innocent line from a poem from 1902 called *Ode on the Day of the Coronation of King Edward VII*, written in rather vague praise of British imperial greatness. "Time, and the ocean, and some fostering star," wrote Sir William Watson, "In high cabal have made us what we are."[78]

Prouty quotes Churchill reciting these lines in *The Secret Team*, but seems to have been so keen to find evidence of elite power that he missed the fact that in the poem the prime minister was quoting, "cabal" is just a metaphor. Perhaps, though, Prouty's misunderstanding makes a kind of intuitive sense. His imagination already contained something like a "high cabal." He latched on to this phrase because it gave another name to his existing way of thinking about how power works.

In his quest to make sense of his Cold War past—which combined with an exaggerated sense of self-importance, a blurring of fact and fiction, and an inability to handle evidence—Prouty blundered into helping Liberty Lobby spread its malignant ideas. And in the post–Cold War America of the 1990s, the idea that Lewin's fiction was authentic—which Prouty promoted with all the authority of his old Pentagon job—was already having much more serious consequences among people who came to believe the book was 100 percent real.

People who were a lot more frightening than even Prouty's far-right friends.

# 7

# BLUEPRINT FOR TYRANNY

At 9:02 a.m. on Wednesday, April 19, 1995, a truck bomb packed with five thousand pounds of fertilizer and racing fuel detonated outside the Alfred P. Murrah Federal Building in Oklahoma City. It killed 168 people, among them nineteen children, and injured more than 680 others. At first, many suspected it was the work of Islamist terrorists, but after the arrest of a right-wing extremist, the awful thought began to dawn that this atrocity had been homegrown. The glare of the media spotlight swung onto the militia movement, which had been springing up across the United States and training its recruits for some kind of political nightmare scenario. That Friday, Robert Tomsho, a Dallas-based reporter for the *Wall Street Journal*, found himself driving out from Oklahoma City to a tiny town near the Arkansas border to try to make sense of what the militias thought was coming, and why.

Tomsho had got hold of the head of the state's Unorganized Citizen Militia, a denture maker named Ross Hullett, after Hullett told the main Oklahoma City paper that "most militia people are Christians" and "only the government could make you believe"[1] they were involved in the bombing. True, one member of his militia had used its stationery to "call for white supremacy and threaten an armed overthrow of the US government,"[2] but Hullett was not at all happy about that. He wasn't available to talk to the *Wall*

*Street Journal* but agreed to arrange for two other members of his group to be interviewed.

One hundred and twenty miles east of Oklahoma City, Tomsho arrived in Eufaula, a secluded little community bordered on three sides by lakes. It was "a beautiful day."[3] He went to the office of the local sheriff, who took him out into the woods, introduced him to the two militiamen—and made his exit. One of the men was a retired welder who'd seen combat in Vietnam. The other, the Oklahoma Militia's cofounder, was a retired fireman but said he went by the nickname "the chaplain." He declined to divulge his name "for fear of government retribution."[4] As far as Tomsho remembers, they weren't armed. At one point, however, they did start talking about how, if the day of reckoning came and the sheriff failed to take their side, they might have to kill him.

They denied all connection to the carnage in Oklahoma City, but it hadn't shaken their commitment to the movement. The Vietnam vet said he wasn't interested in trying to topple the government by force of arms, but still saw it as "the enemy." "I would lay down my life for my country," he told Tomsho, "But I wouldn't spit on a congressman if he were burning to death."[5] As the three of them sat among the trees, the militiamen started setting out the scenario for which they were preparing. It gave the reporter "chills."[6]

The federal government, they explained, had "come under the control and domination of a group of wealthy coconspirators," and was poised to "declare war upon its own citizens,"[7] seize their guns, and crush their liberty. This was just part of a plot to hand the subjugated United States over to the forces of the United Nations. "The day the Russian troops come across the border," the chaplain said, "we'll have the guns and we'll be fighting." They asked Tomsho if he knew about the government's secret concentration camps, built to hold militia people in cells underground and, also, outdoor "tiger cages" like the ones in which American POWs had been held in Vietnam.

When Tomsho asked militiamen how they knew this nightmare was coming, they replied: "Have you read *Iron Mountain*? Have you read *Iron Mountain*?" As one explained, the *Report* was "the plan for the destruction of the U.S."[8]

How had it come to this?

—————

At the height of the Cold War, C. Wright Mills had wanted to show that America could thrive "with the economics of war subtracted."[9] If peace came, he was confident it would not cause the terrible economic and political problems that the "crackpot realists" feared. That was part of what Lewin and Navasky had implicitly argued with *Report from Iron Mountain*. War had become far too dominant; to believe peace would wreck America was insane. Back then, the idea that any of this might ever actually start happening had seemed a utopian dream. But then, in 1989, it did.

Ironically, the men the *Report* was attacking thought they'd won, too. Walt Rostow may have looked like a hubristic fool by the end of his time working for President Johnson, but twenty years on, his belief that the Cold War could be won economically seemed to have come true. By 1990, the Soviet model had irreparably broken down; the American model was sweeping all before it.

Paradoxically, the advent of peace began with America's first officially declared war in decades—the effort to drive Iraq out of Kuwait known as Desert Storm—but it was over almost before it began. And while the operation was led by America, it had the blessing of the United Nations. In the run-up to the invasion in the fall of 1990, with even the dying USSR joining the coalition, President George H. W. Bush felt able to proclaim a "new world order." Ever since the late 1940s, the Soviet Union had been America's supreme enemy. By the end of 1991, it had vanished. Sunny predictions of a new age of worldwide liberal democracy blossomed. Yet Bush—high-born diplomat, ex-head of the CIA—was a somewhat chilly prophet. To many, his new world order sounded less like a promise than a threat.

In the face of the deindustrialization of the 1980s, defense companies had fared better than industries like steel, cars, and tech, because President Reagan had massively hiked military spending. But Reagan had left behind a huge deficit; now, in the face of a recession, with the promise of a "peace dividend," the Pentagon made dramatic cuts. Big bastions of the military-industrial complex finally had to "downsize." A cut in orders for F-16s killed jobs at General Dynamics in Fort Worth; across town, employees at Bell Helicopter faced a similar fate. In 1992, Colt furloughed its workers for two weeks at a time; by 1993 it was pleading for a loan from the Connecticut Development Authority. And in Long Beach, California, defense giant McDonnell Douglas laid off close to thirty thousand workers inside four years.

The Cold War standoff was over, but at home, the sense of conflict spiked. At McDonnell Douglas's "career transition center," the journalist Susan Faludi found the company's high-status aerospace employees confronting a future as clerks in casino pits. "Their faces tense with confusion and anger," she wrote, "they all asked the same question: What enemy had done this to them?"[10] One man told Faludi he wanted a "dictatorship" in America, to bring back "the old 'system.'"[11]

Few of the benefits that had flowed from America's great victory in 1945—the boom-fueled government largesse, the job security, the rising pay—had survived the Cold War. Yet somehow the fearful visions it stirred up continued to thrive. On the day Oliver Stone's JFK opened, newspapers on Long Island and in Texas were worrying about the impact of defense industry layoffs.[12] Yet the film's depiction of a murderous, all-powerful military-industrial complex struck a nerve.

The high-spending postwar state, and 1945's other legacy—righteous military might—had once reinforced each other. But Lyndon Johnson, father of the Great Society, had also lied and lied and led young Americans to disaster. By the 1970s, the postwar economic model was coming apart, too. Those who came home from Vietnam soon found themselves adrift in Reaganland, where the president believed that government was the problem, and that his predecessors had deliberately sabotaged the war effort. Not for the first or last time, the United States had a conspiracy theorist in the Oval Office. Reagan seemed less exercised by the plight of actual veterans than by the phantom POWs and MIAs supposedly left behind, waiting for Rambo. This myth was a magnet for hucksters, eager to defraud desperate families with "evidence" that their loved ones might still be alive. Nonetheless, the story that the men sent to fight in Vietnam had been duped and betrayed by the power elite endured and metastasized.

America had still not come to terms with how it had been transformed into a superpower by the Second World War and how Vietnam had mangled its sense of heroic righteousness—and now the world had lurched again. By 1992, the republic of small farmers was the planet's one remaining super-power. And the new world order brought new treaties, opening up a global-ized economy, pulling American jobs abroad. So who was the enemy now?

It wasn't just autoworkers or aerospace engineers—or Vietnam veterans—who felt that someone had turned against them. In the 1970s, the republic's small farmers had been lured into borrowing heavily to expand, only to be hit, as the decade ended, by shockingly high interest rates, just as property values slumped. On top of that, dependence on multinationals exposed them to the global economy. The journalist Joel Dyer interviewed hundreds of those affected, and in his 1997 book *Harvest of Rage* he pointed out that losing the family farm cut much deeper than losing a job. It tore away a person's identity, their heritage, leaving them angry and ashamed. Many struggled hopelessly for years to stave off losing what was theirs, but through the 1980s and the 1990s a tornado of foreclosures swept across the plains, forcing almost a million people off their land in 1986 to 1987 alone. Huge agribusinesses swallowed the spoils. In Oklahoma, the governor established a task force to try to understand why the suicide rate was so high in his state. The group heard from many people subjected to ill-treatment by banks, while the federal government shrugged. One woman admitted that she'd "written letters to Washington D.C. on brown paper food bags, as I had no other paper to write on," but to no avail: "the greedy Farmers'[sic] Home Administra-tion foreclosed on our only source of livelihood."[13] In western Oklahoma, a common-law jury declared that a woman who'd died of a heart attack from the stress had been murdered by the FHA agent dealing with her case.

The scandalous and cruel neglect of farmers might have led, as it had before, to a left-wing mass movement against a cold, uncaring power elite. As the extremism expert Daniel Levitas has noted, labor union members, liberal Jewish groups, and the Democratic presidential contender Jesse Jackson were among those who stood with the farmers. But where radical anti-government activists succeeded in selling farmers a compelling explanation, they came from the extreme right. The likes of Willis Carto had been retailing their story of power for decades—of evil politicians plotting dictatorship, and evil Jewish bankers using debt to enslave the world. To some farmers who'd worked hard and lost everything, this idea suddenly seemed horribly plausible. And this could all too easily be fused with the story that had driven the Declaration of Independence: of dark forces trying to impose "absolute tyranny." In 1984, the conflict between a Nebraska farmer named Arthur Kirk and his bank ended up in a standoff with state troopers after sheriff's deputies tried to serve papers demanding repayment of a huge loan. Kirk told them: "Farmers fought the revolutionary war and we'll fight this son of a bitch."[14] The siege ended when he was shot dead. In his house, along with his many weapons, they found a copy of *The Protocols of the Elders of Zion*.

By the early 1990s, as taxes rose, unemployment hit 7.8 percent, and disorienting global change ground on, the idea that the enemy was at home had spread beyond the far right and those radicalized farmers. The left certainly felt alienated by long years of Reagan and Bush, but so, it turned out, did many ordinary people of a much more right-wing mindset. Corporate tax breaks, free trade, and foreign wars weren't everyone's top priorities. A patriot movement began to emerge across the country, consciously echoing the American Revolution. It was driven by the fear that the federal government was controlled by a secretive power elite plotting imminent tyranny, maybe on a global scale. This brought together people focused on economic troubles and government abuse of power with much more extreme, overtly racist groups, but it was a much looser, broader, more popular phenomenon than

Liberty Lobby. It sprang from the grass roots—phone-ins, friend groups, gun shows.

The 1992 presidential election was packed with right-wing populists. The conspiracist ex–Green Beret Bo Gritz, champion of the POW/MIA myth, was standing for Carto's Populist Party. Its previous candidate, David Duke, ran for the Republican nomination; so did Pat Buchanan, a former aide to Nixon and Reagan, who attacked Bush and his business elites in proto-Trumpian terms: "He is a globalist and we are nationalists. He believes in some *Pax Universalis*, we believe in the Old Republic. He would put America's wealth and power at the service of some vague New World Order; we will put America first."[15] The *Spotlight* didn't lack for candidates it could support. And then there was Ross Perot, an anti-war, anti-globalization populist billionaire, who stood as an independent, "giving voice to valid grievances and hysterical fears."[16]

Throughout that election year, a fearful patriot on red alert for federal tyranny barely had to leave his or her couch. In April, when riots flared across Los Angeles, President Bush invoked the Insurrection Act and authorized sending federal troops into an American city. In August, deep in the Idaho mountains, the latest standoff began between federal authorities and a right-wing extremist. At a place which became known as Ruby Ridge, U.S. marshals came to arrest a survivalist veteran named Randy Weaver who'd failed to appear in court to face firearms charges. After one of the marshals shot and killed Weaver's fourteen-year-old son, a siege developed. The following day, an FBI sniper shot Weaver's wife, Vicki, in the head as she cradled their baby. Finally, after more than a week, Weaver surrendered. In October, well over a hundred far-right activists met in the Rocky Mountains in Colorado where they agreed to unite against the dictatorial government and foster the creation of militias. Nine days later, Bill Clinton was elected president, promising gun control and preparing to antagonize left and right alike by ratifying the North American Free Trade Agreement, which lifted economic barriers with Mexico.

And then, in February 1993, yet another standoff began between government and extremist outsiders, this time near the Texas town of Waco. The Bureau of Alcohol, Tobacco, and Firearms (ATF) tried to raid the compound of the Branch Davidian religious cult. The group was accused of stockpiling illegal guns but refused to deal with the federal authorities. In the ensuing battle, six cult members died along with four ATF officers. So began a fifty-one-day siege, perpetuated by Branch Davidian leader David Koresh's obduracy and exacerbated by divisions within the FBI. Finally, federal agents rammed holes in the walls with tanks and pumped in tear gas, expecting people to surrender. Instead, the building caught fire—live on TV, on the anniversary of the start of the American Revolution. Seventy-six Branch Davidians, including more than twenty children, were killed. The government saw an abusive cult leader holding his followers hostage; and audiotapes later emerged indicating that Koresh and his lieutenants started the blaze, a conclusion confirmed by an official investigation. Nevertheless, for the many who saw an FBI massacre here was tyranny made visible.

After Waco, the militia movement spread like fire. John Trochmann was an adherent of an extreme racist ideology, Christian Identity, who'd been present at the far-right conclave in Colorado. In February 1994, he started a militia in Montana, a state where jobs in timber and mining had given way to "a low-wage vacation and service economy."[17] He was soon sending out around two hundred "militia start-up packages a week."[18] The Militia of Michigan was set up that April. The Republican triumph in the November 1994 midterm elections even brought the voice of the movement into Congress.

One of the Michigan leaders told a television journalist that he'd been tipped "over the edge" by Clinton taking America into the 1994 General Agreement on Tariffs and Trade. He feared the country faced "economic collapse" and worried about a power elite plot to pull America toward "a socialist program for world government."[19] The militia model had long roots, not only in the memory of the Revolution, but among the latter-day minutemen allied with General Walker in the early 1960s, and William Potter Gale, who founded the California Rangers, a "secret underground guerrilla force," in 1958.[20] Not for nothing had President Kennedy suggested Americans devote "less energy to organizing armed bands of civilian guerrillas."

For men stuck in dead-end work in the Rust Belt, southwestern desert towns, and the edge cities of California, here was the chance to dress in camouflage, wield a weapon, and play a vital part in a righteous, apocalyptic drama. The boring grind of bureaucracy and the diktats of distant politicians were transfigured into a ruthless totalitarian enemy. And for farmers who'd lost everything while Washington ignored them, the militias offered a way to fight back. This was a new declaration of war against the power elite, this time from the disaffected right.

———

As Robert Tomsho would discover in the aftermath of the Oklahoma bombing, some militias were particularly influenced by three key texts. Each told a story about the evils of the power elite.

The first was *The Turner Diaries*, a 1978 novel by a neo-Nazi ex-ally of Willis Carto. The idea that elites tend not to have the population's best interests at heart is useful, if treated judiciously. But *The Turner Diaries* stretched the notion to conspiracist, anti-Semitic extremes, with the aim of triggering a race war. It fantasized a near-future America ruled by Jews. Their oppressive "System" confiscates guns and persecutes white people; an underground resistance movement launches guerrilla war, pogroms, and mass executions of politicians, bureaucrats, judges, businessmen, and journalists. In Oliver Stone's prescient 1988 movie *Talk Radio*, far-right callers enthuse to the horrified Jewish host about the book's visions of vengeful far-right revolution. Early in the book, the protagonist, Earl Turner, blows up the FBI building in Washington, DC, with a truck bomb, with the aim of obliterating a computerized system of internal passports. The narrative ends with Turner deliberately flying a plane equipped with a nuclear warhead into the Pentagon.

Some militias' second guiding text had been written by the televangelist and former Republican presidential candidate Pat Robertson, chief of the highly influential Christian Coalition and Christian Broadcasting Network. Where the *Turner Diaries*' author was a fringe extremist, Robertson was a significant figure on the Republican right. His *The New World Order*, published in 1991, spied conspiracy among bankers, the Rockefellers, the Council on Foreign Relations, the Trilateral Commission, the United Nations, and global elites in general. The book opens with Bush's declaration of a new world order—which, Robertson frowningly informed readers, was a phrase Hitler had used. The advocates of the new world order aimed to "eliminate national sovereignty" in favor of "world government, a world police force, world courts, world banking and currency, and a world elite in charge of it all."[21] As the *Spotlight* had done, Robertson suggests the Gulf War was a setup, a ruse to advance the globalist cause. He condemns the Federal Reserve, meanwhile, as "a secret power center controlling our economy."[22] As critics eventually pointed out, the book drew on anti-Semitic myths about how Jewish bankers had supposedly funded the Russian Revolution; Robertson insisted he wasn't anti-Jewish, and revised the text. A quote from an anonymous reader on the paperback declared that the book "reads like a spy thriller."[23] It doesn't, but the tacit admission of its proximity to fiction is telling.

And the third book inspiring the movement was *Report from Iron Mountain*: a real, firsthand product of the power elite itself. A government document exposing the plot that lay behind all the bewildering changes sweeping the world in the early 1990s, and what the elites were plotting next. The claim that it was a "hoax" was obviously a cover-up. As one Indiana lawyer told the *New York Times*, "To the majority of people in the patriots' community, this is not a piece of fiction." It was being disseminated among patriots "to show the evil."[24] The publisher of a newsletter in Arkansas called *Patriot Report* refused to believe that *Report from Iron Mountain* was satire: "It was an official document, done by the will of the president and secreted away so that it wouldn't be released to the public," he insisted. "It shows that there is a conspiracy against the citizens."[25]

---

For Fletcher Prouty, and his movie doppelganger Mr. X, the overriding revelation of *Report from Iron Mountain* was the power elite's determination to entrench the war system, even to the point of killing the president. But the *Report* also had much to say about what the elite had planned in the absence of war—which was now the disorienting new normal. In Bush's peaceful new world order, attention turned to the eye-catching alternatives to permanent conflict that the Iron Mountain Special Study Group had brought up for consideration: slavery, eugenics, fake alien scares, planned pollution. One figure who pointed people to this aspect of the *Report* was perhaps the militia movement's leading thinker: a strange, intense man named Milton William Cooper.

Like Prouty, Bill Cooper was a veteran of a long stint in the postwar American military and spent the rest of his life struggling to make sense of the power he'd once willingly served: to understand just what, since 1945, his country had become. One way or another, Cooper had absorbed most of the traumas this book traces. He was born in Long Beach in 1943 amid the huge new factories that had sprung up to feed the U.S. war machine. His father was a pilot in the Army Air Corps; not far away, in the Douglas Aircraft Company's endless, windowless, air-conditioned buildings, thousands of workers clanged and riveted and hammered away day and night. A few miles southwest lay the vast naval shipyard on Terminal Island.

Cooper belonged to the same generation as Tom Hayden and Lee Harvey Oswald. He saw his father as a "tyrant";[26] Cooper senior often hit young Bill with a belt. As his biographer Mark Jacobson has charted, Cooper spent his childhood on military bases, imbibing the television version of America in those bases' rec rooms, never staying anywhere long enough to build a home or make friends. He enlisted in the air force and wound up on a Strategic Air Command base in Texas, tending Minutemen missiles during the Cuban missile crisis—and during the red alert when the president was shot. While Hayden was leading protests against the Vietnam war in Chicago, Cooper was fighting it. As soon as he left the air force, he enlisted in the navy and found himself piloting a patrol boat on the river that led inland from the Gulf of Tonkin. He ended up in Naval Intelligence in Hawaii, with, he said, Q-level security clearance, which would have allowed him to access material classified as "Top Secret."[27] His job was briefing an admiral. But then his patriotic trust in his leaders, his willingness to die at their command, was ruptured. At the same time that President Nixon was insisting that the United States wasn't bombing Laos and Cambodia, Cooper was handling documents that showed it was doing exactly that. He was not the only Vietnam veteran who had come to feel he'd been tricked.

He began civilian life in the decay of the 1970s Bay Area. By the late 1980s—his stability diminished by a slew of drunken rages, broken marriages, aborted jobs, and finally a PTSD-induced breakdown—he'd fallen down the rabbit hole of alien-abduction and UFO tales. He slid erratically between fact and fiction, insisting he'd seen evidence of all kinds of outlandish stories in secret naval intelligence papers, just as he "remembered" seeing the Kennedy assassination on TV on the fateful day—when there was no such broadcast. On July 2, 1989, he told a UFO symposium in Las Vegas: "Without the aliens, you can't make sense of anything that has happened in this country for the past forty-four years."[28]

But then he had a revelation. All those UFO stories were just a manipulative trick perpetrated by the elites to cow the populace. He'd certainly shown that he himself was vulnerable to swallowing hoax claims.

Under it all, in Jacobson's judgment, was a man in "anguish" at his nation's "decline."[29] This was entwined with Cooper's revulsion at the way the Constitution had been perverted by a secret government leading a "nation of sheep."[30] No wonder he fell for *Iron Mountain*.

Cooper's ominous stories and calls for the public to do their own research had been building a following. By 1993 he had his own show on shortwave radio and had appeared at London's Wembley Arena; he is one major reason people talk about "sheeple." His biggest breakthrough, though, was his book *Behold a Pale Horse*, published in 1991: an extraordinary compendium of "forbidden knowledge," which became an underground bestseller and was embraced by everyone from Public Enemy and Tupac Shakur to the creator of *The X-Files*. Cooper's book compiled government documents, aerial photos of UFO sites, press releases, letters, and much more. He seems

particularly suspicious of the Federal Emergency Management Agency, calling attention to executive orders that he thought had given FEMA power to
suspend the Constitution and establish a police state. Appallingly, Cooper
also included in his book the full text of *The Protocols of the Elders of Zion.*
He merely added a quick disclaimer that, by "the Jews," the text really meant
"the Illuminati." In the view of one expert on conspiracy literature, *Behold a
Pale Horse* is "among the most influential" of "superconspiracy theories."[31]
It's also a favorite target for shoplifters.

*Report from Iron Mountain* appeared in Cooper's book in two different guises—though he was only aware of one. In appendix E: "New World
Order," between a fragment on the Kennedy assassination and a paper from
the Carnegie Endowment for International Peace, Cooper reproduces four
pages from the *Report.* These outline some of the alternatives to war that
the Special Study Group supposedly discussed: "deliberate environmental
poisoning," space exploration, confecting an alien menace. This section of
the *Report* argues that "however unlikely" these suggestions seem, some sort
of war alternative will have to be found, if the "transition to peace" is not to
trigger "social disintegration."[32]

Cooper opened his book with long excerpts from another document,
dated 1979. It was titled "Silent Weapons for Quiet Wars." This purported to
reveal the elite's "quiet war" on the American people: a permanent campaign
of social, economic, and psychological control being waged with "silent
weapons" like television. The objective was to enslave people in a completely
automated society: better that than letting ordinary people stay free, which
just led to economic chaos and war. Cooper insisted this obvious hoax document was genuine, on the grounds that it "correctly outlines events which
subsequently came to pass," and that people only ignore it because they "are
not ready to admit that they have been cattle."[33]

At the top of the excerpts from "Silent Weapons," he added a title: "The
Illuminati's declaration of War upon the people of America,"[34] and a note.
This asserts that "the peaceful Citizens of this nation are fully justified in
taking whatever steps may be necessary, including violence, to identify,

counterattack, and destroy the enemy."[35] To justify this, Cooper cited "the principles outlined in the Declaration of Independence, the Constitution of the United States of America, and the fully recognized and acknowledged historical precedents that have served as the justification for destruction of tyrants."[36]

He wasn't to know, but it would later become clear that "Silent Weapons" was heavily influenced by *Iron Mountain*—doubling the impact of Lewin's hoax on Cooper's incendiary ideas. According to Mark Jacobson, this opening chapter was "the most influential chapter in *Behold a Pale Horse*."[37] Its story of insidious elite mind control certainly seems to have made a deep impression on a long list of hip-hop artists. In 1997, for instance, the Wu-Tang Clan affiliate Killarmy released a whole album named *Silent Weapons*. The book also took off among Black men incarcerated in the U.S. prison system. As one Harlem bookseller told Jacobson: "The incarcerated African American is the most legitimately paranoid man in the world. When you get to William Cooper, he is one paranoid white man, he speaks the same language."[38]

In 1993, a 140-minute video appeared titled *Iron Mountain: Blueprint for Tyranny*. This was produced by a retired pilot named Stewart Best; it is still much circulated online today. Using arguments very similar to those Cooper used about "Silent Weapons," it insists repeatedly that *Iron Mountain* is real. We learn that the *Report* has a "globalist agenda,"[39] and reaches conclusions similar to those of the Trilateral Commission, the Council on Foreign Relations, and so on. The video works through the Special Study Group's "war alternatives," including the ones highlighted in *Behold a Pale Horse*, to show how each is "now being implemented."[40] Pollution is being deliberately left unsolved, "until it can be manipulated by the world media into a global crisis,"[41] allowing the rich men who own the United Nations to seize the land and enslave the world. Then President Clinton is introducing government health care as one of the *Report*'s economic substitutes for war. Its line about reintroducing slavery, partly for the "control of potential enemies of society,"[42] reveals the fate that awaits opponents of the new world order. The *Report*'s talk of staging "blood games," in the tradition of inquisitions and witch trials, is taken to explain the demonization and killing of the Branch Davidians. Its discussion of trying out eugenics and population control becomes evidence that such things are on their way.

All this points to a single, sinister purpose. *Iron Mountain* is cross-referenced, line by line, with official documents and end-times theology to show that America is months from globalist totalitarian takeover. The global elite has long plotted to re-create the "invisible functions of war" by other means, as the secret plan in the *Report* reveals—including maintaining control of the citizenry. Now that the "war system" is coming to an end, this is coming to pass. Washington is in the process of betraying the American people to a one world slave state under the United Nations.

The video's scenario, very similar to those laid out by the *Spotlight*, Cooper, and other militia thinkers, proceeds something like this:

> *To override Americans' defense against dictatorship—the right to bear arms—shadowy federal agencies are preparing to mobilize. Already, their unmarked black helicopters are showing up all across America. Soon, the Federal Emergency Management Agency will invoke emergency law and take over. A multi-jurisdictional task force, incorporating state police, National Guard, and co-opted street gangs, will conduct house-to-house searches and seize citizens' guns. FEMA will split families, and enslave civilians in work brigades. It will brand dissidents "terrorists" and send them to concentration camps, including a million-acre facility standing ready in Alaska. Civilian disturbances will be crushed with military force, under the UN Charter chapter on dealing with acts of aggression. The USA will be cut into ten regions of the world state, under the heel of foreign troops—Russian, Mongolian, German, Venezuelan.*

This scenario took *Report from Iron Mountain*, and its old 1960s vision of the big, centralized postwar power elite, and escalated it into a truly Orwellian nightmare. As with misreadings of *Nineteen Eighty-Four*, this interpretation missed the point, in a revealing way. The *Report*'s details—its horrific alternatives to war—are there to flesh out Lewin's satire. But *Blueprint for Tyranny* saw them as terrible plots that were coming true. In the video, the voice-over exclaims in horror at the *Report*'s inhuman coldness. Exacerbating all this—as in Orwell's novel—is Lewin's satirical technique of pushing everything to extremes. Read literally, this just seemed to confirm the depths of the elite's evil and its infinite power. Stewart Best went on to produce a further six-hour video series, *Iron Mountain II*.

Through the early 1990s, nightmares of totalitarian global takeover quietly spread through a U.S.-wide virtual community: not just through mail-order videos but through shortwave radio shows, computer disks, and the early internet. Until, exactly two years on from the end of the Waco siege, a young Gulf War veteran drove to Oklahoma City and committed a real act in this imaginary war.

———

Timothy McVeigh grew up outside Buffalo, with a dad stuck in the declining car industry. His mom first left when he was eleven; five years later, she was gone for good. He ended up enlisting in the army and served in the Gulf War, but came to question why it had been fought. He came home to pursue his dream of joining the Special Forces, but didn't make it. He loved guns, and the American dream of liberty. He was horrified by Ruby Ridge, and Waco—he went to watch the siege—and by Clinton's attempts at gun control. He took to living in his car, shuttling from gun show to gun show— Michigan to Kansas to Arizona—selling copies of *The Turner Diaries*. Until finally he decided to strike back against the federal agencies he hated, for what he believed was their massacre of the Branch Davidians and for those same agencies' determination to rule the country by absolute despotism. Exactly two years after the end at Waco—and two hundred and twenty years on from the start of the American Revolution.

When McVeigh was arrested shortly after the explosion, on a minor traffic violation, he was wearing a T-shirt bearing the slogan of President Lincoln's assassin, SIC SEMPER TYRANNIS—"Thus always to tyrants." On the back was a quotation from Thomas Jefferson: "The tree of liberty must be refreshed from time to time with the blood of patriots and tyrants." In the trunk of his car was a thick bundle of papers: the fuel for his nightmarish vision of how power worked in America. This included pages from *The Turner Diaries* about bombing government buildings, articles criticizing the government over Waco, and one of the bumper stickers he'd been trying to hawk when he visited the siege of the Branch Davidian compound: WHEN THE GOVERNMENT FEARS THE PEOPLE, THERE IS LIBERTY. WHEN THE PEOPLE FEAR THE GOVERNMENT, THERE IS TYRANNY. There were quotations about freedom from such thinkers as Jefferson, Churchill, John Locke, and Patrick Henry (that old revolutionary hero of C. Wright Mills). There was also a copy of the Declaration of Independence, with McVeigh's postscript at the bottom: "Obey the Constitution of the United States, and we won't shoot you."[43] In a letter "intended to be found someday"[44] by the federal agency centrally involved in the Waco siege, McVeigh had called them "tyrannical mother fuckers" who "will swing in the wind one day" for their "treasonous actions against the Constitution of the United States."[45]

He had been introduced to some of these ideas by his old army buddy, and later accomplice, Terry Nichols, and Nichols's brother James. Their family had been victims of the farm crisis in Michigan, and they'd turned to the extremes. In part through their influence, McVeigh had tuned in to hard-right shortwave radio and started reading the *Spotlight*, the *Patriot Report* newsletter, and the magazine *Soldier of Fortune*.

And perhaps, somewhere in the swirl of influences, direct and indirect, that shaped McVeigh's dystopian view of America, there lurked the notion that something called *Report from Iron Mountain* revealed the government's terrible plans. In April 1994, an ad for *Iron Mountain: Blueprint for Tyranny* appeared in *Soldier of Fortune* when McVeigh was known to have been reading it: "You have fought in the desert," it read. "You have been betrayed. You are mere cannon fodder for a bigger purpose, an evil purpose, a purpose that will now enslave you." As we saw, the editor of those *Patriot Report* news-letters believed *Iron Mountain* was a suppressed, leaked official document, which revealed the "conspiracy against the citizens."

McVeigh was also an avid listener of William Cooper's talk show, *The Hour of the Time*, which began on WWCR after *Radio Free America* at 10:00 p.m. central time with an eerie cacophony of sirens, screams, barking dogs, and marching feet, meant to evoke the coming of tyranny. We know that in the three months or so before the bombing, McVeigh listened when-ever he could get a signal. During this period, Cooper's rhetoric seemed to be inciting violence, calling on listeners to "go there bodily and rip down the UN building," and to "kick those bastards off our soil," affirming that "we are at war."[46] Michael Fortier, a libertarian Arizona meth head whom McVeigh told about the bombing in advance, was asked in August 1995 about the influences that led McVeigh to carry it out. He said: "We heard lots of tapes and saw videos and read things. There is this guy with a radio station in Arizona, Bill Cooper. He keeps calling people "sheeple" and was mad that they ain't doing anything to change things. Well, we got to think-ing that's right, *things need to change.* Tim really responded to that."[47]

If, on the night of January 19, 1995, McVeigh's dial found WWCR, he would have heard Cooper say this:

We must restore the Constitution because it is not in effect and you better get that through your thick heads, we are under United Nations international law. Right this moment, and have been since 1945. For many years, nobody saw any results of this because they had to promote a *huge* brainwashing and propaganda campaign against the American people, to get them to accept it. Part of that is what's known as the New Age movement. Part of that is the ozone holes. Part of it is global warming. Part of it is pollution, environmental destruction, done on purpose to create this cry for international control. Read the *Report from Iron Mountain.* The *Report from Iron Mountain.* The possibility and probability of permanent peace. All of these things were outlined in that book as contingency plans to bring about world government and do away with wars forever.[48]

---

The scramble to understand McVeigh's motivations revealed just how far *Report from Iron Mountain* had spread through the minds of the militia movement, in ways that have had a lasting influence. In a follow-up to his initial *Wall Street Journal* report from the Eufaula woods, Robert Tomsho broke the story on the front page. Chip Berlet, an expert on the far right, was quoted saying that the *Report* had "taken on a life of its own in the 'patriot movement,'" and that it was "one of their major influences." Samuel Sherwood, founder of the U.S. Militia Association, based in Blackfoot, Idaho, saw the movement as a way to forestall "civil war."[49] He told Tomsho that the *Report* arose because "A group of people got together, and said, 'Here is our blueprint for America.'" It had "caused a great deal of alarm." A cofounder of the Michigan Militia had been watching the *Iron Mountain* video series, and said its message was "There's been no accountability" and "It goes back to Kennedy."[50]

Looking back, Robert Tomsho thinks the kind of deep distrust in government he found after the bombing, as expressed in the belief that *Report from Iron Mountain* was real, had been germinating for a long time—certainly by the time it was published in 1967. Though Tomsho was then still in his teens, he was aware of "the official pronouncements on how the war was going versus what you were seeing on television," and how that undermined belief in what the government said. He was at high school near Kent State University in Ohio when the National Guard shot four students dead there in 1970; he remembers "distrust between parents and their own children" over the anti-war protests. Eighteen months later, he went to Kent State to study, and heard rumors "about various defense intelligence agencies having agents on campus, and disguised as students—there was just crazy paranoia. Well, maybe it wasn't paranoia."[51]

That distrust was there when he moved to Dallas, too. Two decades on from the assassination, there was a feeling in the city that "nothing is what it seems to be," and, also, a tendency to "see a government-manipulated conspiracy behind . . . almost everything."[52]

On April 22, three days after the Oklahoma City bombing, the FBI visited someone who appears to have been a member of the Oklahoma Militia. Two days later, the bureau's agents returned; the man had now "decided to cooperate."[53] He told them which radio shows he listened to, as recommended by militia members, including Cooper's and Liberty Lobby's *Radio Free America*. He gave them the names of four more "radical members," including the Oklahoma Militia leader Ross Hullett, who'd "gone underground" (though he was still talking to the *Oklahoman* later that week), along with someone who was "dangerous and possibly armed." And he passed them a stack of militia-related material: a "Basic Equipment List," manuals, a ticket to see a militia activist from Michigan speak in Tulsa, documents relating to preserving family farms. There were newsletters—one from Montana called *Taking Aim* and the one that McVeigh had read, *Patriot Report*. And there were also six videos, including *Blueprint for Tyranny*, and its three-part, six-hour sequel, *Iron Mountain II*.

To Cooper's fury, the hunt for the ideological wellsprings of McVeigh's atrocity brought much criticism of his broadcasts. It appeared McVeigh had visited him; he told the FBI agent that one day two young men of military bearing had turned up and tried to recruit him for some kind of direct action, telling him to "watch Oklahoma."[54] One had given him a copy of *The Turner Diaries*. Cooper insisted, however, that it wasn't McVeigh.

Likewise, Stewart Best, the producer of *Iron Mountain: Blueprint for Tyranny*, strongly objected to his company being categorized under "Active Patriot Groups"[55] by the extremism watchers of the Southern Poverty Law Center. Best said the militias were telling Americans the truth, but that he had nothing to do with them, or with McVeigh. As a Christian, he was "forbidden by Jesus Christ to take up arms against my government."[56]

That was in April 1997; in September 1995, Best Video Productions had placed an advertisement in a hard-line anti-government magazine called *Media Bypass* to promote the *Iron Mountain* videos—including *Iron Mountain III, The Update*. The ad insisted, over and over again—often in bold, capitalized, underlined text—that the *Report* was "real" and was "being implemented." It was "everything your worst nightmares are made of." Its agenda for the new world order was "being followed to the exact letter," so how could it be a hoax? "Official government documents, public laws, UN documents and treaties ALL PROVE THE AUTHENTICITY OF IRON MOUNTAIN." It had, after all, been "Declared the TRUTH by the editor of DIAL PRESS, and the truth by the author of the forward [*sic*], published as NONFICTION, and collaborated by a well-known author" when it was published. Yet it had been called fake both at the time and now again, on the front page of the *Wall Street Journal*, while "The author of the forward [*sic*] now claims he wrote the whole thing as a hoax." So, the ad demanded:

Why is the establishment media so upset over IRON MOUNTAIN? What information does it contain that they must DEBUNK THE EN-TIRE REPORT? Do they have something they are trying to HIDE FROM THE AMERICAN PEOPLE?[57]

---

One day in May 1996—a long way from Wisconsin, and Arizona, and Oklahoma City—three men met for lunch on the edge of Greenwich Village. The Knickerbocker Bar and Grill looks like Manhattan restaurants used to look, before image mattered more than food—dark browns, glass lampshades, a vintage poster for a victory ball. Here, five minutes from the old *Monocle* office where it all began, Leonard Lewin, E. L. Doctorow, and Victor Navasky had gathered to talk about *Iron Mountain*.

They had much to discuss. When Robert Tomsho's *Wall Street Journal* article about the militias' fascination with their old stunt had appeared a year earlier, Navasky had revealed the *Report*'s real origins in *The Nation*.

That "today's ultraright paranoids" took it seriously was "the scariest propo-
sition" of the whole saga, he concluded. Maybe the only solution was to say:
"Guys, you're right! *Report from Iron Mountain* is a real government document. Remember: You read it here in the pro-Commie, pro-government,
pro-Jewish, pro-African-American *Nation*."[58]

Robert Tomsho had called Lewin to break the news about the militias'
misplaced enthusiasm for his old satire; the now elderly writer had sounded
"really bummed out . . . taken aback and just weary . . . It was like somebody
let the air out of him."[59] Tomsho quoted him as saying, "It never occurred
to me that this was the kind of stuff that would appeal to the sort of people
we're talking about now." It made him "want to throw up."[60] Looking back,
Tomsho reflects that publishing the hoax was "pretty dicey,"[61] given the fact
that many Americans were losing trust in authority. But his article had its
own unexpected side effect. After Lewin's long, fruitless struggle to get his
masterpiece back in print, and his drawn-out battle with Liberty Lobby, he
discovered that Tomsho's piece had revived mainstream publishers' interest
in the *Report*. Lewin found himself with a new agent. An editor at the Free
Press—an alumnus of *The Nation* named Mitch Horowitz—was so intrigued
by the whole story that he agreed to give the *Report* a proper republication.
This gave Lewin a chance to write a new afterword, underlining once again
that the *Report* was "of course, a satirical hoax," done that way to "provoke
debate,"[62] which had duly followed.

So this was the spur for Lewin and Navasky to convene with Doctorow
at the Knickerbocker Bar and Grill: the publication of the new version of
*Report from Iron Mountain*. It was not just a private occasion, though; they
were joined by someone from the *New Yorker*. At this point in 1996, the publication of political books with mysterious authors was already a running
theme. The magazine cast *Iron Mountain* as a forerunner of two anonymous
texts that were currently the subject of much fevered speculation about who
was behind them. One was *Primary Colors*, a farcical roman à clef depicting
characters very much like the Clintons. Two months after the Knickerbocker
lunch, *Primary Colors* was revealed to be the work of the journalist Joe Klein,

who'd spent several months denying it. The other was *Industrial Society and Its Future*, which attacked technology's corrosive effect on liberty and the "power-holding elite of industrial society (politicians, scientists, upper-level business executives, government officials, etc.)."[63] This was the manifesto of the "Unabomber," whose mail bombs had killed three people and injured ten. The author-bomber was finally identified as Harvard star turned reclusive extremist Ted Kaczynski; he ended up in prison in Colorado, where he got to know Timothy McVeigh. According to McVeigh's biographers, they found that "their political views often coincided,"[64] particularly concerning "individual freedom."[65]

At one level the reunion lunch was a celebration, but the underlying reason why the republication had happened cast a shadow. Talking about the irony of the right-wing revival of their decidedly left-wing book, Doctorow invoked the then-fashionable postmodern idea that a text's meaning had nothing to do with its author's intentions. He asked Lewin how it felt to be "deconstructed." "Terrible," Lewin answered, adding, "deconstructed or not, I'm not doing any book tours in Montana."[66]

---

This left the conundrum of why a left-wing satire had ended up as a bible of the far right. In the edition of *The Nation* in which Navasky had explained the hoax's origins, he ran a piece that hinted at a possible answer. One of the magazine's more mulish writers, Alexander Cockburn—who'd attacked his left-wing comrades for buying into *JFK*—had been to Michigan, where he had spent a Saturday at the Gun Stock '95 rally at Freedom Hill County Park, north of Detroit. He reported that, along with denunciations of U.S. troops fighting under the flag of the United Nations, one speaker, a Republican ex-state legislator, preached "radical economic populism, indistinguishable from many speeches I used to listen to back in the sixties." It turned out that this man "had been at the march on the Pentagon and that he hated establishment Democrats and Republicans with equal fervor." Of another speech,

Cockburn wrote, "Most of it could have been delivered by a leftist in the late sixties without changing a comma."[67] He thought the right's populist story was mainly at fault in who it identified as holding power: it should focus not on "'the Jews'" but "the corporations."[68] The left, Cockburn lamented, did not seem interested in offering an alternative story to people like the car plant workers who appeared to make up much of the crowd, preferring to dismiss them as fascists.

This suggests that the popularity of *Iron Mountain* might have been one of the stories filling that absence. And that, perhaps, people could have been persuaded that it still offered a sharp critique of a callous federal government, even if you read it as satire. Just not so callous as to put militiamen in concentration camps—though even that nightmare had precedents in the anti-war movement's old fears.

It can often seem as though a conspiracist vision of those in power is a specifically left- or right-wing problem. But this is never true for long. These nightmares shift, according to which side feels more intensely that they're losing, or are otherwise weakened or disoriented. In the early 1990s, long-standing left-wing fears that the power elite was a frightening autocracy became more audible on the right, in strikingly similar tones.

This extended well beyond the specter of American concentration camps. Johnson's war in Vietnam was often compared to the crimes of the Nazis, long before McVeigh and others made the same parallel under Clinton. Left-wing hostility to the FBI in the 1960s and 1970s is strikingly similar to later right-wing attitudes. C. Wright Mills preferred the autonomous man with a gun to the Pentagon megadeath intellectual; looking back, this has all too obvious parallels on the 1990s right. As we've seen, Noontide Press even co-opted that term "megadeath intellectual," just as the *Spotlight* and the John Birch Society enthusiastically embraced Kennedy conspiracy theories about the military-industrial complex. In that 1960s New Left satire *MacBird!*, one character calls the public "sheep" and demands they "awake"—long before Cooper was talking about "sheeple."

This extended to political violence, too. One armed group that challenged gun control long before the 1990s was the Black Panthers. And one of the bomb-making manuals McVeigh bought was the 1971 counterculture favorite *The Anarchist Cookbook*—ordered from a neo-Nazi catalogue.

This comparison needs to be handled with care. There is no simplistic moral equivalence to be drawn. Even in crude numerical terms, the far right have demonstrably killed far more of their fellow Americans than the far left. The ways in which each side's fears are justified by the evidence varies widely. And as we've seen, organizations like Liberty Lobby sought to exploit the ways in which left-wingers had a similarly critical view of power elites. Nonetheless, the appeal of *Report from Iron Mountain* to people whose politics were a world away from Lewin's and Navasky's forces us to explore the extent to which justified criticism of power elites can become a problem in itself.

The key lies in the fact that *Iron Mountain* was satire, and in what happened when sight of that was lost.

When Navasky agreed to write a new introduction for Lewin's book, its editor, Mitch Horowitz, encouraged him to address this question of why a left-wing satire had inspired the right. Were the two sides getting similar messages from it? Did it "expose a sort of cognitive netherworld or faultline of paranoia"[69] that the two sides had in common? In his introduction, Navasky suggested that Lewin

with his perfect pitch, has stumbled on a netherworld for paranoids— the black hole of government secrecy and deception, where Kennedy assassinationologists today march in lockstep with white supremacists, neo-Nazis, and militiamen. By exposing their exaggerated fears and suspicions, he also taps into our own unresolved political conflicts.

But make no mistake about it. The contradictions in contemporary culture are not confined to paranoids. These days anti-interventionist alumni of the peace movement have found themselves on the same "side" as isolationists like Pat Buchanan in opposing U.S. intervention in Bosnia. Ditto civil libertarians and NRA activists in opposing measures like 1995's counterterrorism bill. *Iron Mountain* speaks to a moment when it is unclear whether such convergences mean political realignment or simply signify confusion.[70]

McVeigh would claim that in perpetrating his bombing, he was "borrowing a page from U.S. foreign policy," citing American attacks on government buildings in Serbia and Iraq.[71] This sounded an echo, too, of an old slogan of a group of far-left militants called the Weather Underground: "Bring the War Home." On March 6, 1970, in the basement of a Greenwich Village town house, three members of the Weather Underground were building a bomb intended to bring the Vietnam war home to a noncommissioned officers' dance at Fort Dix, New Jersey. Glance down West 11th Street on your way from the Knickerbocker Bar and Grill to the old *Monocle* office on Fifth Avenue, and you can see the spot where the bomb accidentally went off, killing the bomb makers and destroying the house. The Village may have been a long way from Oklahoma City, but it wasn't so far from the shadow of political bombing.

———

For Leonard Lewin, the republication had all come very late: he was almost eighty, and, as Julie Lewin recalls, he was beginning to develop Alzheimer's. This time, he was in no position to appear on television or radio—to take the chance to talk freely about *Iron Mountain* as he hadn't been able to do in 1967. Michael Lewin says the afterword was the last thing his father wrote and was "very hard for him to do."[72] Its final lines run like this:

I have no regrets in having written the book: You can never foresee how something you write might be misused, and I hope that the book can serve today as a warning against superficial logic. And if I'm given reason to believe that readers are able to find some useful ideas in the mixture, that might help lead to some real program for a real peace, that will do nicely.[73]

Meanwhile, the Free Press's parent company, Simon & Schuster, had a squad of "electronic detectives" chasing the bootleg version all over the rapidly growing internet, with formal warnings to follow. This was, they told the *New York Times*, the first time they had "encountered a work that multiplied so rapidly."[74] One site host protested that if "militia types" had fallen "for a lie, who is at fault really—the rubes or the liars?"[75] Lewin and Navasky might have countered that the truth had been clear since 1972.

Either way, no sooner had Timothy McVeigh been arrested than a fresh conspiracy theory began to stir. Was he really the perpetrator or a puppet of dark forces? *Report from Iron Mountain* had contributed to the swirl of conspiracy theories that had also laid the ground for the bombing; now the bombing itself became the subject of a new conspiracy theory. And this drew on *Iron Mountain*, too.

# 8

# THE GHOST OF LEE HARVEY OSWALD

Months before the Oklahoma City bombing, William Cooper had told listeners to *The Hour of the Time* to expect false flag–style attempts to smear the militia movement. The night after the atrocity, as the country tried to come to terms with what had happened, Cooper went on air as usual. He dismissed the theory, which was prominent on the news, that the bomb was the work of Middle Eastern terrorists. April 19 was two years to the day since the Branch Davidian fire at Waco and that, he was certain, was the key. At the FBI, a profiler who'd been involved in negotiations during the siege was thinking much the same thing. He told colleagues that the culprit might be a disaffected young right-wing veteran. But to Cooper, the choice of this anniversary showed something even more sinister: that the attack was "part of the agenda to bring about a new world order" by smearing the militia movement. There would be more terror attacks, he told his listeners; the police state would "escalate exponentially,"[1] and the people would be disarmed. The "one-world totalitarian socialist government" was on its way.[2]

The next morning, Thursday, a journalist reached out to John Trochmann of the Militia of Montana, and he said much the same. Trochmann claimed there had been two explosions, and that "there was a black helicopter hovering over the building earlier in the day."[3] By Friday, those Oklahoma militiamen in the woods were airing the same story to the *Wall Street*

*Journal.* This tale that the government had had a hidden hand in blowing up the Murrah Federal Building was soon standard fare on shortwave and in the *Patriot Report* newsletter. For the militias, this was the truth obscured by the "official story"; for their critics, it was the militias' official story, obscuring the truth. Not long afterward, a Democratic senator from Michigan lambasted a militia leader who he said had speculated on television, right after the bombing, that the federal government was behind it. Visibly outraged, he asked, "How's that for a suggestion: that we may have killed our own employees and children?"[4]

On that Friday, two days after the bombing, the news broke that a suspect was under arrest, and the militias' narrative acquired a new aspect. When Timothy McVeigh, clad in an orange jumpsuit, was walked the twenty-odd steps from the police station to a waiting vehicle, he was greeted by a battery of cameras and an audibly furious crowd. One militia propagandist was soon on air suggesting that, unless the authorities were just "showboating," this was "the Lee Harvey Oswald syndrome."[5] For some, the bombing resembled the "plot" to kill President Kennedy, right down to the patsy who'd take the blame, leaving the real conspirators to get away with it. Pursuing the parallel, they thought that, like Oswald, McVeigh might soon be murdered. Invoking two conspiracy theories in eight words, William Cooper declared that McVeigh was "the Lee Harvey Oswald of the American Reichstag!"[6] That reference to the supposed Nazi plot in 1933 to torch the German parliament, blame the communists, and thereby entrench Hitler in power did not take off. But the parallel with Dallas became commonplace, well beyond the fringes. McVeigh's soon-to-be lead attorney, Stephen Jones—a respected pillar of Oklahoma's legal and political circles—watched McVeigh's perp walk, and wrote later that he " 'saw' in him the ghost of Lee Harvey Oswald."[7]

And fourteen hundred miles away from Oklahoma City, a radical journalist began to see things this way, too, and set off in pursuit of the truth—fortified by the horrifying revelations contained in *Report from Iron Mountain.*

David Hoffman was raised in Baltimore, but when the bomb exploded in the heartland, he was living in San Francisco. He was in his mid-thirties, struggling along as the editor-publisher of the *Haight Ashbury Free Press*. This was a revival of a hippieish underground newspaper that had first appeared in 1967, around the same time as *Iron Mountain*, back when the artists, activists, and teenage runaways of the Haight-Ashbury neighborhood were inventing the Summer of Love. By 1994, all that had long faded, but the new version of the *Haight Ashbury Free Press* seemed to be aiming for a similar vibe. The center spread of its first edition was an illustrated poem called "Mystic Moment." Hoffman's version of the paper, however, also had a combative, libertarian edge. The cover for the November 1994 issue shows a man being held upside down by his legs in a huge fist. Notes and coins and what look like joints and a bottle fall from his pockets, as various implacable male authority figures look on: a cop, Robocop, the DEA, the ATF.[8]

In the newspaper's August 1995 edition, less than four months after the bombing, Hoffman turned his attention to the militia movement. He and his magazine were clearly on the left—there were pieces about the war on drugs, the plight of the homeless, the evils of Republican House Speaker Newt Gingrich's likely cuts to welfare. But Hoffman's overriding concern was the overweening power of the federal government, whether through restrictive new laws or what he believed was the FBI massacre at Waco. In the course of a feature on the militias, he recognized kindred spirits, much as Alexander Cockburn had done in *The Nation* a few months earlier. Hoffman was hostile to racism and far-right ideological "spew."[9] But he also suspected that the media was exaggerating all that, to smear what he thought was mainly a movement of honestly concerned Americans, with roots in "anti-government populism."[10] Roots that stretched into left- as well as right-wing soil.

This strange ideological fusion was captured in the startling illustration on the cover. A couple stand outside a wooden barn in the forest. She wears a peace symbol, his long hair is braided. But both wear camouflage and have pistols, and he is holding a rocket launcher. A black helicopter hovers overhead. It's like a hippie version of the extreme-right Randy Weaver and his wife at Ruby Ridge. The barn even looks like the Weavers' outbuilding. This was the anti-government symbolism of the 1960s left and the 1990s right, fused in a single image.

At times, in Hoffman's pieces from this edition of his magazine, he begins to sound a little like C. Wright Mills, critiquing the way elite groups "interlock at the highest levels of government and business"[11] and how they strive to "narrow consensus, and define the parameters of public debate within the strictest of terms—mainly, those of the international capitalists."[12] Hoffman quotes one of the founders of the Michigan Militia, denouncing the CIA as having been "in the business of killing Americans and killing people around the world since 1946."[13] He seems conscious, as Mills once was, of not totalizing all this into conspiracy theory. He puts it to one militia leader that some of the mutterings about "UN troops disarming citizens, microchips, and ID cards" and the socialist one world government "seem pretty crazy."[14] But there is also talk of the Great Depression as a manipulation,[15] of elites pulling strings, of "the Rockefellers and the Rothschilds."[16] He sees militia videos as creating "an aura of Orwellian paranoia and Strangelovian doom-saying," yet thinks "much of the evidence bears thoughtful and careful investigation."[17]

Overshadowing everything was the atrocity in Oklahoma. Hoffman thought there was "strong evidence" that it was "not the result of a lone bomber."[18] At some point in the year or so after he wrote those articles, Hoffman decided to move from the colorful streets of the Haight to the quiet roads of Oklahoma City, determined to track down those who were really behind the bombing. On March 10, 1996, he signed a book deal with an alternative publisher called Feral House. And he set up an office, under the banner of "Americans for Responsible Media," just to the north of Lake Hefner.

---

Charles Key, at the time a Republican state congressman in Oklahoma, was also unconvinced by the official investigation. He was distrustful of the government and aware from history, he says, that things go on that "aren't always what it looks like on the surface."[19] Under an unusual aspect of Oklahoma state law, citizens can petition for the creation of a county grand jury, and Key decided to try this route. The district attorney, Robert Macy, was among those in Oklahoma City who considered this a futile exercise, but after sixteen months of legal battles, the state supreme court upheld Key's case. He and his allies, including a man who'd lost two grandsons in the bombing, set about gathering more than thirteen thousand signatures—more than twice the minimum required—and on June 30, 1997, the citizens' grand jury was duly empaneled. It would convene in the basement of the county jail, a few blocks west of the site of the bombing. If a majority of the jurors could be persuaded of the theories advanced by Key, Hoffman, and others, they might indict new suspects. This would shatter the government narrative that McVeigh and his accomplices acted alone. Broadly, there were three main entities who some theorized had been involved: Islamic extremists, the far right, and the government itself.

McVeigh had consistently maintained that he alone had carried out the bombing. Earlier that June, after a trial that had lasted over a year, he'd been found guilty by a federal jury, despite the defense case that the government had prior knowledge of the attack. Nonetheless, Key had set up his own investigation team, and one of those who worked with him was David Hoffman. Key recalls that not everyone was convinced by Hoffman's standards of evidence; indeed, some felt that "he would go maybe a little bit too far, or wouldn't have the kind of stuff you'd really like to have to back up what you're claiming."[20] For himself, though, Key "never took it as [Hoffman] was wrong" and "got along with him fine to work with."[21]

To assist the grand jury in its inquiries, Macy assigned one of his staff investigators, an ex–highway patrol lieutenant named Larry Dellinger. When the bomb detonated, Dellinger had been a block away and had rushed to join the rescue effort; he still vividly remembers what he saw inside. Macy instructed him to work hard to find evidence of conspiracy, despite doubting that there was any to find. As Dellinger puts it today, "If

I could have found a conspiracy and proved it—would I not have been *the* investigator?"[22]

He found himself spending the next eighteen months serving subpoenas and checking out a wide range of claims from witnesses—some very shaky. He was also tasked with collecting witnesses from the county courthouse and escorting them the few blocks west to appear before the grand jury at the jail, where two assistant district attorneys led the questioning. The process meant Dellinger had some strange encounters. In McVeigh's federal trial, the defense had been keen to call a witness named Carol Howe, a former informant for the ATF on the Oklahoma extreme right—some of whom, she claimed, she'd heard talking about bombing. The judge ruled that this was too insubstantial to admit as evidence. Nonetheless, the story was given play by a journalist from the John Birch Society's magazine who argued that Howe had given the government warning of the bombing. And when the grand jury called her to testify, Dellinger found the journalist, one William F. Jasper, in an "unauthorized" area of the building, intent on showing Howe some pictures.[23] (Jasper said he'd been escorted to the area by jail staff.) A few weeks later, Dellinger found himself escorting the Oklahoma representative of William Cooper's "intelligence service"—a local ballet instructor named Michele Marie Moore—to testify to the grand jury.

---

By March 1998, David Hoffman's investigation had borne fruit, yielding a book called *The Oklahoma City Bombing and the Politics of Terror*. This account won some strikingly good reviews: one appraiser judged it "a convincing compilation of federal blunders, red herrings, half-truths, and evasions."[24] It would even win high praise from one of America's most famous writers.

The book strongly suggested the bombing was "deliberately engineered" because "the Plutocracy required a tragedy to manipulate public opinion."[25] Hoffman admitted it was not certain that the bombing was "part of a preconceived plan to create the illusion of a domestic terrorist threat within America—as a foundation for destroying political dissent," but insisted that "it is clear that the investigation was crafted for just that purpose."[26] The aim was to crush dissent by smearing the militia movement with an unthinkable crime. "The government feels it has got to stop political dissidence," he told the *Baltimore Sun*. "It will do anything to reinforce the image to the American public that the militia movement is dangerous."[27]

But why did they think this was necessary? And why did they think it would work? To answer these questions, Hoffman drew heavily on *Report from Iron Mountain* and its argument that war is "an indispensable controller of dangerous social dissidence and destructive antisocial tendencies" and provides "an external necessity for a society to accept political rule." Now that the threat from the Soviet Union had evaporated, the national security establishment needed what the *Report* called an "alternate enemy," which would have to be compelling enough to imply "a more immediate, tangible, and directly felt threat of destruction."[28] That, Hoffman argued, was the real reason for the bombing. The "massive media campaign" linking the militia movement to the bombing had made it America's new enemy.

This was psychological manipulation by the "ruling elite," refocusing "the war spirit"[29] through what the *Report* called a "fictive model." Hoffman quotes its argument that such a model would create a "sociomoral conflict" as compelling as war, which would "justify the need for taking and paying a 'blood price' in wide areas of human concern."[30] Then Hoffman makes a remarkable leap. He puts this "shocking revelation"[31] from the 1960s together with something written much more recently, by Arthur M. Schlesinger Jr., one of Kennedy's old advisers and a bête noire of C. Wright Mills. Schlesinger had suggested that "We are not going to achieve a new world order without paying for it in blood as well as in words and money."[32] Was this, Hoffman wondered, "the 'blood price' carried out on April 19, 1995?"[33]

He was aware that *Iron Mountain* had been categorized as a satire but pointed out that it had been quoted from by Fletcher Prouty in *The Secret Team*. He noted that Galbraith had said *Iron Mountain* was authentic, and that the *Wall Street Journal* had been "seriously debating its merits," even if *The Nation* was "still denigrating the report as a 'hoax.'"[34] None of that was entirely accurate. But it was apparently enough to convince Hoffman that the *Report* revealed why the power elite had probably orchestrated the murder of American children and its own employees. As for McVeigh, Hoffman echoed some of the militiamen's theories, drawing extensive parallels between the convicted bomber and Lee Harvey Oswald. He argued that both were patsies, who may well have been brainwashed by the CIA or some other element of the government to carry out an act of terror.

---

The famous writer who was so taken with Hoffman's book was that old left-wing aristocrat, anti-war veteran, and sharp-witted, much-feted novelist, essayist, and screenwriter Gore Vidal. In 2002, in the wake of 9/11 and the launch of the war on terror, Vidal published a book titled *Perpetual War for Perpetual Peace: How We Got to Be So Hated, Causes of Conflict in the Last Empire*, which would sell over a hundred thousand copies in the United States alone. It was a collection of his essays on the Oklahoma City bombing, the war on terror, and what he saw as the frightening rise of an American police state. In a long piece originally published in *Vanity Fair* in September 2001, titled "The Meaning of Timothy McVeigh," he wrote: "Thus far, David Hoffman's *The Oklahoma City Bombing and the Politics of Terror* is the most thorough of a dozen or two accounts of what did and did not happen on that day in April."[35]

Vidal also wrote for *The Nation*; some years earlier, he'd suggested in his column that a neoconservative Jewish writer, Norman Podhoretz, should register as an agent of Israel, and he'd been attacked as anti-Semitic. His editor Victor Navasky wrote later that, had Vidal meant what he said literally, he would have been guilty as charged, but that he was "a satirist, an ironist, a man from Iron Mountain."[36] So you might have expected him to spot that Hoffman's book had treated a satire as a genuine text—either because those references to *Iron Mountain* backed up startlingly extreme charges against the government, or because the satire in question was the brainchild of Vidal's own editor. How did he not notice?

Vidal was another military veteran struggling to make sense of what his country had become since 1945, and especially since 1991. *Perpetual War for Perpetual Peace* offers detailed, reasoned takedowns of America's endless military interventions, and of the federal intrusions on liberty that emerged in the "wars" on drugs and terror—from draconian anti-terror laws to people killed by police in no-knock drug raids. But Vidal also veers repeatedly into nightmares of a dystopian American power elite exerting total control. He lambasts the "Pentagon Junta"[37] supposedly programming the president. He declares that "for more than half a century" America's rulers "have made sure that we are never to be told the truth about anything that our government has done to other people."[38] He is convinced the fire at Waco was an FBI massacre and that the United States is "under metastasizing martial law."[39] And then there's his book title—which had also been the name of a work by Harry Elmer Barnes, whose antipathy to "perpetual war" led him to become a pioneer of Holocaust denial and an inspiration to Willis Carto.

Vidal corresponded with McVeigh and saw the bombing as an expression of his theory that the dictatorial federal government was provoking blowback. He quotes McVeigh's contention that his crime was less heinous than Truman's use of the Bomb. In the essay that praises Hoffman, Vidal makes the parallel between McVeigh and Oswald. And he insists that the evidence is "overwhelming" that the bombing was a plot "to create panic in order to get Clinton to sign that infamous [1996] Anti-Terrorism Act."[40] Hoffman's *Iron Mountain*–informed thesis fitted Vidal's nightmarish vision of government power all too well.

In reality, Timothy McVeigh was a disillusioned young veteran from a broken family. A bright, angry young man convinced he was bound for greatness who suffered crushing disappointment. A lonely figure, lost at the joyless edge of American society, who sought affirmation in the power of guns—and who found in extremist politics a story that explained why his humiliation was the fault of those in power. In each of those respects, he *did* have something in common with that other autonomous man, Lee Harvey Oswald. McVeigh was another would-be lone guerrilla, though he turned right rather than left—and his crime was far, far worse.

So in a way, the bombing did repeat the Kennedy assassination—but only in the conspiracy theories each spawned. The assassination was perpetrated by a left-wing extremist, but some on the left preferred to blame a conspiracy of the power elite. The bombing was perpetrated by a right-wing extremist, but some on the right preferred to blame a conspiracy of the power elite.

David Hoffman was right that *Iron Mountain* suggested that the vanishing of the Soviet Union would lead people to invent an enemy within. But the government didn't do that to the militia movement. It was the militia movement that refocused the "war spirit" and cast government as an insidious foe—full of dastardly schemes to carve up the republic and hand it to the new world order.

———

By the fall of 1998, Larry Dellinger had ferried many witnesses to the grand jury chamber and had personally testified at least eighteen times. In the course of his investigations, he'd had cause to research David Hoffman, visiting him at his apartment in north Oklahoma City and providing evidence about this to the grand jury. He told them it was like being back in the sixties. As he remembers, Hoffman "had love beads hanging across the door."[41] This transported Dellinger back to 1969 when he was a military policeman at Fort Dix, New Jersey, at the height of the protests against the war in Vietnam. But what also struck him, as Dellinger remembers it today, was the picture of Dellinger's boss, District Attorney Bob Macy, that Hoffman had up on his wall with "a target on his head."[42] At one point Hoffman reportedly appeared on a cable TV show and called Macy "a two-faced liar and a coward."[43] Hoffman feared the DA and his assistants were trying to steer the grand jury process. Finally, Hoffman was summoned to appear before them himself.

In late September 1998, Dellinger returned from a trip to Kansas to subpoena an out-of-state witness—and found a mangled box on his desk in the DA's courthouse offices. He was told it had been mailed to a grand jury member, who alerted prosecutors that he'd received a "suspicious package";[44] the bomb squad had dealt with it accordingly. Inside, Dellinger found a copy of Hoffman's book and a note saying, "If you don't want this, please give it to Vicki Ann,"[45] another member of the jury. At some point, the juror who received the package had also been sent an anonymous letter. It read: "Do not let them tell you what to do, and do not take your cues from them"—evidently a reference to the assistant DAs interrogating witnesses for the grand jury. "If you do," the message continued, "you will be making a grave mistake, and short-changing the people of this nation."[46]

On October 7, Dellinger escorted Hoffman to the county jail to testify under the basement ceiling's low fluorescent squares. Including two alternate jurors, there were six women (four white, two Black) and eight men (seven white, one Hispanic); among them, a teacher, a police officer, an electrician, people working in computing and medicine, employees of the state and the city. They sat around three sides of some pushed-together tables, their pads and pens before them, a model of the downtown area propped against the wall. As Hoffman was questioned under oath, could he convince the jurors to indict the perpetrators of the conspiracy? He arrived pulling a trolley stacked with copies of his book. He was in there for three and a half hours. One of the things they questioned him about "at length"[47] was the mailing of that book to at least one of their number. They took this as a coercive attempt to influence them.

Whoever could the sender have been? Charles Key denied it, saying he'd advised his fellow investigator not to send the jury his book. (As Key recalls it, the two men weren't always in sync; they'd already had a dispute over Hoffman's use of a speech by Key as the foreword to his book, without asking Key's permission.) Hoffman said it wasn't him either—but investigators soon determined that it was. The assistant DA who'd interrogated Hoffman before the grand jury took what the author had done seriously. He'd previously served five days for stalking a woman; the implication was that he'd tried to intimidate the jury into accepting the argument of his book.

---

At last, at the end of 1998, after hearing from 117 witnesses, the grand jury delivered its report. On the morning of December 30, the hitherto anonymous jurors gathered in open court, along with Charles Key and a host of other interested parties, to hear the district judge William Burkett read the grand jury's findings. This would reveal how many people they'd indicted for conspiring to bomb the Murrah Building. Larry Dellinger remembers the local TV news shows interrupting their programming to go live to the courtroom. The findings would be reported on CBS and in papers from the *Los Angeles Times* to the *Washington Post*.

As Burkett read out their report, it became clear that, as had occurred at the federal trial, the grand jury had found no evidence of a wider conspiracy. The jurors didn't believe the federal government had "prior knowledge" of the bombing. They'd found "no credible evidence that the bombing was linked to white supremacists or foreign terrorists, and they found no additional conspirators."[48] Rather, they "found several cases of the same misinformation being used repeatedly by bombing conspiracy theorists."[49] Judge Burkett added a lengthy personal statement of his own:

> Remember that there were seven U.S. Secret Service Agents, six U.S. Customs agents, five agents of the ATF and many other federal employees in the building, many of whom lost their lives. What reasonable person could believe that there were those other than McVeigh, Nichols and Fortier who knew about this and deliberately withheld the knowledge, condemning 168 to die, or that such a conspiracy could possibly be kept secret?

A wise man has said that there are two ways to slide easily through life: to believe everything and to doubt everything. Both ways save us from thinking.[50]

Alas, he added, there were some who would "now simply include these jurors as the newest members of the conspiracy."[51]

A disappointed Charles Key countered that he hadn't been criticizing the emergency services. Moreover, he suggested that the district attorney had exercised more control over the grand jury than was proper and that key witnesses hadn't been called. And he promised to publish his own report on his investigation's findings. His committee's *Final Report* maintained that there had been a conspiracy.

Hoffman's efforts to get someone indicted did bear fruit, however. There was one sealed indictment. The name wouldn't be revealed until the person concerned had been taken into custody, a job that fell to Larry Dellinger. Hoffman discovered that the person the grand jury had indicted was . . . himself, for attempting to influence them by sending one of their number his book and that letter. Dellinger went to Hoffman's apartment, but his quarry had already skipped town. Dellinger left Hoffman a voicemail: "I know where you're at, I'm right behind you."[52]

From his refuge in Colorado, Hoffman protested that he hadn't done anything wrong by mailing his book to the grand jury—and maintained that his notes were intended to be "inspirational."[53] He denounced the jurors for not returning "more indictments." It was, he declared, "the biggest cover-up since the Kennedy assassination";[54] he was the victim of "a political prosecution."[55] For his part, Charles Key thought this was all "very petty"; Hoffman posed "no real threat."[56] As the *Baltimore Sun* put it, Hoffman—and his book—had suddenly landed in the "national spotlight,"[57] but perhaps not in the way he might have wanted. In the end, he went back to Oklahoma City and turned himself in to Dellinger, claiming the DA was prosecuting him "for speaking the truth about a crime [DA Macy] was charged to investigate" but had failed to do so.[58] Hoffman was reported to be facing two counts of jury tampering, with a potential sentence of two years. But his hopes of turning the case into a political trial were dashed; he was given community service.

All along, Larry Dellinger had wondered how Hoffman had managed to fund his investigation. In the course of the press hullabaloo, the answer emerged. A Chicago property tycoon named Alexander B. Magnus had heard about the independent investigations into the bombing and had offered a slice of his largesse. Here was Hoffman's point about anti-government left and anti-government right uniting in action. Magnus had once run for vice president on the Taxpayers Party ticket, was angry about Waco, and had been involved in attempts to prove the government was involved in the 1993 World Trade Center bombing and the 1996 crash of TWA Flight 800.[59] He also thought the Oklahoma City bombing needed investigation— it could not have just been one bomb, he believed. From August 1997 to May 2000—more than a year after Burkett read out the grand jury's verdict— Magnus funded Hoffman's writing, which included a planned second book, to the tune of almost $68,000, through his group Americans for Responsible Media. Which is why Hoffman set himself up in an office under that name. In the Acknowledgments section of *The Oklahoma City Bombing and the Politics of Terror*, he thanks a mysterious "Mr. 'M'" for his "generous financial support."[60]

In the aftermath of the indictment, Hoffman spent ten days touring Oklahoma, Arkansas, and Texas to check out sites of alleged FEMA concentration camps pinpointed by a New Age writer. He came back laughing, having found nothing sinister at all, mocking the New Ager's failure to check his facts. Hoffman reported this online, along with a link to his book. But the sequence of unfortunate events that had befallen him wasn't quite over.

Had anyone decided to take up Vidal's 2001 recommendation in *Vanity Fair* and read *The Oklahoma City Bombing and the Politics of Terror*, they would have struggled. The book had suggested that an FBI officer knew that the bombing of Pan Am Flight 103 in December 1988 was coming and pulled his son and his daughter-in-law off the plane at the last minute. This was untrue, and the officer sued for libel. In December 1999 Hoffman's publisher agreed to pulp all its copies of his book—though the case was eventually dismissed on the grounds that Hoffman had shown neither malice nor "reckless disregard for the truth."[61] Today, *The Oklahoma City Bombing and the Politics of Terror* survives online, thanks in part to white nationalists.

---

Timothy McVeigh wasn't the patsy of an *Iron Mountain*–informed scheme to scapegoat the militias and to manipulate the masses, but the idea didn't go away. A few years later, a prominent conspiracy theorist named Texe Marrs asked: "Was the Oklahoma City atrocity plotted out in advance as part of a '*Blood Games*' agenda?"—before revealing that "there is such an agenda":[62] *Report from Iron Mountain*.

More broadly, those corrosive fears of a shadowy power elite that had sprung up in the 1960s, as captured in the *Report*, survived on the left and right alike. In 1999, even as Hoffman's book was condemned to the shredder, the World Trade Organization met in Seattle, behind closed doors. This attracted mass protests against high-handed globalization, uniting labor activists and environmentalists with the kind of right-winger who feared the WTO was a harbinger of one-world rule. Pat Buchanan praised the protesters, declaring "we stand against global government and an undemocratic new world order."[63] Meanwhile, movies like *The Matrix* were providing additional leftish images of total, invisible, elite control—which, once again, were seized on by the far right.

Often these fears spoke to real concerns. Across a remarkable range of them, Leonard Lewin's old satire was used to "prove" that exaggerated versions of those fears were all too real.

On a site called biblebelievers.au, a conspiracist named Joan Veon published a transcript of an interview she'd managed to conduct with Harlan Cleveland, a diplomat and university chief, who in the late 1960s had been President Johnson's ambassador to NATO. She was concerned that the

*Report*'s "Orwellian goals and objectives just happen to be the same goals and objectives as the United Nations today." When she got a chance to talk to Cleveland, she tried to "get him to either affirm or deny *The Report from Iron Mountain*," and she concluded that he had indeed "affirmed it by the way he answered my questions." What her transcript actually suggests is that he had no idea what the *Report* was. At the time of the fuss about it in Washington, he'd been based in Brussels. This dialogue is a fascinating glimpse of an encounter between utterly different worlds: neither sees who the other person actually is. Veon added a long appendix to the transcript, taken directly from Hoffman's book. Where Hoffman had written that *Nineteen Eighty-Four* was coming true, she added in square brackets: "and *The Protocols of the Learned Elders of Zion*."[64]

Lewin's satire was also misinterpreted by at least one writer with far more substantive worries. In his 1995 book *Black Lies, White Lies: The Truth According to Tony Brown*, the African American writer and broadcaster attacked *Iron Mountain* as a "precursor to *The Bell Curve*,"[65] a hugely controversial study published in 1994 that toyed with the notion that ethnicity plays a role in intelligence. Brown acknowledged that the *Report* was fiction but found its talk of reinstituting slavery "ominous" nonetheless. There were just too many other things it seemed to chime with, from America's long history of "real plots against Blacks"—slavery, FBI spying, syphilis experiments[66]— to fears stoked by the racial tensions of the 1990s. In this context, Brown expressed himself unsurprised by the popularity of *Iron Mountain* among white supremacists. He decided that both Lewin's best-known book and his novel *Triage* "offer blueprints for a sophisticated and diabolical culling of undesirable population groups."[67] Lewin assured him that he found the far right's embrace of his work outrageous, but Brown wasn't convinced, and concluded that both books warranted "paranoia and alarm in the Black community."[68]

Meanwhile, Jim Keith, a radical libertarian and conscientious objector against the Vietnam War, became a leading promoter of one of the key elements of militia movement folklore: that the mysterious black helicopters sighted all across the United States were the "strikeforce" of the new world order's totalitarian takeover. His 1996 book *Okbomb! Conspiracy and Cover-Up* was cited by Gore Vidal. In *Mass Control: Engineering Human Consciousness* (1999) Keith referred to the *Report* as satire, but still used it to warn of the imminent dangers of "the cybernetics approach to world management" which would soon give "the ruling elite . . . total control over the minds and bodies of mankind."[69]

A zine called *Steamshovel*, where Keith was an editor, ran a piece soon after the *New Yorker* reported on Navasky, Lewin, and Doctorow's meeting at the Knickerbocker, suggesting the magazine's account of the reunion was merely the "cover story"[70] for how the *Report* had really come about. The *Steamshovel* piece saw Lewin's book as prophesying everything from the U.S. role in Somalia to UFO movies to the proposed "Star Wars" missile shield. This being the mid-1990s, the most resonant thing for which *Steamshovel* thought the *Report* had provided a "blueprint" was "the popularization of the Environment Movement."[71] This was one of the most fertile misunderstandings of the *Report*—it's audible in the *Blueprint for Tyranny* video, too.

And then there was that John Birch Society journalist who'd arrived at the Oklahoma City county jail determined to show some pictures to one of the witnesses. In 1992, William Jasper had published a book called *Global Tyranny . . . Step by Step* which featured long quotations from *Iron Mountain* to bolster arguments echoing that old Bircher General Walker. Jasper presents the *Report* as "evidence to demonstrate that the entire environmentalist 'movement' and all of its phony 'crises' have been created, promoted, and sustained by the Insiders for the singular purpose of conjuring up a credibly terrifying menace to replace the fear of nuclear holocaust as the impetus for world government."[72] Jasper misread Galbraith's old tongue-in-cheek admission that he was "a member of the conspiracy"[73] that created the hoax. He thought it proved the *Report*'s sinister authenticity, which he saw in the context of his reading of geopolitical history. The first attempt at world order began after the First World War, the second after the Second; for forty years the threat of nuclear war served "to keep America tied to the

United Nations."[74] With the end of the Cold War, the fear of nuclear war was suddenly much less potent, but the "Insiders" were so brilliant that they'd already started plotting a new bogus threat in the 1960s.

Like Hoffman, Jasper zeroed in on the *Report*'s talk of alternate enemies, fictive models, and the paying of a "blood price," but where Hoffman thought this explained the Oklahoma City bombing, Jasper thought it explained the Green movement (much as he thought the bombing was the work of a conspiracy, too). As he pointed out, the *Report* suggested that "gross pollution of the environment can eventually replace the possibility of mass destruction by nuclear weapons as the principal apparent threat to the survival of the species," though it would take "a generation and a half" before it was "sufficiently menacing, on a global scale, to offer a possible basis for a solution."

Jasper puts this together with the *Report*'s call for alternatives to war that are similarly economically wasteful. "With this diabolical thought in mind," Jasper concludes, "seemingly insane" environmental policies that destroy jobs for the sake of supposedly endangered species "begin to make sense."[75] From there, he moves on to warn of the "New Green World Order," and something called "Agenda 21."

On January 28, 1999, Leonard Lewin died at the age of eighty-two. To clear out the piles of pirated editions of the *Report* left over from the lawsuit, Julie Lewin placed classified ads in *The Nation*, giving them away to universities and peace groups. She put a sticker on each, making clear it was a hoax.

In the new millennium, the cracks in the old confident postwar America would only grow wider. And new voices would find in *Iron Mountain* the evidence that sinister forces lay behind their troubles.

# 9

# THEY WANT TO KILL EVERYBODY

Broadcasting from Waco a week after the fire at the Branch Davidian compound, William Cooper told listeners he'd predicted a massacre, and that it would now be escalated across America. "Folks," he warned, "you're next!"[1] Eight years later, on November 5, 2001, after a protracted dispute over his taxes, his behavior had become threatening and erratic. After Cooper waved a gun in the face of the local doctor in his little Arizona town, sheriff's deputies came to arrest him at his hilltop home, on charges of aggravated assault. There was another standoff, another shootout. A deputy was shot in the head. Cooper was killed.

This meant he never discovered the real story behind the text that had such an influence on his thinking, and that he'd done so much to promote: *Silent Weapons for Quiet Wars.* Nor did he find out how it sprang from that other dubious document he'd repeatedly invoked: *Report from Iron Mountain.* But through Cooper's unwanted, horribly successful successor, a young "investigative journalist" named Alex Jones, *Silent Weapons* would keep the phantoms raised by Lewin's hoax on the move. To trace how the *Report's* influence has spread right up to the present—and what that reveals about how attitudes toward the power elite have sharpened, even since the 1990s—we first need to go back.

The title page of *Silent Weapons for Quiet Wars* declares it to be an "Operations Research Technical Manual," classified "Top Secret."[2] In 1981, excerpts from *Silent Weapons* appeared in the letters column of a libertarian Ohio newspaper, accompanied by some worrying contextual remarks about the Rothschilds, and "the Beast."[3] No one appears to have noticed. But five years later, the text was reportedly published by America's Promise Ministries—a far-right church and publishing business, then based in Phoenix, that preached the racist beliefs of the Christian Identity movement—and was advertised in its newsletter.[4] Its newsletters retailed nightmares about the coming suppression of right-wing patriots, the malignancy of the Federal Reserve, and the supposed omnipotence of the Jews; and it sold anti-Semitic literature, including *The Protocols of the Elders of Zion*.[5] In such a publication, *Silent Weapons* and its supposed revelations of an elite plot to control the American people had found a home. According to Mark Jacobson, *Silent Weapons* was also published in an obscure Arkansas newspaper, the *American Sunbeam*, that published similarly grim content and whose owner may have received his copy from William Cooper.[6] More mentions and excerpts would occasionally surface in other newspapers' letter columns, sent in by readers anxious to spread the word.

Like *Report from Iron Mountain*, this text came complete with a bizarre origin story. It had supposedly come to light as the result of an auction of surplus office equipment from McChord Air Force Base, forty miles south of Seattle. A Boeing employee had apparently attended the auction and purchased a photocopier to strip down for parts. Inside the machine, as luck would have it, he came upon a copy of the elite's secret manual. One of their minions had evidently left it there by accident.

By the 2000s, as a result of William Cooper's championship, *Silent Weapons for Quiet Wars* had become an influential underground text. In the fall of 2003, a conspiracy magazine called *Paranoia* published an article asking for information about its origins. This elicited a letter from a federal prison, from a man named Hartford Van Dyke. He claimed he'd written it. He also insisted it was genuine.

Van Dyke had inherited a conspiracy theory about Pearl Harbor from his father, which in the early 1970s, the younger Van Dyke had written up and posted to the nation's politicians. He appears to have had links with the Liberty Lobby–affiliated Holocaust deniers at the Institute for Historical Review. He was also a "sovereign citizen": a movement that, by 2016, U.S. law enforcement considered the country's "top domestic extremist threat."[7] Sovereign citizens hold to the theory that the true, constitutional government of the United States was overthrown by corrupt bankers after the Civil War, who allegedly conspired to make U.S. currency worthless—hence the creation of the Federal Reserve in 1913—and to turn Americans into economic slaves. Understanding this can supposedly liberate sovereign citizens from such federal shackles as taxation. This sort of pseudolegal conspiracism was what had landed Van Dyke in prison. He was serving eight years for printing and circulating millions of dollars of false currency: what U.S. law calls "fictitious obligations."[8]

From his cell, Van Dyke revealed that he read the *Report*—or the first half, anyway—around 1973. And then, going through his old college algebra textbook, he had an epiphany. He noticed that one of the footnotes "exactly corresponded to the ideas in *Report from Iron Mountain*." This was it! He'd "discovered the mathematical methodology of the Silent Weapons System."[9] The footnote led him to the work of Wassily Leontief, a Nobel Prize–winning Soviet-American economist. (During the war, Leontief had worked for the Office of Strategic Services, the forerunner of the CIA.) In the late 1940s and early 1950s, he'd made pioneering use of computers to model the structure of the American economy, in a project funded by the Rockefeller Foundation. Here were the silent weapons that were being used to wage the quiet war revealed in *Report from Iron Mountain*. There must be a secret manual setting out how to do this, so Van Dyke set himself to expose it—by writing it.

The influence of Lewin's hoax is evident from the start, in Van Dyke's echoing of the *Report*'s thriller-plot frame. *Silent Weapons* informs the new recruit to the quiet war that "You have qualified for this project because of your ability to look at human society with cold objectivity"—which sounds rather like the instructions supposedly given to the Iron Mountain Study Group. Likewise, the dire need for secrecy is stressed: on no account must the citizenry discover that the elite has declared war on them. The publication of *Report from Iron Mountain* is even folded into the backstory, through a warning that the silent weapons system was almost exposed when the *Report* was "leaked" in 1967.

From there, *Silent Weapons* fleshes out the *Report*'s aim of finding a way to maintain economic stability in the absence of war through alternative means of social control. It details how this is achieved with computers, TV, and advertising, based on techniques imported from warfare. A silent weapon, Van Dyke writes, "shoots situations, instead of bullets," weakening citizens' self-discipline through everything from calculated economic shocks to sex-and-violence on TV. The aim is a populace enslaved in a completely automated society, as predictable as a guided missile. This, the manual instructs, is better than letting ordinary, ill-disciplined people stay free, which would just lead to economic chaos and war. Instead, welfare reduces its recipients to "a standing army for the elite," as the responsible, wealthy few accrue all economic power. One thing that is particularly troubling about this text and its vision of a cruel, omnipotent elite is its claim that the basis for the supposed means of total social control was discovered two centuries ago, by a member of the Rothschild family.

The key to Van Dyke's world view seems to lie in the many electrical diagrams that adorn his curious document. The elite's great, secret insight, we learn, is that the economy can be controlled as completely as electricity, and so, too, can the population. This is the totalizing, everything-is-connected logic of conspiracy theory, and of fiction. But it does speak to real, widespread fears about conformism, advertising, the influence of television and so on: the worries that drove C. Wright Mills's talk of "cheerful robots." And it does build on a grain of truth. As we've seen, the postwar power elite did have astoundingly grandiose ambitions to use approaches developed during the war to plan the economy and the future. This was the mindset that Lewin was lampooning. But his lampoon apparently convinced Van Dyke that the power elite had actually succeeded.

Contradicting himself, but still echoing the *Report*, Van Dyke has his manual describe war as "the primary economic flywheel," and the draft as a means of social control through "human behavior modification." The manual even has the elite planning for genocide. This echoes one of the darkest parts of Lewin's satire—the *Report*'s suggestion of culling the public. But here, it's not satire; it's straight-up dystopia. As we'll see, this particular nightmare is still alive and well today.

There are some flashes of prescience in *Silent Weapons*, such as the prediction that "every individual element of the structure" will come "under computer control through a knowledge of personal preferences": shades of today's social media and its determination to learn and shape our every whim. Nonetheless, this document is a poorly spelled, none-too-coherent fake, hacked out on a typewriter. Much of it is a haphazard salad of jargon. And unlike Lewin, Van Dyke seems to keep forgetting that he is supposed to be creating an "official" document and falls instead to ranting. One section is about men being "pussy-whipped."

So why then, given that Van Dyke admitted he wrote the manual himself, based in significant part on *Report from Iron Mountain*, did he feel able to claim it was genuine? One of his answers was that he'd really just compiled it from other texts. Another, in his letter to *Paranoia*, was that: "It is not a 'hoax' any more than any other presentation of a scientific process could be deemed a hoax merely because it was not presented with the endorsement of its original discoverer."[10] A third was that Leontief confirmed it in one of his later articles.

As with the story of the *Report*, this suggests the nature of truth for conspiracy theorists: a document along these lines must exist, so if I have created it, then it must, effectively, be genuine. *Silent Weapons* is an attempt to create a strategy manual that might have existed, if *Report from Iron Mountain* had been real. On that basis, Van Dyke created a second hoax as "evidence" for the hoax that had taken him in.

He even adds a missing piece to the origin story. In 1980, he wrote, he'd picked up a "military person" who was hitchhiking in uniform on Interstate 5, in a hurry to get from Van Dyke's hometown of Vancouver, Washington, to McChord Air Force Base two hours upstate.[11] Van Dyke recounts how he drove this person all the way, telling him about *Silent Weapons* en route, and how, as the man got out of the car and headed into the base, Van Dyke gave him a copy. So perhaps it really was left in an old photocopier. That makes more sense as the fate of a fantastical pamphlet than if the document really were the power elite's top secret blueprint for tyranny.

*Silent Weapons* is far less credible than *Report from Iron Mountain*. Yet, somehow, it persuaded people anyway, even after Van Dyke had revealed he wrote it, partly based on a hoax. And one of those convinced by its assertions was a figure who'd take this whole *Report*-inflected world view far beyond the audience that either Cooper or Van Dyke had ever captured for it.

———————

As a teenager in Austin, Texas, Alex Jones was captivated by a story about power. *None Dare Call It Conspiracy* was a propagandistic bestseller by a man named Gary Allen, a spokesman of the John Birch Society; along with *Iron Mountain*, Allen's book appears to have influenced *Silent Weapons*. *None Dare Call It Conspiracy* opened young Alex's eyes to the big secret: it was the world's bankers, not the politicians, who really controlled America. Alex was nineteen when, a hundred miles to the north, the Branch Davidian compound at Waco went up in flames. Here were the dark forces of the power elite in action! He dropped out of community college and started a call-in show on public access television. He discovered William Cooper and *Silent Weapons*—more compelling tales of malevolent elites—and began trumpeting the nightmares we've been tracing. In 1996, he landed a job hosting a radio talk show and exulted one day when his hero, Cooper, called him, on air, to swap conspiracist memes. By 1998, Jones was making "documentary" films like *America Destroyed by Design*, in which he echoed the theory that the Oklahoma City bombing was the work of the government—specifically, "military black ops squads"—and was a plot "to scare the American public into submitting" to Clinton's new police state. *Police State 2000*, a 1999 follow-up, criticized the militarization of the police—a common enough complaint—but then cast them as "thugs and bullies for the bureaucrats and their foreign banker globalist controllers." When Jones was fired, he simply set up online.

It was Jones, as much as anyone, who carried the nightmares nursed by the militia movement through into the new millennium, even if on the night of Y2K itself, his escalating nonsense frenzy—"'Cash machines are failing in Britain. . . . Hundreds of thousands are dead in Chechnya"[12]—made him look ridiculous. After the release of yet another film about elite evil, *Dark Secrets Inside Bohemian Grove*, he'd made his name. Following Cooper's death, Jones appointed himself the dead guru's successor, entirely unabashed by Cooper's having branded Jones a fearmonger, a "bold-faced, miserable, stinking little coward liar" and a "sensationalist bullshit artist" whose behavior was "especially not good for militias and patriots."[13] In Cooperish mode, Jones responded to the almost-fatal shooting of Arizona Congresswoman Gabrielle Giffords in 2011 by declaring, "My gut tells me this was a staged mind-control operation."[14]

According to the podcaster Dan Freisen—whose show *Knowledge Fight* is dedicated to highly skeptical but incredibly detailed analyses of Jones's theorizing—the inspiration for much of it can be traced to *Silent Weapons* and its vision of an elite deliberately confecting economic shocks and terror attacks to keep the people shaken and subdued. After countless hours of listening to Jones's on-air fantasizing, Freisen reports that *Silent Weapons* is one of the few sources the host cites and that he does so regularly.

In his debt to Cooper and *Silent Weapons*, Jones isn't alone. The British conspiracy theorist David Icke has also done much to preach the nightmare scenarios of the American far right—he once praised the *Spotlight* for its "long and proven record of accuracy"[15]—though he maintains more of a distance from that world than Jones does. In his 2013 book *The Perception*

*Deception*, along with references to Orwell and *The Matrix*, Icke cites *Silent Weapons* repeatedly and in detail. He pays particular attention to its assertions about how people are kept ignorant and distracted through the media, the education system, and economic shocks, with the help of information gleaned about them via technology. In a new age of economic uncertainty following the 2008 global financial crisis, and of real fears about unseen forces harvesting our data, it's not hard to see why some people might be drawn into Icke's story of power.

Adopting the attitude that has so often found its way into assessments of *Report from Iron Mountain*, Icke eventually admits that he "can't say for sure" if *Silent Weapons* "is genuine," but continues to cite it anyway, on the basis that it's very detailed and that "what it describes is now blatantly happening by the hour."[16] But this is the logic that takes you over the line from critical skepticism to conspiracism. "This text bears some resemblance to reality" becomes "this text is uncannily similar to reality" becomes "this text created that reality." *Silent Weapons* may be prescient in places, but so are many texts that don't harangue the reader about pussy-whipping or invoke the Rothschilds. Likewise, just because someone claims to have perfect control of society—even in a genuine document—doesn't mean they actually do. *Silent Weapons* is a product of America in the 1970s, hardly the model of a perfectly controlled society. But then, all that pales into insignificance given Icke's signature addition to 1990s right-wing conspiracism. At the apex of his "pyramid of manipulation" lurk extraterrestrial, part-reptilian overlords.[17]

In February 2023, something of this narrative, minus the lizards, made a bizarre appearance on British television. Neil Oliver, one of the hosts on the right-wing channel GB News, delivered a long monologue that warned of "the silent war waged by parliament against we the people. Some learned souls," Oliver continued, "will tell you it's been the stuff of decades, if not centuries, passed between generations of politicians and others. The strategic objective is total control of the people. This has been achieved not by bullets and bombs but by stealth, sleight of hand, and the misuse of legislation."[18]

As the journalist Matthew Sweet noted, Oliver was then joined by a guest who "gives talks about the Bavarian Illuminati and secret societies who control the world" and who "is associated with groups that circulate conspiracy theories about Rothschilds, 9/11, 5G, covid [*sic*]."[19] Around all these stories, however ludicrous, lurks the very unfunny ghost of the *Protocols of the Elders of Zion*: the forgery that has long provided a template for tales of malicious power elites exercising invisible, long-planned control. Icke has insisted that while he believes the *Protocols* are genuine, he doesn't believe they were written by Jewish people but, rather, reptilians. Jones, for his part, has insisted he is not anti-Semitic but, even so, denounces a "Jewish mafia."[20] In response to the Oliver incident, GB News said it "abhors racism and hate in all its forms and would never allow it on the channel."[21]

Jones and his fellow fabulists take us into the biggest, most bizarre reality distortion yet: the belief that the globalist elite wants to depopulate the earth, cutting humanity down by 80 percent or more. It didn't take Sweet much searching to find one of the groups Oliver's guest belonged to using the phrase "silent weapons for quiet wars" with reference to "the Covid chimera" and "the ever present digitalised EMF radiation frequencies continuously manipulating and denaturing human brain cells." There was also a warning of coming "slaughter."[22]

This is partly a conspiracist riposte to another long-standing apocalyptic idea, which was mainstream in the 1960s and 1970s: the fear that a massive overpopulation crisis would soon engender worldwide famine. This led to various proposed solutions, including a 1974 report by Henry Kissinger, Walt Rostow's successor as national security adviser. Alex Jones has been talking about such matters since at least his 2007 film *Endgame: Blueprint for Global Enslavement*. This film cited real historical wrongs—such as America's widespread use of eugenics and the horrific Tuskegee experiment, which deliberately withheld treatment from African American men with syphilis from 1932 to 1972 to see what happened—along with Jones's usual outrageous claims. In an eerie echo of *Iron Mountain*, he also claimed, wrongly, that Kissinger's memorandum had recommended that "instigating wars was also a helpful tool in reducing population"[23] in the Third World. At one point we see him taking up a megaphone and bellowing at a hotel where the Bilderberg Group is meeting that he will not stand for this.

Unsurprisingly, given that Lewin's satire was written in 1967, overpopulation is one of the themes on which it draws. The un-satirical *Silent Weapons for Quiet Wars*, meanwhile, just goes ahead and accuses the elite of plotting genocide. And so both texts have been used to wildly overinterpret measures to avoid overpopulation. As recently as 2015, the producer of *Iron Mountain: Blueprint for Tyranny* was invoking both Lewin's and Van Dyke's works, along with *The Protocols of the Elders of Zion*, as genuine documents showing the elite's plans for depopulation under martial law.[24] So it isn't surprising that, when the pandemic hit, these notions were pressed into service to explain what was happening—giving the theory a huge boost. Jones turned to his abiding fascination with the idea of *Silent Weapons for Quiet Wars* to cast vaccines as the newest phase of the elite's depopulation drive.[25] On his show on March 16, 2021, for example, he warned:

> They want to kill everybody. But they want to kill you in a year or six years, ten years—every person's different—and they'll just claim it's something else causing it. It's called a "Soft Kill Weapon." *Silent Weapons for Quiet Wars*. There's Pentagon papers on that if you'd like to go look that up.[26]

Perhaps, somewhere in the depths of Jones's mind, the fake "leaked document" *Silent Weapons* had merged with the real leaked documents published as the *Pentagon Papers*.

Another example, from February 21, 2022, shows Jones evoking, from *Silent Weapons*, the idea of ordinary people as the elite's farm animals, under perfect, technological control:

> But now we're going into World War Four that is economic, that is psychological, that is cyber, that is radiological, that is electromagnetic,

that is chemical, that is covert. *Silent Weapons*. *Silent Weapons for Quiet Wars*. *Silent Weapons for Quiet Wars*—just look these terms up. And it's what the globalists are obsessed with, and they brag how you're dumb animals, and they brag how they're going to annihilate you and they're going to slowly take all our resources, but make you love it while they brainwash you, using Pavlovian behavioral psychology. These are the worst villains the earth has ever seen.[27]

As the journalist James Ball has charted, the ruptures of the pandemic—lockdowns, sudden mass vaccines, mask mandates, the simultaneous arrival of 5G cell phone towers—provided an array of components for conspiracists to assemble to make the case that the elite were planning to depopulate the planet. Vaccines would, they claimed, cause infertility. Or death. Or they were said to contain a microchip that would allow Bill Gates to control people via 5G. Or the chips would be "activated by a 5G signal, meaning billions will drop dead all at once."[28] And so on.

Much of this was reinforced by the metastasizing cluster of conspiracy theories known as QAnon that spread online during the pandemic from one isolated individual to the next.

Here too, *Silent Weapons* found a role. QAnon began with cryptic messages from "Q," a supposed intelligence officer inside the "deep state" who was supporting a virtuous President Trump in his battle with the cabal of Democrats and other evil liberals who ostensibly run the world—and, in their spare time, a satanic pedophile ring. In Q circles, this came to be known as the "silent war."[29] One Q "drop" concluded "Think depopulation. The Silent War continues."[30] Another, in February 2018, endorsed *Behold a Pale Horse*, which appears to have sent Cooper's book, complete with its extracts from *Silent Weapons* and *Iron Mountain*, up Amazon's bestseller charts. The notion of an intelligence officer blowing the whistle on the evil machinations of the elite echoes Cooper's backstory; as the *Arizona Republic* noted, he even claimed he had "Q clearance." Having spent time interviewing Trump supporters in 2016, the author Jared Yates Sexton observed:

"The narrative of *Behold a Pale Horse* has infected America's right wing in totality. But where its head has bobbed out of the surface is in the QAnon movement."[31]

Meanwhile, in December 2023, in what may have been one more case of pandemic radicalization, an Australian conspiracist murdered two police officers and a neighbor. A search of his many online posts unearthed one that talked of having "been trying to reach people as individuals for the past twenty-five years and convince them of the WWO, UN, WHO, Reset, 1%ers plans and the use of silent weapons for quiet wars."[32] The shooter was not a supporter of the QAnon movement, however; he seems to have thought it was a "psyop."[33]

———————

*Report from Iron Mountain* continues to be widely read and alluded to, not least by some of those warning about depopulation. On the finance website Zero Hedge, on January 9, 2024, one poster informed readers that *Iron Mountain* was a "monstrous" document, which spoke of "the ruling establishment's need for permanent warfare and large-scale destruction of life (depopulation)," not to mention advocating the return of slavery.[34] In fact, the *Report* pops up all over, not least through several of Alex Jones's associates. It underpins conspiracy theories in books, DVDs, podcasts, and online videos. On social media platforms like X (formerly Twitter), it's been described as the playbook for elitist evil.

The range of mischievous "alternatives to war" Lewin came up with means his satire has become an all-purpose way to claim that a malign, all-powerful, manipulative, or deceptive force hovers behind anything that resembles those alternatives. Indeed, the *Report* is so all-purpose that it's used to back both sides of a given argument. It allows a conspiracist to take something they dislike or fear and either argue it is being faked by elites . . . or that it is being deliberately perpetrated by them. And the book's supposed authenticity allows advocates of any such theory to claim that it is "documented." This is bolstered by combining it with real documents in which apocalyptic threats are detected.

Since the nineties, one of the most important theories that leans on the *Report* concerns the environment. As we saw in Chapter 8, this is prompted by the Special Study Group's recommendation that "gross pollution of the environment" might "eventually replace the possibility of mass destruction by nuclear weapons as the principal apparent threat to the survival of the species." This, the *Report* cautions, would likely only be viable once pollution had grown much worse, which might take another "generation and a half." By this math, the elite's ability to wield the pollution threat would manifest in the early 1990s—exactly the interpretation that started to appear. By confecting a climate crisis, the *Report*'s 1990s interpreters warned, the elite would be able to enforce global unity and conformism. On this basis, the measures needed to tackle climate change are transformed into a sinister trick that will usher in tyranny.

This theory—which seems to have had a significant impact on many Americans' attitude toward environmentalism—began to spread after the Earth Summit, held in Rio de Janeiro in 1992. One of the theory's earliest proponents was William Jasper, the John Birch Society journalist who that year set out the idea in his book *Global Tyranny . . . Step by Step*. In 1993, the idea was expounded in detail in that video *Iron Mountain: Blueprint for Tyranny*, which still circulates online. In 2001, Jasper returned to the theory in a new book, *The United Nations Exposed: The Internationalist Conspiracy to Rule the World*, in which he adds chilling details about the Special Study Group and their evil tricks: "The available evidence indicates that Herman Kahn and his CFR-laden Hudson Institute may have formed the core of the SSG, or that the SSG may have been entirely a Kahn/Hudson operation."[35] (Jasper credits this conclusion to Gary Allen, the author of that Bircher tract Alex Jones devoured as a boy.) While casting the *Report* as just a "delightful joke,"[36] Jasper warns, the elite were quietly putting it into action. They were "furiously building the threat of environmental destruction"[37] to construct the *Report*'s recommendation: "a credible substitute for war capable of directing human behavior patterns in behalf of social organization."[38] It could hardly be a coincidence that, just three years after the *Report* was leaked, "the first Earth Day was held."[39] (This highlights another logical mistake that *Iron Mountain* often triggers: even if what is happening in the world is *exactly* the same as what a fictional group of people talk about, you can't use that as evidence of anyone's intent. Because it's fiction.)

Jasper contends that the *Report* is not alone in arguing that its fake environmental threat had to be "immediate, tangible, and directly felt." The "Iron Mountain gang" were just following existing thinking—as shown by a 1962 Institute of Defense Analyses paper for the State Department that makes a similar argument. So, here, Lewin's satire is corroborated by its target. Jasper thinks Lewin's parody of think tank speak is real . . . because it sounds like real think tank speak. The unintended consequences of Lewin's uncanny accuracy were still spreading in the new century. They help Jasper to conclude, drawing on the *Report*, that climate change is a hoax: the claims that "our planet faces imminent, cataclysmic consequences unless immediate, global action is taken" are "doomsday propaganda" to usher in "*global* government with *global powers*."[40]

To show what the elite is planning, Jasper—who attended the Rio Summit as a reporter—is able to point to something called "Agenda 21." This was a very long document setting out a strategy for sustainable development. Jasper insists that it is a "mammoth program for global social engineering and eco-tyranny" and "a massive blueprint for regimenting all life on Planet Earth in the 21st century—in the name of protecting the environment."[41] Today, it is more obvious even than it was in 2001 that we need to change how we live, and how we use land, to avoid global heating; it is also true that, like any movement, environmentalism has its extremists. Nevertheless, this 1992 UN action plan is *not mandatory*. For good or ill, we are a lot further from a one-world government than we were in 2001.

For twenty years, the Agenda 21 conspiracy theory remained on the margins with the Birchers, but in 2012, it was suddenly everywhere, amid terrifying warnings that it heralded a "new Dark Ages of pain and misery yet unknown to mankind."[42] The theory even stirred that specter of coming planetary depopulation, on the grounds that the elite thought humans were bad for the environment and would largely have to go. Agenda 21 was promoted by a range of voices, not all on the right, and not all of whom echoed Jasper's arguments about *Iron Mountain*. But one of its most tireless promoters has done exactly that.

In his 2010 book *Rescuing a Broken America: Why America Is Deeply Divided and How to Heal It Constitutionally*, Michael Coffman,* a scholar of ecosystems analysis, casts the "cold, calculating"[43] Study Group and their "amoral"[44] *Report* as the first in a series of elite moves to "shift control of property rights from the individual to the state or federal government"[45] under the guise of sustainability. The next elite move was the Club of Rome's famous 1972 report, *The Limits to Growth*. According to Coffman, this called "for severe limits on human population and the control of all development."[46] Agenda 21, he concluded, brought this long-nurtured process to fruition. Like Jasper, Coffman was aware that when the *Report* leaked, "the major media" had "immediately denied its authenticity."[47] This wasn't surprising—but its authenticity had since been admitted, he wrote, by Harlan Cleveland, in that 1999 encounter with Joan Veon—the one we heard about in Chapter 8.

The Tea Party movement, which appeared in reaction to the global financial crisis and the bailouts that followed as well as the election of Barack Obama, seized on Agenda 21—as did its noisiest mainstream media cheerleader. Glenn Beck used his platform on Fox News—while it lasted—to hammer home the idea that Agenda 21 was the playbook for global totalitarian takeover. Senior politicians jumped aboard: from Newt Gingrich and Texas governor Greg Abbott to a host of state legislators. Ted Cruz, a first-time candidate for the U.S. Senate in Texas, popped up on Beck's radio show to warn that Agenda 21 was an attempt "to undermine property rights and undermine our economic liberty." It was "part of a pervasive movement . . . to undermine our sovereignty and to use international bodies like the UN to

---

* Not to be confused with the Colorado Republican politician of the same name.

push a leftist agenda that couldn't get through our own legislatures."[48] The end result would be "pushing away from private property, pushing away from single family homes, farming and ranching, because all of those are deemed contrary to the UN decree of sustainable development."[49] It was "putting the tentacles of the United Nations into the very foundations of our government throughout this nation."[50] According to the Southern Poverty Law Center, the Senate majority leader in Georgia "organized a four-hour, closed-door anti–Agenda 21 briefing in October 2012 for fellow Republicans," delivered by a conspiracy theorist, at which those present learned that "President Obama was using 'mind control' techniques to push land use planning, and that the UN planned to force Americans from suburbs into cities and also was implementing mandatory contraception to curb population growth."[51]

Beck was so aghast at all this that he even wrote a dystopian novel to bring the threat to life. In *Agenda 21*, constitutional democracy has been replaced by the rule of the Authorities, and humans live in grim communal concrete quarters with rationed food and water, forced to tread boards daily to generate energy. Women must procreate with whoever is assigned to them; their children are whisked away, growing up to pledge themselves "To the Earth and its preservation."[52] (The book's editor announced that Beck did not actually write the book. It appears that he paid the real author, a retired nurse named Harriet Parke, for the right to put his name on the cover, with his company as copyright owner, and she agreed to a coauthor credit.[53]) The fear of Agenda 21 caused political pushback across the country. In Alabama, a law was passed banning any encroachment on property rights "without due process, as may be required by policy recommendations originating in, or traceable to 'Agenda 21.'"[54] By August 2012, the official Republican platform announced that "We strongly reject the U.N. Agenda 21 as erosive of American sovereignty, and we oppose any form of U.N. Global Tax."[55] The Iron Mountain Study Group must have been furious.

Even long after the hullabaloo had subsided, these claims of Agenda 21's dark intent were still appearing online, sometimes invoking *Report from Iron Mountain* as evidence. Such notions are interlocked with "chemtrails" theories: the baseless suspicion that airplane vapor trails are being used to spread toxins across the planet, to enslave people to Big Pharma, say, or to enforce mind control. Ted Cruz's reference to Agenda 21's alleged hostility to farming and ranching suggests that, to some extent, the UN action plan was becoming intertwined with real concerns among farmers about federal restrictions, some of which were designed to protect endangered species. But the decrying of Agenda 21 was clearly also driven by flagrant overinterpretation, as a way to fuel a decades-old conspiracy narrative that is always hungry for new "evidence." Ironically, there is even a self-published pastiche of the original *Report* available online, called *Second Report from Iron Mountain*, which uses Lewin's original format to lampoon *anti*-environmentalists. But this, too, argues that population control is a hidden motive: it's just that here, it is climate change deniers who are the guilty men.

Needless to say, when Covid began, Agenda 21 rapidly resurfaced. The plan to exterminate "just over 90 percent of the global population" for the benefit of the planet seemed to be coming to life.[56]

---

Among the promoters of depopulation and Agenda 21 theories, it's not hard to spot the militias. And tracing their return from the margins soon leads back to the *Report*, by which they set so much store in the 1990s. After 9/11, during the Bush presidency, the hard right had found itself divided. Many hard-right polemicists joined more moderate Republicans in embracing the Patriot Act, the Department of Homeland Security, and the War on Terror, leaving the likes of Alex Jones, who saw only false flags and police states, on the fringe. The militia movement lost much of its momentum.

But with the rise of Barack Obama to the presidency, the right had a common enemy once more. And the America First side of right-wing politics, championed by the patriot movement, now had a stronger case. As America's industrial base continued to rust, that old 1990s hostility to free trade began to look prescient. Then the financial crisis and its waves of foreclosures were met with a bailout for the banks that had caused the trouble in the first place.

As the journalist David Neiwert has charted, the militia movement doubled in size between 2007 and 2008. "Birtherism"—the baseless claim that Obama wasn't a native-born American—was folded into the old talk about the new world order. Right-wing violence began to rise again. Then, in May 2009, a conference was held at a place called Jekyll Island, on the Georgia coast. This brought together representatives of a wide range of right-wing groups and delivered a huge boost to the resurgence of the broader patriot movement.

The reason to meet in this odd location was that, in 1910, the Jekyll Island Club had played host to the secret meeting that created the Federal Reserve: America's private central bank and the bête noire of the far right for decades. Indeed, the right-wingers—described in a report for the Southern Poverty Law Center as "radical tax protesters, militiamen, nativist extremists, anti-Obama 'birthers,' hard-line libertarians, conspiracy-minded Patriots with theories about secret government concentration camps, even a raging anti-Semite"[57]—gathered in what is now memorialized as the Federal Reserve Room. There, they reportedly "held an elaborate ceremony meant to symbolically 'supplant the secretive deliberations' of 1910."[58]

One reason the radical right was aware of this place was an influential book, written by one of the meeting's organizers. *The Creature from Jekyll Island: A Second Look at the Federal Reserve* was first published in 1994, at the peak of the militias' previous rise. Its author, Edward Griffin, is a stalwart of the John Birch Society. He was a friend of its founder, Robert Welch, the man whom Richard Hofstadter once mocked as the embodiment of the paranoid style. In 1968, when George Wallace ran for president as an independent segregationist, with Kennedy's old foe General Curtis LeMay as his running mate, it was Griffin who wrote LeMay's speeches. He reportedly believes that HIV is fake—and has said that chemtrails are real.[59]

In *The Creature from Jekyll Island*, he makes the familiar case that the Fed is a plot against America. To help substantiate his arguments, he turns to *Report from Iron Mountain*—the "origin of many of the stratagems"[60] that he traces in a chapter called "Doomsday Mechanisms." As ever, he acknowledges that the *Report* is said to be a satire, but points to Galbraith's various remarks to suggest it is probably authentic, and then argues that it doesn't matter either way, because the book describes reality. Indeed, it is being implemented in "almost every detail."[61] Once you realize this, it makes many "incomprehensible" issues "suddenly become clear."[62] Why else, if not for the evil plans of the Iron Mountain Study Group, could anyone possibly want to introduce foreign aid, gun control, or a world bank? *Iron Mountain* also explains wasteful spending and the destruction of American industry. It is, Griffin warns, "shaping our future."[63]

Generally, Griffin's reading of the *Report* is the familiar one, but there are some intriguing new details. He takes up the idea that the *Report* was a product of the Hudson Institute, which he says is "located at the base of Iron Mountain in Croton-on-Hudson";[64] the two locations are roughly eighty miles apart. He dismisses the articles in *Time* and the *Washington Post*, which said the *Report* was a satire or hoax, by pointing out the affiliation of the founder of *Time* and the owner of the *Post* with the dreaded Council on Foreign Relations. We learn that total disarmament would involve . . . a world army, that dissidents "would face heavy fines" for being "politically incorrect,"[65] and that "a primary model"[66] for the *Report* is Orwell's *Nineteen Eighty-Four*. This last claim might actually be true, but not in quite the way Griffin means.

*The Creature from Jekyll Island* won a laudatory blurb from the libertarian congressman Ron Paul. In 2011, Glenn Beck could be heard endorsing the book, too.[67] According to reporting by Heidi Beirich of the Southern Poverty Law Center, in his opening speech at Jekyll Island, Griffin told the gathered right-wing leaders that putting "large numbers of people in the street" was insufficient, declaring "We must achieve power."[68]

Shortly before the Jekyll Island conclave, in March 2009, the return of the militias had already taken another step forward with the launch of an organization called the Oath Keepers, a "national group of veterans who openly subscribe to the Patriot movement conspiracy theories regarding the

New World Order,"[69] which they believed President Obama was planning to impose. The group soon revived the nightmares of the 1990s in some detail.

Representatives from the Oath Keepers attended some of the meetings set in motion at Jekyll Island. As Sam Jackson, an academic expert on the far right, puts it, "heavily armed members" have repeatedly "put themselves in situations where they might shoot at law enforcement."[70] When a stand-off developed between farmers and the federal government in Oregon in 2015, the Oath Keepers chose not to participate; nonetheless, founder Stewart Rhodes reportedly warned that if law enforcement acted as they had at Waco, they risked "starting a conflagration so great it cannot be stopped, leading to a bloody, brutal civil war."[71] Several of the Oath Keepers' leading figures, including Rhodes, went on to play a key role in the attack on the Capitol, and were sentenced to long prison terms.

In this sphere, too, *Report from Iron Mountain* is occasionally visible. Until November 2016, a Vietnam veteran named Franklin Shook who goes by the name "Elias Alias"—apparently a long-time associate of Rhodes[72]—was editing the Oath Keepers website. Sam Jackson told the congressional inquiry into the Capitol attack on January 6, 2021 that "As editor, Alias wrote many articles promoting conspiracy theories that used rather apocalyptic language."[73] On the site, the *Report* was mentioned to back up the argument that the militarization of law enforcement was part of the federal government's "statist authoritarianism."[74] More recently, having left the group, Alias edited a piece that cites the *Report* at length, and he explained why Lewin's book is worth reading despite being described as a hoax—by citing Edward Griffin. (There is no suggestion that Alias was involved in the attack on the Capitol.)

Given the end of the Cold War, most of the invocations of *Iron Mountain* we've been tracing relate to its proposed substitutes for war. It is striking that the conflict in Iraq, for all the profits made by private companies, seems to have provoked little reference to Lewin's book. But with the outbreak of the war in Ukraine, and disputes over the provision by the Biden administration of military aid to President Zelensky's troops, the original focus of Lewin's satire has returned to the fore. Retired U.S. army colonel Lawrence Wilkerson, a veteran of the war in Vietnam, could be found insisting that it was "still undetermined" whether the *Report* was really a satire or "or a genuine report of a special study group composed of luminaries as disparate as E. L. Doctorow and John Kenneth Galbraith," and that its claim that "War itself is the basic social system" remained of "fundamental relevance."[75] He argues that the *Report*'s claim that war is "the principal basis of organization on which all modern societies are constructed" is shown to be true by the war in Ukraine.

Wilkerson served as chief of staff to Colin Powell, both when Powell was chair of the Joint Chiefs of Staff and as secretary of state. In that role, Wilkerson researched the deeply flawed presentation to the United Nations in which Powell made the case for the 2003 invasion of Iraq. Wilkerson now says he inadvertently took part in a hoax; he has become a sworn enemy of the neoconservative "cabal."[76] The embrace of Lewin's hoax by a conservative opponent of the war machine brings together the themes we've been exploring.

"*Report From Iron Mountain* will never die," observed Chip Berlet in despairing tones in 1996.[77] Almost thirty years on, he is still correct.

# CONCLUSION: AS IF

The conspiracy theories that *Report from Iron Mountain* has been used to "prove" generally center on an evil cabal in the heart of power. Such fears are red warning lights flashing on the dashboard of democratic governments. Today, the phrase most associated with this fear is "deep state." And if many Americans feel there's a deep state that couldn't care less about them, or even means them harm—it shouldn't really be surprising.

In recent years, criticism of excessively centralized power has come from left and right at once, not least in the wake of the wars in Iraq and Afghanistan. In her 2012 book *Drift: The Unmooring of American Military Power*, Rachel Maddow was one of those calling out the executive branch's tightening grip on the power to declare war, the close ties between defense companies and the federal government, and the ever-more-intrusive national security state. In 2015, the historian Christian Appy spied a "profound disconnect between the ideals and priorities of the public and the reality of a permanent war machine."[1] More recently, in the long aftermath of the 2008 crash and the bank bailouts that followed, a range of other writers[2] have concluded that, since the 1980s, economic power has been pulled ever further away from ordinary people, into the hands of huge, monopolistic corporations, to the point of endangering democracy.

These writers argue that such concentrations of power, in national security and the economy alike, have been justified to the American people with all sorts of dubious tales. Tales about imminent terrorist attack, and about the inherent evil of government; about how safety regulations and employment rights are suffocating obstructions, and giant corporations need the same protections as individuals.

Put together, all this sounds rather like the postwar phenomenon that C. Wright Mills skewered in *The Power Elite*: individual citizens left disempowered by the centralization of power and the orthodoxies that protect it. Except this time, it's worse. Compared with the 1950s and 1960s, the social fabric of the country is in worse repair, and inequality much more glaring—widening the gap between the empowered individual of the American ideal and what many people's lives are actually like. As George Packer writes in *Last Best Hope: America in Crisis and Renewal*:

> overwhelmed by unfathomably large forces, Americans can no longer think and act as fellow citizens. We look for answers in private panaceas, fixed ideas, group identities, dreams of the future and the past, saviors of different types—everywhere but in ourselves. When none of these sets us free, we turn against one another.[3]

Government, he adds, "which did so little for ordinary Americans, was still the enemy, along with 'governing elites,'" but the ideal of freedom had degenerated into "a defiant and armed loneliness."[4] So perhaps it is not surprising that this time the conspiracy theories are more widespread and more extreme.

Finally, one writer sought to do what Mills had once done in *The Power Elite*, and pull all these issues—governmental, economic, and military—into a single analysis of what had gone wrong. The result, published in 2016, was a book called *The Deep State*. The author was a former congressional staffer named Mike Lofgren, who'd spent twenty-eight years working on Capitol Hill, "the last sixteen as a senior analyst on the House and Senate budget committees." During this period, he grew more and more horrified by the "fantasy math" of the Iraq War and the "sausage making" of the post–crash Troubled Assets Relief Program.[5] He'd been an Eisenhower-style Republican, but left the party disillusioned by what he'd seen unfold. His book

similar happened to *Report from Iron Mountain*—a satire on the thinking of the real power elite that was purloined by fascists. So perhaps the bizarre story that we've been uncovering in this book can offer us an answer.

———————

Like *The Deep State*, the sociologist Arlie Russell Hochschild's book *Strangers in Their Own Land: Anger and Mourning on the American Right* was published in that fateful year, 2016. In the aftermath of Trump's shock victory that November, it became one of the explanatory texts through which people sought to make sense of what had happened. The book is a report on five years of fieldwork that took Hochschild deep into the inner landscapes of conservatives in Louisiana. Midway through, she writes:

> Behind all I was learning about bayou and factory childhoods and the larger context—industry, state, church, regular media, Fox News—of the lives of those I had come to know lay, I realized, a deep story.
>
> A deep story is a *feels-as-if* story—it's the story feelings tell, in the language of symbols. It removes judgment. It removes fact. It tells us how things feel. Such a story permits those on both sides of the political spectrum to stand back and explore the *subjective prisms* through which the party on the other side sees the world.[15]

Hochschild is clearly right. It is vital that we acknowledge, understand, and respect each other's deep stories. But this is difficult territory. Those deep stories are not simply interior narratives. At some level, they're about power, which means they have much wider, political consequences. The risk lies in the way that, as Hochschild puts it, much as a person's deep story will generally have roots in reality, it "removes fact." Overriding the vexing restrictions imposed by accuracy is what makes it a satisfying narrative.

These stories can become public in various ways. They may show up as movies, plays, and novels (and it would be worth asking whose deep stories those tell, and whose they scorn). They may show up as TikTok clips, urban myths, jokes, and folktales (which is maybe where the stories Hollywood ignores can be found). And, especially when these *feels-as-if* stories are about power, they manifest as conspiracy theories, as with Trump's version of the "deep state." This is where things get sticky, because a conspiracy theory, unlike a novel or a joke, is making factual claims.

Deciphering how this works is difficult if every fact is disputed, which is where the story of *Report from Iron Mountain* is so revealing. What differentiates the *Report* and the thinking it inspired from most conspiracy theories about nefarious power elites and deep states is that at the core we have a document that we know as a matter of absolute, unarguable fact, was concocted as a satirical hoax. This is another genre of *feels-as-if* story about power that makes factual claims—but with the crucial distinction that, once revealed, we know it is fictional. Tracing how people interpreted the *Report*, after Lewin had confessed, allows us to see with unusual clarity how a certain kind of thinking unfolds.

As we've seen, the logic visible in these responses says that it doesn't matter if the *Report* is fabricated. If it feels real, it is real. And for some, if it matches reality, it must have *caused* that reality. It is taken to explain the intentions behind any phenomenon mentioned in the text, from climate change to the ending of wars. Some responses also reveal the belief that the first version of a story is always true, and that the follow-up is always a cover-up. The basic principle here is that "nothing is accidental." No one ever makes, and then corrects, a mistake. No one ever plays a prank, then reveals it. One online analysis of *Report from Iron Mountain* in 2014 followed this logic to the point of concluding that when Leonard Lewin later wrote a novel, it "may easily have been" a case of "sheep-dipping":[16] building a cover story retrospectively, to help substantiate his eventual claim that he was a writer of fiction, the *Report* included.

Much of this is based on a resolute refusal to distinguish fact from metaphor—for example, between criticizing those in power for behaving *as if* they would consider reintroducing slavery, and believing that they're actually planning to enslave real Americans. The *feels-as-if* story, with fact removed, is itself transformed into fact. *Report from Iron Mountain* so compellingly confirmed some people's deep stories that they painlessly slid over this line.

That this blurring of fact and fantasy began in the late 1960s and flourished in the decades that followed is understandable. The whole idea that there was a neat, reassuring thing called "fact" had long been under pressure, not least because of the way those in power had conducted themselves. Beyond the all-out disinformation blizzards stirred up by Hitler and Stalin, the idea that you could trust democratic leaders had long been in doubt. Lyndon Johnson and the endemic lies and self-delusions produced by the Vietnam War are often blamed, but as C. Wright Mills had shown, John F. Kennedy and others had mastered these arts years earlier.

This is visible in the origins of the *Report* itself. Lewin said his aim was to draw attention to the normalized absurdity of the war system "in a *provocative* way." As he wrote in 1972, "If the 'argument' of the Report had not been hyped up by its ambiguous authenticity—is it, just possibly for real?—its serious implications wouldn't have been discussed. At all."[17] By blurring the line between fact and fiction, you could break through the dominance of the "official narrative" and get people to see the truth. Provided people still recognized the distinction between satire and reality.

In the years after the *Report* was published, telling the two apart became more complicated. E. L. Doctorow, who was instrumental in ensuring the *Report* was taken seriously, went on to become one of the greatest American novelists of the century through works that put a fictional spin on real historical events, like *Ragtime* (1975), in which Sigmund Freud and Henry Ford rubbed shoulders with characters Doctorow had invented. In 1977, in response to criticism that his work blurred the line between fact and fiction, Doctorow wrote an essay called "False Documents" in which he argued that supposedly factual writing—journalism, history, social science—was "regime language." This led him to a revealing conclusion: history was really "a kind of fiction." "There is no fiction or nonfiction as we commonly understand the definition," he concluded: "there is only narrative."[18] It was this essay that the screenwriter Nora Ephron was quoting in that Town Hall debate in 1992, in defense of Oliver Stone's *JFK*.

Doctorow's argument bore the influence of the radical ideas of the 1960s New Left, those disciples of Mills, and their theories about the power elite and false consciousness. Supposedly factual writing, Doctorow insisted, must be subverted by imaginative writing—"the language of freedom." The "human mind," he argued, "has to be shocked, seduced, or otherwise provoked out of its habitual stupor."[19] Doctorow had done this in *The Book of Daniel*, which dramatizes the idea that the official Cold War narrative covered up the U.S. government's crackpot realism. And he'd helped Lewin do it more subversively with the *Iron Mountain* hoax.

Decades later, when Doctorow teased Lewin at the Knickerbocker Bar and Grill by asking him what it felt like to be "deconstructed," he was playfully alluding to a radical idea that was then popular in academia. Like allied ideas such as post-structuralism and postmodernism, deconstruction involved dissecting language to the point where the idea of meaning itself seemed suspiciously conservative. Not long before the reunion at the Knickerbocker, Victor Navasky had been concerned enough about these ideas to spend a semester at Harvard wrestling with them. During this hiatus from *The Nation*, Navasky hoped to "gain insight into the opportunity for magazines of critical opinion to provide what the language I didn't really speak called a counternarrative." But he soon concluded that his professor, "who was at home with . . . deconstruction" could all too easily "give his students the illusion that we understood what he was talking about."[20]

This set of ideas has had a huge impact, for good and ill. The argument that a given person can only ever see the world from a subjective point of view was a powerful tool for undermining the claims of sexists, racists, and homophobes. But like most powerful tools, it could do damage in the wrong hands. As Deborah Lipstadt has argued, casting doubt on the concept of objective truth was a "reminder that the interpretations of the less powerful groups in society have generally been ignored. But it also fostered an atmosphere in which it became harder to say that an idea was beyond the pale of rational thought."[21] Deconstruction encouraged "permissiveness toward questioning the meaning of historical events."[22] Strikingly, one of the first examples she cites is Oliver Stone's *JFK*.

In 1986, picking up on some of these trends, the philosopher Harry G. Frankfurt wrote a paper in an obscure academic journal. Two decades later, in the era of the Iraq War, it was published as a book, *On Bullshit*, which caught the moment. Frankfurt argued that bullshit was different from lying because the bullshitter "does not reject the authority of the truth, as the liar does, and oppose himself to it." Rather, he "pays no attention to it at all." Donald Trump and his way of moving through the world comes to mind.

This indifference to reality meant that bullshit was "a greater enemy of the truth than lies are."[23] As many lost confidence in the very idea of objective reality, Frankfurt saw that the old ideal of *correctness* had been largely cast aside for a new ideal: *sincerity*. All that seemed to matter was whether you believed it when you said it. This is one way that *feels-as-if* becomes unmoored from *is*.

Once the compulsions of the deep story are used to override a fealty to fact, malign possibilities open up. Much of the discussion in recent years about "disinformation" has tended to interpret it as spreading information that is factually wrong. But as Frankfurt's distinction between lying and bullshit suggests, the aim is less to misinform than to degrade the whole idea of information, of shared trust in truth, itself. When in 2018 the British government accused Russia of attempting to murder an ex-agent, Sergei Skripal, in the little English city of Salisbury, claims began to appear that the poisoning had really been carried out to make Russia look bad, or to divert attention from Brexit, or that Ukraine did it, or Sweden, or MI6, or that it was to interfere with the Russian elections, or that it was to distract from Russian "peacekeeping" in Syria, or that the Skripals weren't poisoned at all. Likewise, as Deborah Lipstadt wrote in her study of Holocaust deniers over thirty years ago: "Certain computer networks have been flooded with their materials. Their objective is to plant seeds of doubt that will bear fruit in coming years, when there are no more survivors or eyewitnesses alive to attest to the truth."[24] In his 1977 essay, arguing that all was narrative, Doctorow emphasized that the Holocaust was real. But by 1980, Holocaust denial, with its "challenge" to the "official narrative," was becoming a significant problem (with the groups that later pirated *Iron Mountain* leading the way).

As President Trump's former chief strategist Steve Bannon once advised, the task is to "flood the zone with shit": to discharge so much dubious data into the atmosphere that no one knows what to believe. This is strikingly reminiscent of a moment in *JFK*. The Fletcher Prouty figure, Mr. X, advises Jim Garrison that, to combat his enemies, "the best chance you got is come up with a case, something, anything, make arrests, stir the shitstorm."[25] And this is not a bad description of the proliferating Kennedy conspiracy theories. The intention of the assassinationologists is not at all like that of Russian disinformers—most of the former sincerely seek the truth—but the effect is much the same. Researchers have generated more detail, more speculation, and more mutually contradictory theories than any one person could fully process in a lifetime.

What seems to be at work here is the process we've been tracing: the overriding of fact by *feels-as-if*. When *JFK* came out, the leading New Leftist Tom Hayden argued that Oliver Stone was being attacked for shattering the media's "fairy tale notion of democracy," and many have contended that there is a desire to believe that it was simply Oswald because that is more comforting than thinking Kennedy was murdered by conspiracy. But the immense energy that has been put into trying to show the murder was anything but the work of a lone assassin suggests that the idea that it *was* just Oswald is as unbearable as the idea that it *wasn't*. If your deep story of power is predicated on a version of American exceptionalism—on the idea that the American state, however malign, is all-powerful—why would the Oswald story comfort you? As for Hayden, he also wrote that whether it was a lone assassin or an elite plot, "Either notion was enough to unsettle my world."[26]

Something of this phenomenon is visible in the response of voices like Alex Jones to school shootings. Jones became notorious for insisting that such incidents could not be the work of armed individuals and must rather be "false flag" operations by the deep state. Among those whose deep story this fits, this has led to what Richard Hofstadter called "strivings for evidence to prove that the unbelievable is the only thing that can be believed." This has come at terrible cost to bereaved families, who have been tormented for years with accusations that they're just pretending to have lost their children—that they're "crisis actors." In the case of the 2012 shootings in Sandy Hook, Connecticut, this famously culminated in Jones's being sued successfully for well over a billion dollars.

---

*Report from Iron Mountain* is not the only case of satirical hoaxes and fictions being absorbed into conspiracy theory and supposedly revealing the truth about power. In 1997, as the *Report* was spreading through the militia movement, Hollywood made a film called *Wag the Dog*. This was a satire on the media manipulations of the Gulf War, which satirically extended the media's power to the point where it successfully tricks the entire U.S. population into believing that a war is taking place in Albania while it is actually being staged in TV studios. When President Clinton ordered a series of military actions in the midst of the Lewinsky scandal, the film's premise was stripped of its satire and used to accuse the president of having gone to war to distract from his difficulties. More recently, in Italy, an obscure far-right politician's pronouncement that "I'm Giorgia, I'm a mother, I'm a woman, I'm Italian, I'm Christian" was turned into a dance track, as a way of satirizing her opposition to LGBT rights. But it made Giorgia Meloni's name. In 2022 she became prime minister.[27] In 2016, when the emails of John Podesta of the Democratic National Committee were hacked and leaked, they turned out to contain little of interest . . . until a couple of posters messing around on 4chan made up a "code" that they pretended was used in the leaked emails—"hotdog" meant "boy," and so on.[28] Thus was born the Pizzagate conspiracy theory, which absurdly accused Podesta, Hillary Clinton, and others of running a pedophile ring out of a Washington, DC, restaurant. This went on to provide the foundation for QAnon.

The most notorious example of this phenomenon, with which QAnon has much in common, is the nineteenth-century French novelist Maurice Joly's *Dialogue in Hell Between Machiavelli and Montesquieu* (1864). This imagines the ghost of Machiavelli cynically explaining how to manipulate the gullible public, as a coded satire on the populism of the dictatorial French emperor Napoleon III. This was a worthy target, just as the 1960s U.S. war machine was for Lewin and Doctorow. But in 1903, Joly's long forgotten book was surreptitiously plagiarized wholesale by the anonymous creator of the anti-Semitic smear *The Protocols of the Elders of Zion.* Joly's text was taken and falsely presented as though it were a real record of the meetings of a secret Jewish cabal, plotting to manipulate the gullible public and create a world tyranny. When this blatant misrepresentation of a piece of fiction was revealed, it did little to stop the spread of the *Protocols*, which was feted by the Nazis and has been a staple of conspiracist Jew-hatred ever since.

The horrible irony is that *Report from Iron Mountain* was crafted with such ingenuity and insight that Lewin, Doctorow, and Navasky accidentally created another multipurpose, undying conspiracy theory that could be used to substantiate the craziest claim about the elite's schemes. Both *Protocols* and *Report* seem to confirm the same deep story about invisible elite conspiracy. The 1990s far right promoted both books—and even sold Lewin's satire as new "Secret Protocols." Today, some racist conspiracists use the fact of Navasky and Lewin's Jewishness as "evidence" that their hoax really does reveal an evil plot.

And yet *Report from Iron Mountain* also shows us how to counter this problem. In his afterword to the 1995 edition, Lewin says he intended his book as a challenge to superficial logic, which is one reason for its enduring relevance. It is a reminder that there's a difference between the fact that politicians sometimes tell lies and act out emotions they don't really feel, and the story that politicians are being played by actors and are working to a script. There's a difference between the charge that the media sometimes tells lies and is manipulative and unfair, and the claim that it's a perfectly designed system of mind control. There's a difference between finding truths expressed in fiction, and thinking fiction is factual evidence. And finally, there's a difference between Lofgren's "deep state," and Trump's, or Truss's. Lewin's *Report* is a test of whether you would cross that line—of how superficial or substantial your logic is.

Shared stories are certainly vital to democracy. As George Packer has argued, "nations require more than just facts—they need stories that convey a moral identity."[29] As Phillips and Milner put it, "Merely yelling at someone about how wrong they are . . . isn't going to tell the sort of alternative story that might, just might, get them to start seeing, or at least start being open to the possibility of seeing, things differently."[30] And stories are crucial to challenging power and pushing for political change. But today, politicians at points across the spectrum are retailing fiction-filled world views that fuel mutual incomprehension and hostility. In such a world we really need to be able to distinguish between fact and fiction. We no longer have the luxury of seeing everything as narrative. The tale of *Report from Iron Mountain* offers a warning about the consequences that await if you don't keep an eye on the line between your deep story about how power works, and what the facts support. Between what *feels-as-if* and what is.

# AUTHOR'S NOTE

This book began one Saturday afternoon in summer 2022. Instead of going outside like a sensible person, I was sitting at my iMac, searching old political science books for mentions of the military industrial complex. My first book had just come out, and I had an idea for a new one—about the real stories that feed the conspiracy theory movie we all carry around in our heads. I found a run of mentions of an odd-sounding volume called *Report from Iron Mountain*. One writer talked about it as though it were real, but another seemed unsure. And the third thought it was fake. I looked up the *Report*, and nearly fell off my chair. I had been searching for something like this for years. I wrote at the top of my notes, *This is a good story.*

At first, I thought this would make a great chapter in the book I was planning. But as I kept researching, it began to remind me of that trick where the illusionist pulls a string of knotted handkerchiefs from their empty sleeve, and they never seem to stop. This wasn't just a chapter. I saw that telling the story of the *Report*—its roots, its flowering, and its bizarre afterlife—would give me a way to explore themes that had been tugging at my sleeve for a long time.

But you would not be reading this were it not for the editors who opened the door. I will always be grateful to Andrew Gordon and George Lucas, my agents in the UK and the US, for bringing this project to the attention of Rick Horgan at Scribner in New York, and Neil Belton at Head of Zeus in London, and to Neil and Rick for each taking a chance on me, and expertly guiding me through every step of the process that ensued. You changed my life. Thank you.

This commission allowed me to jump through the screen of my iMac into the worlds I'd been researching. One of those worlds was the literary, satirical New York of the 1960s, the land of *Esquire* and Dial Press, as seen through the lens of *Monocle*. A particular thank you to Anne Navasky for sharing her memories of this story, and the extraordinary man who launched it, Victor Navasky, and to Richard Lingeman, who was present at the creation of the idea—and who let me rummage through his copies of the *Outsider's Newsletter*. I'm grateful too for the chance to hear the recollections of Calvin Trillin, Kitty Krupat, Eleanor Foa Dienstag, Carole Baron, Arthur Waskow, Howard Junker, Raymond Heard, Jeremy Baker, and everyone else I spoke to, and to the inheritors of that generation—Jamie Kitman, Mary Kaye Schelling, and Maria Margaronis—for their help. And to Tony Cavin, not just for sharing his memories of his father, but for a great evening over an old-fashioned or two at the Algonquin. And also to my old friend Leo Carey, for a similarly splendid evening at the Knickerbocker Bar and Grill, for giving me the perfect line to describe it, and for introducing me to McKenna Stayner, who was kind and helpful as well. I'm honored that Kai Bird—who, as he writes, knew four of those involved—set the seal on my foray into this world with his wonderful Foreword. Likewise, I very much appreciate the contributions of everyone I spoke with in Oklahoma City, especially Charles Key and Larry Dellinger, and of Robert Tomsho, who broke the second half of this story in the first place, and shed fascinating further light on it when we spoke. Writing about two periods—the 1990s and the 1960s—that are each receding into history, albeit at different speeds, involved trying to contact more people than I was able to reach, and still fewer who felt able to talk to me. I'm grateful to everyone who did so.

But most of all, my heartfelt thanks go to Michael Lewin and Julie Lewin for giving this project their blessing, and for so generously sharing their memories of their father, and also to Julie for her hospitality, for giving me a copy of the pirated edition of the *Report*, and for a lift back to New Haven in the rain. I deeply appreciate the trust you both put in me.

The research for this book relied on the work of unfailingly helpful staff in archives and libraries both in the United Kingdom, at the British Library and the Harmsworth and Bodleian Libraries in Oxford; and in the United States, at the Tamiment Library and Robert F. Wagner Labor Archives at New York University and the Dolph Briscoe Center for American History at the University of Texas at Austin, both of which I was able to visit; and at the Rare Book & Manuscript Library and the Center for Oral History at Columbia University, Dartmouth College Library, the Dwight D. Eisenhower Presidential Library, the Kenneth Spencer Research Library Archival Collections at the University of Kansas, the Special Collections & University Archives at the University of Massachusetts Amherst, the Bentley Historical Library at the University of Michigan, Stanford University, the Archival Research Center at Tufts University, the Z. Smith Reynolds Library at Wake Forest University, and the Wisconsin Historical Society Archives at the University of Wisconsin–Madison. My thanks to Isabel Dorval for her kindness in offering to pay what turned out to be a very fruitful visit to the Library of Congress. Chapter 5 would be the poorer without it.

For their calm and expert work on turning my Word document into this splendid object, and for taking it safely out into the world, I would like to thank the teams at Head of Zeus—Neil, Karina Maduro, Dan Shutt, Katherine Wands, Amy Wong, and Jessie Price—and at Scribner: Rick, Mark LaFlaur, Martha Schwartz, Vic Hendrickson, Kathryn Kenney-Peterson, Colleen Nuccio, Kassandra Engel, and Sophie Guimaraes. I was pleased to learn that this is the first book Sophie has worked on from start to finish, but I would never have guessed it: like everyone at both Scribner and Head of Zeus, she is a professional.

For their advice, expertise, and generosity, I would also very much like to thank Jonathan Freedland, Dan Freisen, Sharon Ghamari-Tabrizi, Andrew McKenzie-McHarg, Anthony Julius, Rick Perlstein, John Summers, Elizabeth Varon, Jesse Walker, Bruce Weber, and all those who read an early draft in whole or in part, and gave me such good guidance: Alex Goodall, Steven Gillon, William Hitchcock, Dorian Lynskey, Rana Mitter, and Matthew Sweet. Thanks also to Helen Lewis, who gave me the most spectacularly bracing note I've had since my wife Sam told me that fifteen pages of my first book were unreadable. If my Introduction hooked you, we both have Helen to thank.

I'm grateful to Adam Smith, not only for inviting me to deliver a version of Chapter 1 as a lecture at Oxford's Rothermere American Institute, and hosting a wonderful dinner at which I met several of the people mentioned in this note, but for the evenings we spent concocting documentary ideas in the Somers Town Coffee House near King's Cross, which turned into adventures around the United States, chasing *The Day of the Locust* in Los Angeles, *Invasion of the Body Snatchers* in Sierra Madre, the dream of paradise in San Francisco, *The Killers* in Chicago, the robber barons in New York harbor and on the railroad to Washington, and the fate of the Fourteenth Amendment in the 2016 summer of Trump in North Carolina. This book would never have happened without all that. I was learning all the way.

But finally, like most writers, I owe most to the people who were nearest when I was busiest: my family. To my parents, Ed and Sue—I'm sorry for the missed weekends, and to Sam, Amy, and Polly—I'm sorry for working on Christmas Day. And to Polly, I'm sorry too for interrupting your first-ever visit to New York with my insistence that we go hunting around Greenwich Village for the shade of C. Wright Mills, when this project was still only the ghost of an idea.

# NOTES

## INTRODUCTION: WHAT HAPPENED?

1. Seymour Martin Lipset and William Schneider, *The Confidence Gap: Business, Labor, and Government in the Public Mind* (New York: Free Press, 1983), 15–17.

## CHAPTER 1: THE POWER ELITE

1. Cong. Rec., 6556 (June 14, 1951).
2. Report of the Tydings Committee, quoted in Larry Tye, *Demagogue: The Life and Long Shadow of Senator Joe McCarthy* (New York: Houghton Mifflin Harcourt, 2020), 185.
3. C. Wright Mills, *Letters and Autobiographical Writings*, ed. Kathryn Mills with Pamela Mills (Berkeley: University of California Press, 2000), 313.
4. Mills, *Letters and Autobiographical Writings*, 134; see also 135, 231, 232.
5. Mills, *Letters and Autobiographical Writings*, 89.
6. Mills, *Letters and Autobiographical Writings*, 251.
7. Mills, *The Power Elite* (New York: Oxford University Press, 1956), 178.
8. Mills, *The Power Elite*, 186.
9. Mills, *The Power Elite*, 184.
10. Mills, *The Power Elite*, 220.
11. Mills, *The Power Elite*, 323.
12. Mills, *The Sociological Imagination* (New York: Oxford University Press, 1959), 175; see also 171, 176. Mills first used the phrase "cheerful robots" in *White Collar: The American Middle Classes* (New York: Oxford University Press, 1951), with regard to the world of work.

13. Mills, *The Power Elite*, 315.

14. Mills, *The Power Elite*, 216, 202.

15. Mills, *The Causes of World War Three* (1958; repr., London: Secker & Warburg, 1959), 62.

16. Mills, *The Causes of World War Three*, 63.

17. Mills, *The Causes of World War Three*, 89.

18. Mills, *The Causes of World War Three*, 146.

19. Mills, *The Causes of World War Three*, 123, 140.

20. Mills, *The Power Elite*, 292.

21. Richard Hofstadter, *The Age of Reform: From Bryan to F.D.R.* (New York: Alfred A. Knopf, 1955), 71–72.

22. John F. Kennedy, quoted in Robert Dallek, *John F. Kennedy: An Unfinished Life* (2003; repr., London: Penguin Books, 2013), 31.

23. Kennedy was in hospital for surgery at the time of the vote, but as his biographer Fredrik Logevall points out, "he did not give his legislative assistant, Ted Sorensen, guidance on how to proceed in his absence"— as he could have done. (Logevall, *JFK*, vol. 1 [2020; repr., London: Penguin Books, 2021], 589.)

24. Kennedy, speech in Senate, April 6, 1954, quoted in Logevall, *JFK*, 576.

25. Mills, *The Power Elite*, 250–51n.

26. Hubert Humphrey, quoted in Dallek, *John F. Kennedy*, 249.

27. *Washington Post*, quoted in "U.S. in Worst Peril in History, Secret Gaither Report Says," *Wilmington Morning News*, December 20, 1957, 4.

28. Mills, *Letters and Autobiographical Writings*, 311.

29. Mills, *Listen, Yankee: The Revolution in Cuba* (1960; repr. New York: Ballantine Books, 1960), 33.

30. James Reston, "The Managerial Revolution Hits Politics," *New York Times*, July 31, 1960, 8E.

31. Mills, *Letters and Autobiographical Writings*, 231.

32. Mills, *Letters and Autobiographical Writings*, 319.

33. Mills, *Letters and Autobiographical Writings*, 319.

34. "Yankees Won't Listen, Mr. Mills," *Charlotte News*, December 6, 1960.

35. Mills, *Letters and Autobiographical Writings*, 320.

36. James Ledbetter, *Unwarranted Influence: Dwight D. Eisenhower and the Military-Industrial Complex* (New Haven, CT: Yale University Press, 2011), 44.

37. "Reminiscences of Malcolm Moos, 1972," oral history interview, Eisenhower administration project, Columbia Center for Oral History Research.

38. Memo: "Conversation with Dr. Moos this morning produced following preliminary guidelines" for State of the Union, Ralph E. Williams Papers 1958-60, A87-6, box 1, Eisenhower Presidential Library.

39. "Interview with Captain Ralph Williams," 1988, Dwight D. Eisenhower Library, quoted in Ledbetter, *Unwanted Influence*, 121.

40. Dwight D. Eisenhower, "January 17, 1961: Farewell Address," Miller Center, University of Virginia, https://millercenter.org/the-presidency /presidential-speeches/january-17-1961-farewell-address.

41. "The Monster We Can No Longer Control," *I. F. Stone's Weekly*, January 23, 1961, 1.

42. Mills Papers, box 4B402, folder: The Capitalist Bloc, Kennedy Administration; December 10, 1960.

43. James Reston, "The Problems to Come: Kennedy's Solutions, in Long Run, Are Deemed Likely to Be Radical," *New York Times*, January 20, 1961, 1, 16.

44. Mills, *Letters and Autobiographical Writings*, 324.

45. Mills, *Letters and Autobiographical Writings*, 326.

46. Mills, *Letters and Autobiographical Writings*, 328.

47. R. Hart Phillips, "Cuba in 'Death' Fight with U.S., Guevara Tells Workers' Rally," *New York Times*, March 29, 1961, 10. A cutting of this article is preserved in Mills Papers, Box 4B379, folder: Cuba 1959–1961.

48. Mills, *Letters and Autobiographical Writings*, 330.

49. Evan Thomas, *The Very Best Men: The Daring Early Years of the CIA* (New York: Simon & Schuster, 1995, 2006), 246.

50. See, for example, "Anti-Castro Base in Guatemala Laid to US," *Fort Worth Star-Telegram*, November 19, 1960, 2, reporting that the London

*Daily Mail* was implying "that the United States has created a $1,000,000 base in Guatemala for training anti-Castro Cuban revolutionaries."

51.  Telegram to President Kennedy, April 17, 1961, quoted in "Urge Neutral Stand in Cuba," *Chicago Tribune*, April 18, 1961, 3.

52.  "An Appeal to Americans," Fair Play for Cuba Committee advertisement, *New York Times*, April 21, 1961, 23.

53.  "San Francisco Cuba Rally Heckled," *San Francisco Examiner*, April 23, 1961, 11.

54.  C. Wright Mills, Telegram in Personals column dated April 19, 1961, in *Daily Palo Alto Times*, April 21, 1961, 29.

55.  Mills, *Letters and Autobiographical Writings*, 227.

56.  Mills, *Letters and Autobiographical Writings*, 341.

57.  Hayden, *Reunion* (New York: Random House, 1988), 80.

58.  Hayden, *Reunion*, 79–80.

59.  Hayden, *Reunion*, 79.

60.  Hayden, *Reunion*, 78.

61.  Marcus T. Raskin, "The Megadeath Intellectuals," *New York Review of Books*, November 14, 1963, 6–7.

62.  Marcus Raskin, quoted in Brian S. Mueller, *Democracy's Think Tank: The Institute for Policy Studies and Progressive Foreign Policy* (Philadelphia: University of Pennsylvania Press, 2021), 2.

63.  Hayden, *Reunion*, 80.

64.  "The Port Huron Statement," in Richard Flacks and Nelson Lichtenstein, eds., *The Port Huron Statement: Sources and Legacies of the New Left's Founding Manifesto* (Philadelphia: University of Pennsylvania Press, 2015), 241.

65.  Flacks and Lichtenstein, *The Port Huron Statement*, 249.

66.  Flacks and Lichtenstein, *The Port Huron Statement*, 271.

67.  Hayden, *Reunion*, 81.

68.  "JFK on the First Hundred Days," *Newsweek*, May 8, 1961, 24.

69.  Fred Kaplan, *The Bomb: Presidents, Generals and the Secret History of Nuclear War* (New York: Simon & Schuster, 2021), 63.

70. Robert F. Kennedy, quoted in Thomas, *The Very Best Men*, 270.

71. Kaplan, *The Bomb*, 68.

72. Edwin Walker, quoted in Peter Adams, *The Insurrectionist: Major General Edwin A. Walker and the Birth of the Deep State Conspiracy* (Baton Rouge: Louisiana State University Press, 2023), 66.

73. Walker, quoted in Adams, *The Insurrectionist*, 31.

74. Adams, *The Insurrectionist*, 69.

75. Dan Smoot, *The Invisible Government* (Belmont, MA: Western Islands, 1965), xi.

76. Walker, quoted in Bill Minutaglio and Steven L. Davis, *Dallas 1963: The Road to the Kennedy Assassination* (2013; repr., London: John Murray, 2014), 84.

77. Kennedy press conference, April 22, 1961, quoted in Adams, *The Insurrectionist*, 41.

78. Walker, quoted in "More About Gen. Walker," *Santa Ana Register*, November 3, 1961, 4.

79. John F. Kennedy, "Address in Los Angeles at a Dinner of the Democratic Party of California," November 18, 1961, American Presidency Project, https://www.presidency.ucsb.edu/documents/address-los-angeles-dinner-the-democratic-party-california.

80. "Gen. Walker Sees 'Release' of U.S. Sovereignty to U.N.," *Baltimore Sun*, December 13, 1961, 8.

81. Walker, quoted in Cliff Seasons, "Walker Flails UN, Calls Dag Red Tool, Lauds Mississippi for Americanism," *Sacramento Bee*, December 30, 1961, 2.

82. Walker, quoted in Adams, *The Insurrectionist*, 54.

83. "Walker Demands a 'Vocal Protest,'" *New York Times*, September 30, 1962, 69.

84. Lee Harvey Oswald, quoted in Vincent Bugliosi, *Reclaiming History: The Assassination of President John F. Kennedy* (New York: W. W. Norton, 2007), 559.

85. Dr. Renatus Hartogs, quoted in *Warren Commission Report*, 380,

https://www.archives.gov/research/jfk/warren-commission-report/chapter-7.html#newyork.

86. Norman Mailer, quoted in Michel Jacques Gagné, *Thinking Critically About the Kennedy Assassination: Debunking the Myths and Conspiracy Theories* (Milton Park, UK: Routledge, 2022), 236.

87. James P. Cannon, "The Coming American Revolution," speech delivered at the Twelfth National Convention of the Socialist Workers Party, November 15 to 18, 1946, https://www.marxists.org/archive/cannon/works/1946/comamrev.htm.

88. "Monday, February 3, 1964: Testimony of Mrs. Lee Harvey Oswald," in *Hearings Before the President's Commission on the Assassination of President Kennedy*, vol. 1 (Washington, DC: U.S. Government Printing Office, 1964), 1, https://www.govinfo.gov/content/pkg/GPO-WARREN COMMISSIONHEARINGS-1/pdf/GPO-WARRENCOMMISSION HEARINGS-1.pdf.

89. *Daily Worker*, October 2, 1962, quoted in Jean Davison, *Oswald's Game* (New York: W. W. Norton, 1983), 115. (Davison gives the source as the *Worker*, but given that October 2, 1962, was a Tuesday, that the *Worker* was a weekend paper, and that she doesn't distinguish between the two titles, the source here must be the *Daily Worker*.)

90. *Dallas Times Herald*, March 6, 1963, cited in Davison, *Oswald's Game*, 129.

91. Bugliosi, *Reclaiming History*, 686a.

92. Corliss Lamont, *The Crime Against Cuba* (Basic Pamphlets, 1961), 27.

93. The letter appears in *The Militant*, March 11, 1963. It is signed "LH" and is identified as being from Oswald in Minutaglio and Davis, *Dallas 1963*, 207.

94. Warren Commission, vol. 22, Commission Exhibit No. 1412, 803, accessed at https://www.history-matters.com/archive/jfk/wc/wcvols/wh22/pdf/WH22_CE_1412.pdf.

95. Bugliosi, *Reclaiming History*, 947n.

96. Lamont, *The Crime Against Cuba*, 31.

97. Patricia Johnson McMillan, *Marina and Lee* (1977; repr., Glasgow: William Collins Sons & Co., 1978), 270.

98. Hofstadter, "The Paranoid Style in American Politics," 35, in "Guard-book containing typescript copies of Oxford University lectures," MS. Top. Oxon. d. 360, fols. 395–434, Bodleian Libraries, University of Oxford; the lecture was published in a "revised and updated" version in 1964.

99. Hofstadter, "The Paranoid Style in American Politics," 37.

100. Hofstadter, "The Paranoid Style in American Politics," 39.

101. Hofstadter, "The Paranoid Style in American Politics," 25, 35.

102. Alan F. Westin, "The John Birch Society: 'Radical Right' and 'Extreme Left' in the Political Context of Post World War II," in *The Radical Right*, ed. Daniel Bell (Garden City, NY: Doubleday, 1963).

103. Senator Paul Douglas, BBC TV interview, December 2, 1963, excerpted in *Conspiracies: The Secret Knowledge*, "Narrative Graphs," episode 2, BBC Radio 4, March 19, 2021. See also Rick Perlstein, *Before the Storm: Barry Goldwater and the Unmaking of the American Consensus* (New York: Nation Books, 2009), 248–49.

104. Kathryn S. Olmsted, *Real Enemies: Conspiracy Theories and American Democracy, World War I to 9/11* (2009; repr., New York: Oxford University Press, 2010), 119.

105. Todd Gitlin, *The Sixties: Years of Hope, Days of Rage* (1987; repr., New York: Bantam, 1993), 212, 213.

106. Hayden, *Reunion*, 114.

107. Hayden, *Reunion*, 114.

108. Hayden, *Reunion*, 115.

109. "The Left and the Warren Commission Report," *I. F. Stone's Weekly*, October 5, 1964, 1.

110. This depended on whether the limit of North Vietnam's territorial waters was regarded as three miles from shore, as was the international standard, or twelve miles, which was the norm for some communist states, including China. (See Stanley Karnow, *Vietnam, A History: The First Complete Account of Vietnam at War* [New York: Viking Press, 1983], 366).

111. President Johnson, quoted in I. F. Stone, "Excerpt: 'The Best of I. F. Stone'" NPR, September 5, 2006, https://www.npr.org/templates/story/story.php?storyId=5769066.

## CHAPTER 2: THE UNTHINKABLE

1. Leonard C. Lewin, unpublished journal (1965), April 14, 1965, 9, Leonard Lewin Papers, University of Massachusetts, Amherst.

2. Leonard C. Lewin, Foreword to *Report from Iron Mountain on the Possibility and Desirability of Peace* (New York: Dial Press, 1967), viii.

3. Reston, "The Problems to Come: Kennedy's Solutions, in Long Run, Are Deemed Likely to Be Radical."

4. Herman Kahn, *Thinking About the Unthinkable* (New York: Horizon Press, 1962), 35.

5. Kahn, *Thinking About the Unthinkable*, 27.

6. Peter Perla, quoted in Sharon Ghamari-Tabrizi, *The Worlds of Herman Kahn: The Intuitive Science of Thermonuclear War* (Cambridge, MA: Harvard University Press, 2005), 165.

7. Emile Benoit, et al., *A Report of the Panel on Economic Impacts of Disarmament* (Washington, DC: U.S. Arms Control and Disarmament Agency, January 1962). For details of the other studies referred to, see sources cited in note 9.

8. John W. Finney, "US-Financed Panel Scores Government's Disarmament Plan," *New York Times*, July 11, 1966.

9. These two paragraphs are based on the following reports and articles: Benoit et al., *A Report of the Panel on the Economic Impacts of Disarmament*; US Government, *The Economic and Social Consequences of Disarmament*, U.S. Arms Control and Disarmament Agency, July 1962; Gerard Piel, "Can Our Economy Stand Disarmament?," *Atlantic*, September 1962, 35–40; Hubert Humphrey, speech, Congressional Record, 22558-22562, October 6, 1962; Kenneth E. Boulding, "Can We Afford a Warless World?," *Saturday Review*, October 6, 1962, 17–20; Ben B. Seligman "Disarmament & the Economy," *Commentary*, May

1963; Murray L. Weidenbaum, "Obstacles to Conversion," *Bulletin of the Atomic Scientists* 20, no. 4 (April 1964), 10–14; Wassily Leontief, "Alternatives to Armament Expenditures," *Bulletin of the Atomic Scientists* 20, no. 6 (June 1964), 19–21; "Arms Cut Is Held No Peril to Boom," *New York Times*, June 23, 1964, 43; "The Economy: Who's Afraid of Peace?," *Time*, September 17, 1965.

10. Lewin, Foreword to *Report from Iron Mountain*, viii.

11. Lewin, Background Information, *Report from Iron Mountain*, xxiii.

12. Lewin, Foreword to *Report from Iron Mountain*, ix, xiv.

13. Lewin, Foreword to *Report from Iron Mountain*, xii.

14. Lewin, Background Information, *Report from Iron Mountain*, xx.

15. *Report from Iron Mountain*, 38.

16. *Report from Iron Mountain*, 31.

17. *Report from Iron Mountain*, 29.

18. *Report from Iron Mountain*, 44.

19. *Report from Iron Mountain*, 40.

20. *Report from Iron Mountain*, 41.

21. *Report from Iron Mountain*, 64.

22. *Report from Iron Mountain*, 47.

23. *Report from Iron Mountain*, 84.

24. *Report from Iron Mountain*, 66.

25. *Report from Iron Mountain*, 71.

26. *Report from Iron Mountain*, 87–88.

27. "What the Others Saw: the year through the eyes of the world's great magazines," *Sunday Times Magazine* (London), January 2, 1966, cover, quoted in Carol Polsgrove, *It Wasn't Pretty, Folks, But Didn't We Have Fun?: Esquire in the Sixties* (New York: W. W. Norton, 1995), 159.

28. Frank Digiacomo, "The *Esquire* Decade," *Vanity Fair*, January, 2007; Polsgrove, *It Wasn't Pretty Folks, But Didn't We Have Fun?*.

29. Harold Hayes, quoted in Felix Kessler, "Who Wrote It? A Fad in Political Comment Is Using Pseudonyms," *Wall Street Journal*, November 13, 1967, 1.

30. "Hoax or Horror? A Book That Shook the White House," *US News & World Report*, November 20, 1967, 48.

31. Irving Kristol, "'Iron Mountain' Lies beyond Credibility Gap," *Fortune*, January, 1968, 185.

32. Howard Junker, "Is Peace Possible?," *Newsweek*, December 4, 1967, 102.

33. See, for example, "Vietnam 1966," audio archive, UPI, https://www.upi .com/Archives/Audio/1966/Vietnam-1966/, and Ted Lewis, "Can Statements Be Trusted?," *Abilene Reporter-News*, May 8, 1966, p. 38 (syndicated column); see also Christian G. Appy, *American Reckoning: The Vietnam War and Our National Identity* (2015; repr., New York: Penguin Books, 2016, 86).

34. Advertisement in *National Review*, December 12, 1967, 3.

35. *Report from Iron Mountain*, 40.

36. H. Rap Brown, quoted in Malcolm McLaughlin, *The Long Hot Summer of 1967: Urban Rebellion in America* (New York: Palgrave Macmillan, 2014), 122.

37. Quoted in Rick Perlstein, *Nixonland: The Rise of a President and the Fracturing of America* (New York: Scribner, 2008), 214.

38. In his account of the march, Norman Mailer uses the term repeatedly. See Norman Mailer, *The Armies of the Night: History as a Novel/The Novel as History* (1968; repr., London: Penguin Books, 2018), 237–39.

39. Mailer, *The Armies of the Night*, 232, paraphrasing Jerry Rubin.

40. "Capitol Security Measure Passed," *St. Louis Post-Dispatch*, October 20, 1967, 2.

41. Raymond Heard, "10,000 Men Will Meet the Anti-Viet March," *Montreal Star*, October 20, 1967, 1.

42. Raymond Heard, "Hippie's Teeth Go Flying," *Montreal Star*, October 23, 1967, 1.

43. Raymond Heard, interview with the author, July 4, 2023.

44. Raymond Heard, "Darker Days Ahead for U.S. dissidents," *Montreal Star*, October 26,1967, 8.

45. Mailer, *The Armies of the Night*, 4.

46. Mailer, *The Armies of the Night*, 234.

47. Mailer, *The Armies of the Night*, 235.

48. Price Daniel to W. Marvin Watson, October 27, 1967, folder "Walt Rostow, vol. 49, November 1–7, 1967 [2 of 2]," 52, Memos to the President, NSF, box 25, Discover LBJ, LBJ Presidential Library, accessed December 21, 2023, https://www.discoverlbj.org/item/nsf-memos-b25-02.

49. This deduction is based in particular on the highly unusual V-shaped hook at the top of the *C* of "Call me," which is visible both in the way Johnson sometimes writes a *C*, and in the *L* of "Lyndon" in his signature. There is no recording of a Johnson-Rostow call in the Johnson Library, but only nine such recordings exist for the year, and there were likely significantly more; not all calls were recorded. Given the frequency of Rostow's meetings with Johnson, it is also possible this issue was addressed face-to-face. Either way, it is clear from a subsequent memo that Rostow and Johnson had some sort of exchange about *Report from Iron Mountain*.

50. Johnson, quoted in Doris Kearns Goodwin, *Lyndon Johnson and the American Dream* (London: Deutsch, 1976), 316, 311.

51. Quoted in David Milne, *America's Rasputin: Walt Rostow and the Vietnam War* (New York: Hill and Wang 2008), 144.

52. James Thomson, "Minutes of a White House Meeting, Summer 1967," *Atlantic*, May 1967, 67.

53. Laurence Stern, "A Spasm of Gullibility," *Washington Post*, November 30, 1967, A22.

54. Edward R. Fried to Walt Rostow, November 2, 1967, folder, "Walt Rostow, vol. 49, November 1–7, 1967 [2 of 2]," 51, Memos to the President, NSF, box 25, LBJ Presidential Library, Discover LBJ, accessed December 21, 2023, https://www.discoverlbj.org/item/nsf-memos-b25-02. See also Stern, "A Spasm of Gullibility."

55. The Editors, "Comment: Social Science Fiction," *Trans-action*, January–February 1968, 8.

56. From Vice President Humphrey to President Johnson, November 1,

1967, folder, "Walt Rostow, vol. 49, November 1–7, 1967 [2 of 2]," 110, Memos to the President, NSF, box 25, LBJ Presidential Library, accessed December 21, 2023, https://discoverlbj.org/item/nsf-memos-b25-f02.

57. From Walt Rostow to President Johnson, October 28, 1967, folder, "Walt Rostow, vol. 48, October 25–31, 1967 [1 of 2]," 133, October 28, 1967, Memos to the President, NSF, box 24, LBJ Presidential Library, accessed December 6, 2023, https://www.discoverlbj.org/item/nsf-memos-b24-05.

58. From Walt Rostow to President Johnson, "Anti-War Demonstrations Given 'Second Look,'" October 30, 1967, folder, "Walt Rostow, vol. 48, October 25–31, 1967 [1 of 2]," 116, Memos to the President, NSF, box 24, LBJ Presidential Library, accessed December 6, 2023, https://www.discoverlbj.org/item/nsf-memos-b24-05.

59. Jeremy Campbell, "Beware the Horrors of Peace!," *Evening Standard*, November 1, 1967, 7.

60. Edward R. Fried to Walt Rostow, November 2, 1967, folder, "Walt Rostow, vol. 49, November 1–7, 1967 [2 of 2]," 51, Memos to the President, NSF, box 25, LBJ Presidential Library, Discover LBJ, accessed December 21, 2023, https://www.discoverlbj.org/item/nsf-memos-b25-02.

61. Stern, "A Spasm of Gullibility."

62. Walt Rostow to President Johnson, November 2, 1967, folder, "Walt Rostow, vol. 49, November 1–7, 1967 [2 of 2]," 50, Memos to the President, NSF, box 25, LBJ Presidential Library, Discover LBJ, accessed December 21, 2023, https://www.discoverlbj.org/item/nsf-memos-b25-02.

63. "Hoax or Horror? A Book that Shook the White House," *US News & World Report*, November 20, 1967.

64. The Editors, "Social Science Fiction."

65. Mueller, *Democracy's Think Tank*, 5. See also 37–38.

66. John Leo, "'Report' on Peace Gets Mixed Views," *New York Times*, November 5, 1967, 1, 40.

67. Leo, "'Report' on Peace Gets Mixed Views," 1.

68. "On the Possibility and Desirability of Peace," *Esquire*, December 1967, 129–37, 222–23.

69. Lewin, quoted in "Peace Games," *Time*, November 17, 1967, 44.

70. *Public Broadcast Laboratory*, episode 102, aired November 12, 1967, on WNET, American Archive of Public Broadcasting, http://american archive.org/catalog/cpb-aacip-516-0k26970r2w.

71. *Public Broadcast Laboratory*, episode 102.

72. *Public Broadcast Laboratory*, episode 102.

73. Clark Mollenhoff, "'Iron Mountain' Peace Study a Hoax, Pentagon Declares," *Des Moines Register*, November 16, 1967, 2.

74. Richard Fryklund, "Most Significant Book on Military Affairs," *Sunday Star*, December 11, 1960, C5.

75. Louis Menand, "Fat Man," *New Yorker*, June 27, 2005.

76. Junker, "Is Peace Possible?"

77. Mollenhoff, "'Iron Mountain' Peace Study a Hoax, Pentagon Declares."

78. Richard Baron, quoted in Mollenhoff, "'Iron Mountain' Peace Study a Hoax, Pentagon Declares."

79. John Leonard, "Iron Mountain Pseudonymology," *New York Times Book Review*, November 26, 1967, 70.

80. Karnow, *Vietnam: A History*, 506.

81. "Hoax or Horror?" *US News & World Report*.

82. Walter Cronkite script, *Dimension*, CBS Radio Network, November 16, 1967, Lewin Papers, b6-01.

83. "Hoax or Horror?" *US News & World Report*.

84. Herschel McLandress [John Kenneth Galbraith], "News of War and Peace You're Not Ready For," "Book World," *Washington Post*, November 26, 1967, 5.

85. Walter Cronkite script, *Dimension*.

86. James Burnham, "A World Without War?," *National Review*, December 12, 1967, 1388.

87. Richard H. Rovere, "Letter from Washington," *New Yorker*, September 23, 1967, 157.

88. Rovere, "The American Establishment," *Esquire*, May 1962; reproduced in Harold Hayes, ed., *Smiling Through the Apocalypse*: Esquire's History

*of the Sixties* (New York, Crown, 1967), 245. Rovere later developed this theme in a book of the same title.

89. Reproduced in Noam Chomsky, *American Power and the New Mandarins* (1969; repr., Harmondsworth, UK: Pelican Books, 1969), 256–57.

90. Chomsky, *American Power and the New Mandarins*, 271, 284.

91. Walt Rostow to President Johnson re Press Contacts (November 6–11), November 11, 1967, [specific call dated to November 6], folder, "Walt Rostow, vol. 50, November 8–15, 1967 [1 of 2]," 112, Memos to the President, NSF, box 25, LBJ Presidential Library, accessed September 23, 2022, https://www.discoverlbj.org/item/nsf-memos-b25-03.

92. Menand, "Fat Man."

93. Campbell, "Beware the Horrors of Peace!"

94. Leo, " 'Report' on Peace Gets Mixed Views."

95. Bob Mackenzie, "The PBL Sleeper," *Oakland Tribune*, November 13, 1967, 18.

96. Richard N. Goodwin, *Remembering America: A Voice from the Sixties* (Boston: Little, Brown, 1988), 396.

97. Richard N. Goodwin, "The Shape of American Politics," *Commentary*, June 1967, https://www.commentary.org/articles/richard-goodwin/the-shape-of-american-politics/.

98. Campbell, "Beware the Horrors of Peace!"

99. John Kenneth Galbraith, *The New Industrial State*, 2nd ed. (1972; repr., Harmondsworth UK: Pelican Books, 1974), 313.

100. John Kenneth Galbraith, *How to Get Out of Vietnam* (New York: Signet, 1967), 19, 15, 26.

101. Raymond Heard, "Report from the Iron Mountain—the Real Thing or Just a Hoax?," *Montreal Star*, November 18, 1967, 44.

102. It looks from Lewin's journal as though one did: Ivan Schidlof of the *Insider's Newsletter* asked him whether Iron Mountain could really have been used earlier than late in 1965. See Lewin, unpublished journal (1967), November 15, 1967, 11, Leonard Lewin Papers.

103. Eliot Fremont-Smith, "Peace—It Could Be Horrible," *New York Times*, November 20, 1967, 45.

104. Robert Lekachman, "In Praise of War," *New York Times*, November 26, 1967, 71.

## CHAPTER 3: THE CONSPIRATORS

1.  Goodwin, *Remembering America*, 451.

2.  Mills, *Letters and Autobiographical Writings*, 302.

3.  Alfred Carl, "This Square Is Not for Squares," New York *Sunday News*, January 23, 1966, C3.

4.  Victor S. Navasky, *A Matter of Opinion* (London: New Press, 2005), 43.

5.  Bob Bone, "Hallelujah I'm a Bomb, or Singing in the Bathtub," *Monocle*, Winter 1957–58, 5; Navasky Papers, NYU, box 17, folder 8.

6.  Richard Lingeman, interview with the author, September 17, 2023.

7.  Mike Nichols and Elaine May, "Watercooler Talk," in *The Fabulous Fifties*, January 29, 1960; viewable at https://www.youtube.com /watch?v=P6R-q0jJLuk.

8.  Mort Sahl, *Mort Sahl 1960, or Look Forward in Anger*, Verve, 1959.

9.  Dick Gregory, *Dick Gregory Talks Turkey*, Decca/Vee-Jay Records, 1962.

10. Navasky, *A Matter of Opinion*, 66.

11. Navasky, *A Matter of Opinion*, 68.

12. Stephen E. Kercher, *Revel With a Cause: Liberal Satire in Postwar America* (Chicago: University of Chicago Press, 2006), 256–57.

13. Ed Koren, "Super-Kahn," *Outsider's Newsletter* 1, no. 36 (undated, c. 1963), 10–11.

14. Lingeman, email to Stephen Kercher, July 29, 2002, Navasky Papers, box 17, folder 6.

15. Irving Kristol, "A twinkle in Yale's eye," London *Observer*, November 10, 1963, 12.

16. Anne Navasky, interview with the author, September 20, 2023.

17. Eleanor Foa Dienstag, interview with the author, July 1, 2023.

18. Richard Lingeman, interview with the author, September 17, 2023.

19. *Monocle* 6, no. 4 Special Issue, *Vietnam Speak-Out or, How We Won the War*, c. January 1966, Navasky Papers, box 18.

20. Mills, *The Causes of World War Three*, 62.

21. Piel, "Can Our Economy Stand Disarmament?," 37.

22. Victor S. Navasky, "Conspiracy Theory Is a Hoax Gone Wrong," *New York*, November 15, 2013.

23. Navasky, introduction to *Report from Iron Mountain* by Leonard C. Lewin (New York: Free Press, 1996), x. All subsequent references to *Report from Iron Mountain* are identified by the date of the edition if other than the first.

24. Navasky, "Conspiracy Theory Is a Hoax Gone Wrong."

25. Richard Lingeman, interview with the author, September 17, 2023.

26. Lewin was worrying about his writing in 1965–66; by the following winter he was hard at work writing the *Report*. See Lewin, unpublished journal (1965) and unpublished journal ("1968" [1966–70]), Leonard Lewin Papers. Lewin's "1968" journal actually covers 1966 to 1970.

27. Navasky, introduction to *Report from Iron Mountain*, x–xi.

28. Lewin, unpublished journal ("1968" [1966-1970]), January 21, 1966, 1.

29. Lewin, "Affidavit of Leonard C. Lewin in Support of Plaintiff's Motion for Summary Judgment," December 2, 1993, 3, Lewin Papers, b7-02.

30. Leonard Lewin, interview with Matt Biberfeld, *Listen!*, WRVR Riverside Radio, broadcast March 25, 1968, American Archive of Public Broadcasting, https://americanarchive.org/catalog/cpb-aacip-528-w08w951z3s.

31. Anne Navasky, interview with the author, September 20, 2023.

32. Michael Lewin, interview with the author, October 6, 2023.

33. Michael Lewin, interview with the author, October 6, 2023.

34. Michael Lewin, interview with the author, October 6, 2023. Lewin's first book, *How to Beat College Tests: a Practical Guide to Ease the Burden of Useless Courses*, was published by Dial in 1970.

35. Richard Baron, Abe Baum, and Richard Goldhurst, *Raid!: The Untold Story of Patton's Secret Mission* (New York: G. P. Putnam's Sons, 1981), 64.

36. E. L. Doctorow, quoted in Sam Roberts, "Richard Baron, Who Published Baldwin and Mailer, Dies at 98," *New York Times*, June 22, 2021.

37. Bruce Weber (Doctorow's biographer), interview with the author, July 2, 2024.

38. Lewin, unpublished journal ("1968" [1966–70]), January 28, 1966, 1.

39. Richard Lingeman, interview with the author, September 17, 2023.

40. Navasky, introduction to *Report from Iron Mountain*, xi.

41. Leo, "'Report' on Peace Gets Mixed Views."

42. Rabbi Arthur Waskow, interview with the author, October 10, 2023.

43. Rabbi Arthur Waskow, interview with the author, October 10, 2023.

44. Arthur Waskow, "Toward the Unarmed Forces of the United States," Waskow Papers, University of Wisconsin, box 3, folder 2, 3.

45. Rabbi Arthur Waskow, interviews with the author, October 10 and September 12, 2023.

46. Lewin, unpublished journal ("1968" [1966–70]), April 20, 1966, 4.

47. James A. Ward *Ferrytale: The Career of W. H. "Ping" Ferry* (Stanford, CA: Stanford University Press, 2002), 81.

48. Rabbi Arthur Waskow, interview with the author, October 10, 2023.

49. Victor S. Navasky, "The Happy Heretic," *Atlantic*, July 1966, 55.

50. W. H. Ferry, "Masscomm as Educator," *American Scholar* 35, no. 2 (Spring 1966): 297.

51. Ferry, "Masscomm as Educator," 298.

52. Raymond Heard, interview with author, July 4, 2023.

53. Galbraith, *The New Industrial State*, 333.

54. Galbraith, *The New Industrial State*, 325.

55. Galbraith, *The New Industrial State*, 338.

56. Michael Lewin, interview with the author, October 6, 2023.

57. Michael (and Julie) Lewin, interview with the author, June 26, 2023. Michael was interviewed by a state congressman, who agreed he was sincere in his beliefs, but in the end, he managed to win deferments.

58. Lewin, unpublished journal ("1968" [1966–1970]), October 21, 1966, 8.

59. Lewin, unpublished journal ("1968" [1966–1970]), November 24, 1966. (See also "UCCC Professor Attends Seminar," *Kingston Daily Freeman*, November 19, 1966, 6. (Lewin refers to the event as a "GE" seminar; this

event is the only publicly reported match. His entries often cover several previous days; the entry for November 24 is the first for ten days.)

60. Julie Lewin, interview with the author, September 18, 2023.

61. Heard, "Report from the Iron Mountain—the Real Thing or Just a Hoax?"

62. Anne Navasky, interview with the author, September 19, 2023.

63. Lewin, unpublished journal (1967), "IM memo," December 7, 1967, 20.

64. Michael (and Julie) Lewin, interview with the author, June 26, 2023.

65. Leonard Lewin, interview by Matt Biberfeld, *Listen!*.

66. Leonard Lewin, interview by Matt Biberfeld, *Listen!*.

67. Julie (and Michael) Lewin, interview with the author, June 26, 2023.

68. Heard, "Report from the Iron Mountain—the Real Thing or Just a Hoax?"

69. Raymond Heard, interview with the author, July 4, 2023.

70. Heard, "Report from the Iron Mountain—the Real Thing or Just a Hoax?"

71. Jeremy Baker, interview with the author, August 21, 2023.

72. Stephen Vizincey, quoted in Jeremy Baker, "A War Book to End All Peace," *Stanford Daily Magazine*, January 26, 1968, 5.

73. *Ronald Reagan at Yale, Public Broadcast Laboratory*, episode 106, WGBH, December 1967, produced by Austin Hoyt, American Archive of Public Broadcasting, https://americanarchive.org/catalog/cpb-aacip-15-94hmh6vt.

74. Gerald Nachman, *Seriously Funny: The Rebel Comedians of the 1950s and 1960s* (New York: Pantheon Books, 2003), 503.

75. Mort Sahl, *The Hollywood Palace*, October 19, 1968, viewable at https://www.youtube.com/watch?v=EB03-_9zp7M.

76. "Playboy Interview: Jules Feiffer" *Playboy*, September 1971, 92.

77. George Case, *Calling Dr. Strangelove: The Anatomy and Influence of the Kubrick Masterpiece* (Jefferson, NC: McFarland, 2014), 23.

78. Jody C. Baumgartner, ed., *American Political Humor: Masters of Satire and Their Impact on U.S. Policy and Culture*, vol. 2 (Santa Barbara, CA: ABC-CLIO, 2019), 314.

79. Martin Orans, "On Serving Your Fellow Man," *ETC: A Review of General Semantics* 19, no. 4 (January 1963): 390.

80. Richard Schechner, introduction to Megan Terry, *Viet Rock: Comings and Goings; Keep Tightly Closed in a Cool Dry Place; The Gloaming, Oh My Darling: Four Plays* (New York: Touchstone, 1967), 12.

81. Barbara Garson, *MacBird!* (1966; repr., Harmondsworth, UK: Penguin Books, 1967), 56–57.

82. Goodwin, "The Shape of American Politics."

83. "Cat Simril interviews Paul Krassner," *Adbusters: Journal of the Mental Environment* 3, no. 3 (Winter 1995), 85.

84. Quoted in Diana Shaw, "The Temptation of Tom Dooley," *Los Angeles Times Magazine*, December 15, 1991, 46.

85. Albert Hadley Cantril, quoted in Charles R. Acland, *Swift Viewing: The Popular Life of Subliminal Influence* (Durham, NC: Duke University Press, 2012), 5.

86. Lewin, unpublished journal (1967), November 20, 1967.

87. Howard Junker, interview with the author, July 10, 2023.

88. Lois Wallace, letters to Harold Hayes and Richard Baron, 27 July 1967, Harold T. P. Hayes Papers, box 10, folder 15, Wake Forest University.

89. Rebecca Bartlett, memo to Harold Hayes (undated), Hayes papers, box 10, folder 15.

90. Lewin, unpublished journal (1967), November 6, 1967, 6.

91. Times Diary, *Times* (London), January 24, 1968, 8.

92. J. K. Galbraith, quoted in Times Diary, *Times* (London), February 5, 1968, 8.

93. Richard Lingeman, interview with the author, September 17, 2023.

## CHAPTER 4: IRON MOUNTAIN

1. In full, the sign on the road to Iron Mountain reads: RESTRICTED AREA—NO TRESPASSING, SOLICITING, DISTRIBUTION OF LITERATURE. PERSONS ENTERING THESE PREMISES WITHOUT PRIOR AUTHORIZATION FOR SCHEDULED WORK OR VISIT WILL BE PROSECUTED TO THE FULLEST EXTENT OF THE LAW. WARNING—THIS AREA UNDER ELECTRONIC SURVEILLANCE—ALL ACTIVITIES RECORDED ON VIDEO TAPE

24 HOURS PER DAY BY NATURAL & INFRARED LIGHT—KEEP OUT. Repeated requests for authorization to visit the site for this book were declined. The facility is now owned by a data storage and records management company called Iron Mountain, which bought it, along with the name, in 1975. It therefore has no connection to the story traced in this book.

2. Russell Watson, "Taking No Chances: More Companies Build Alternate Headquarters as H-Bomb 'Insurance,'" *Wall Street Journal*, January 12, 1966, 1.

3. Watson, "Taking No Chances: More Companies Build Alternate Headquarters as H-Bomb 'Insurance.'" The article's estimate of the distance from Iron Mountain to New York City is a little on the optimistic side: as the crow flies, it's around 100 miles.

4. Watson, "Taking No Chances: More Companies Build Alternate Headquarters as H-Bomb 'Insurance.'"

5. Watson, "Taking No Chances: More Companies Build Alternate Headquarters as H-Bomb 'Insurance.'"

6. Al Lara, "The Secrets in Iron Mountain: Internal Vaults Guard Records of Living and Dead," *Hartford Courant*, February 22, 1999, B7.

7. Alex H. Faulkner, "Firms' Atomic Hideaway, Deep in Heart of N.Y. Hill," *Des Moines Tribune*, March 28, 1966, 11.

8. Watson, "Taking No Chances: More Companies Build Alternate Headquarters as H-Bomb 'Insurance.'"

9. Faulkner, "Firms' Atomic Hideaway, Deep in Heart of N.Y. Hill."

10. Russell Watson, "Taking No Chances: Firms Dig In, Disperse as H-Bomb Protection," *Wall Street Journal*, January 12, 1966, 12.

11. Newsfronts, *Life*, March 1, 1954, 40; quoted in Bradley Garrett, *Bunker: Building for the End Times* (New York: Scribner, 2020), 51.

12. Richard Lyons, "War in Heavens? We Have A-Answer," New York *Daily News*, January 27, 1966, 2.

13. Richard Wilson, "A Secret Government Site and Russians Near-By," *Des Moines Register*, May 4, 1966, 14.

14. See for example: Walter Cronkite script, *Dimension*; Leonard Sanders, "'Iron Mountain' to Raise Uproar," *Fort Worth Star-Telegram*, November 8, 1967, 2-E; Heard, "Report from Iron Mountain—the Real Thing or Just a Hoax?"; Fremont-Smith, "Peace—It Could Be Horrible"; Junker, "Is Peace Possible?."

15. Walter Cronkite script, *Dimension*.

16. George Orwell, "You and the Atom Bomb," *Tribune*, October 19, 1945; reproduced *Orwell in* Tribune: *"As I Please" and Other Writings, 1943–7*, ed. Paul Anderson (London: Politico's Publishing, 2006), 248.

17. Orwell, "You and the Atom Bomb."

18. Lewin interview, WRVR Riverside Radio, March 25, 1968.

19. Mills, *The Power Elite*, 179–80.

20. Orwell, "You and the Atom Bomb," 249. Mills was critical of *The Managerial Revolution*, too; he was more skeptical than Orwell about the idea that "technical indispensability" would hand power to expert managers. See C. Wright Mills, "A Marx for the Managers," in *Power, Politics and People: The Collected Essays of C. Wright Mills*, ed. Irving Louis Horowitz (New York: Oxford University Press, 1963), 57.

21. [Leonard C. Lewin,] *Report from Iron Mountain*, 70.

22. *National Review*, December 12, 1967, 1388–89. As this was a few days before the formal publication date of Burnham's review in the *National Review* of December 12, it is possible that Lewin was not referring to Burnham's review.

23. Lewin, unpublished journal (1967), December 6, 1967, 20.

24. [Lewin,] *Report from Iron Mountain*, 39.

25. Ledbetter, *Unwarranted Influence*, 72.

26. Thomas Jefferson, "A Summary View of the Rights of British America," *Basic Writings*, 15, quoted in Edwin Gittleman, "Jefferson's 'Slave Narrative': The Declaration of Independence as a Literary Text," *Early American Literature* 8, no. 3 (Winter 1974): 241.

27. Gittleman, "Jefferson's 'Slave Narrative,'" 248.

28. Edmund S. Morgan, ed. *The American Revolution: Two Centuries of Interpretation* (Englewood Cliffs, NJ: Prentice-Hall, 1965), 3, quoted in Gittleman, 249.

29. R. Lamb, *An Original and Authentic Journal of Occurrences During the Late American War, from Its Commencement to the Year 1783*, 8, quoted in Jesse Walker, *The United States of Paranoia: A Conspiracy Theory* (New York: Harper, 2013), 116.

30. Mills, *The Power Elite*, 176.

31. Alex H. Faulkner, "U.S. Companies Head for Hills, Set Up Nuclear-War Hideaway," *Buffalo Evening News*, March 5, 1966, 16; the identity of the site's owner is indicated in Watson, "Taking No Chances: Firms Dig In, Disperse as H-Bomb Protection." Carnegie sold his steel company to J. P. Morgan in 1901, who merged it into the new U.S. Steel.

32. Steve Fraser, *Mongrel Firebugs and Men of Property: Capitalism and Class Conflict in American History* (London: Verso, 2019), 121.

33. Fraser, *Mongrel Firebugs and Men of Property*, 117.

34. Olmsted, *Real Enemies*, 31.

35. John T. Flynn, *As We Go Marching* (New York: Doubleday, 1944), 252, quoted in David Aaronovitch, *Voodoo Histories: The Role of the Conspiracy Theory in Shaping Modern History* (London: Jonathan Cape, 2009), 85.

36. Jessie Bernard, "Comment: Social Science Fiction," *Trans-action*, January–February 1968, 12.

37. Jim Garrison, quoted in advertisement for *The Trial of Lee Harvey Oswald*, *New York Times*, November 1, 1967, 40.

38. Irving Kristol, " 'Iron Mountain' Lies beyond Credibility Gap," *Fortune*, January 1968, 185.

39. Peter Richardson, *A Bomb in Every Issue: How the Short, Unruly Life of* Ramparts *Magazine Changed America* (New York: New Press, 2009), 58.

40. Advertisement for *The Realist* in *The Nation*, March 13, 1967. Stevenson, the Kennedy-era UN ambassador attacked by Walker's supporters in 1963, collapsed and died of a heart attack in a London street in 1965.

41. Mort Sahl, *Heartland* (New York: Harcourt Brace Jovanovich, 1976), 106.

42. James Phelan, "The Vice Man Cometh," *Saturday Evening Post*, June 8, 1963, quoted in Olmsted, *Real Enemies*, 139.

43. "*Playboy* Interview: Jim Garrison," October 1967, 178.

44. Memorandum for director, FBI, March 1, 1968, "Garrison and the Kennedy Assassination: Interview of Garrison on Dutch TV by William L. Oltmans," 2, box 85, HSCA/CIA Collection, JFK NARA, https://www.archives.gov/files/research/jfk/releases/104-10067-10080.pdf. Quotes are from the FBI's summary; the only direct quote given from Garrison is the phrase "military-industrial complex." See also Max Holland, "The Lie That Linked CIA to the Kennedy Assassination," *Studies in Intelligence* 45, no. 5 (2001), 13.

45. John F. Kennedy, Address at California Democratic Party Dinner, Los Angeles, November 18, 1961; John F Kennedy Presidential Library and Museum, https://www.jfklibrary.org/asset-viewer/archives/jfkpof-036-020#?image_identifier=JFKPOF-036-020-p0001.

46. Westin, "The John Birch Society," in *The Radical Right*.

47. Edward Jay Epstein, "A Reporter at Large: Garrison," *New Yorker*, July 13, 1968, 60.

48. "Corporations Plan 'Nuclear Proof' Headquarters," York *Gazette and Daily*, May 31, 1966, 17.

49. "Corporations Plan 'Nuclear Proof' Headquarters."

50. Watson, "Taking No Chances: Firms Dig In, Disperse as H-Bomb Protection."

51. Watson, "Taking No Chances: Firms Dig In, Disperse as H-Bomb Protection."

52. Rostow, quoted in Milne, *America's Rasputin*, 214.

53. Dan Wakefield, *Supernation at Peace and War: Being Certain Observations, Depositions, Testimonies, and Graffiti Gathered on a One-Man Fact-and-Fantasy-Finding Tour of the Most Powerful Nation in the World* (Boston: Little, Brown, 1968), 1.

54. Brad Hills, "McCarthy Warns Arms-Industry Power Growing," *Valley News*, West Lebanon, NH, February 7, 1968, 3.

55. Paul Goodman, *Drawing the Line: The Political Essays of Paul Goodman*, ed. Taylor Stoehr (New York: Free Life Editions, 1977), 166, quoted in Jeremy Varon, *Bringing the War Home: The Weather Underground, the Red Army Faction, and Revolutionary Violence in the Sixties and Seventies* (Berkeley: University of California Press, 2004) 137.

56. Richardson, *A Bomb in Every Issue*, 137.

57. Mark Kurlansky, *1968: The Year That Rocked the World* (London: Jonathan Cape, 2004), 282.

58. "Daley Draws Orators' Fire," *Orlando Sentinel*, August 29, 1968, 7.

59. Hayden, *Reunion*, 253.

60. Hayden, *Reunion*, 256–57.

61. John Lindsay, quoted in Appy, *American Reckoning*, 183.

62. Leonard Lewin, "'Report from Iron Mountain,'" *New York Times Book Review*, March 19, 1972, 47.

63. Lewin, interview, WRVR Riverside Radio, March 25, 1968.

64. Lewin, "'Report from Iron Mountain,'" 47.

65. Lewin, "'Report from Iron Mountain,'" 47.

66. Lewin, "'Report from Iron Mountain,'" 47.

67. Lewin, "'Report from Iron Mountain,'" 47.

68. Leonard C. Lewin, *Triage* (London: Macdonald, 1972), 131, 153.

69. Lewin, *Triage*, 212.

70. Michael Lewin, interview with the author, October 6, 2023.

71. Lewin, *Triage*, v.

72. At the time, many on the left believed that the Rosenbergs were innocent; evidence has since emerged that Julius was not. Either way, their trial was a travesty of due process.

73. E. L. Doctorow, *The Book of Daniel* (1971; repr., London: Penguin Classics, 2006), 28.

74. Senator Vandenberg, quoted in Doctorow, *The Book of Daniel*, 290.

75. Doctorow, *The Book of Daniel*, 320.

## CHAPTER 5: THE LOBBY

1. Warren Hough, James Harrer, "Plans for Mass Arrests of U.S. Citizens Exposed," *Spotlight*, September 17, 1990, 1.
2. "Everything You Need to Know About the Trilateral Commission: the World Shadow Government," advertisement in *Spotlight*, March 26, 1990.
3. "Who's Who of Global Elitists at Bilderberg Conference," *Spotlight*, July 22, 1991, 14–15.
4. "Comeback Attempt," *Spotlight*, September 17, 1990, 2.
5. "Experts on the Issues . . . on Audio Cassette Tape," advertisement in *Spotlight*, October 1, 1990, 14. (The advertisement for Lewin's book in this edition is on page 14.)
6. Julie (and Michael) Lewin, interview with author, June 26, 2023.
7. "Personal . . . from the Editor," *Spotlight*, September 17, 1990, 2.
8. Martin Burns, "Perpetual War Engineered," *Spotlight*, September 10, 1990, 6.
9. Burns, "Perpetual War Engineered."
10. Deborah Lipstadt, *Denying the Holocaust: The Growing Assault on Truth and Memory* (London: Penguin, 2016), 160.
11. Lipstadt, *Denying the Holocaust*, 159.
12. Lipstadt, *Denying the Holocaust*, 29.
13. Lipstadt, *Denying the Holocaust*, 25.
14. Lipstadt, *Denying the Holocaust*, 161.
15. Thomas J. Marcellus, Institute for Historical Review, newsletter, January 1990 (Lewin Papers, b7-01).
16. Marcellus, letter to supporters, Institute for Historical Review, March 1991, 1, (Lewin Papers, b7-01).
17. Marcellus, letter to supporters, Institute for Historical Review, March 1991.
18. [Lewin,] *Report from Iron Mountain*, pirated edition, courtesy of Julie Lewin.
19. [Lewin,] *Report from Iron Mountain*, pirated edition.

20. Lewin, "Affidavit," December 2, 1993, 15.

21. Julie Lewin, interview with author, September 18, 2023.

22. "Editorial: Consistency," *Spotlight*, February 11, 1991, 1.

23. "This Is Another No-Win War," *Spotlight*, February 4, 1991, 24.

24. "This Is Another No-Win War."

25. "This Is Another No-Win War."

26. "Videotapes/Audiotapes from The Tenth International Revisionist Conference," advertisement in *Spotlight*, February 11, 1991, 13.

27. Neil Sheehan, review of "Conversations With Americans," *New York Times Book Review*, December 27, 1970, 5.

28. Fred Kaplan, "Parallax View: Political Paranoia," *Jump Cut: A Review of Contemporary Cinema*, no. 3 (September–October 1974): 4–5.

29. Mark Lane, press conference, Georgetown, September 20, 1978, quoted in Tim Reiterman, *Raven: The Untold Story of the Rev. Jim Jones and His People* (New York: Dutton, 1982), 440.

30. Reiterman, *Raven*, 541.

31. Hunt had the distinction of being both a Kennedy conspiracy theorist himself and a suspect in other people's conspiracy theories.

32. Marcellus, letter to supporters, Institute of Historical Review, March 1991, 4.

33. Lane, letter to Handman, March 4, 1991, 1 (Lewin Papers, b7-01).

34. Lane, letter to Handman, March 4, 1991, 1.

35. Handman, letter to Lane, March 12, 1991, 3 (Lewin Papers, b7-01).

36. Handman, letter to Lane, March 12, 1991, 2.

37. Handman, letter to Lane, March 12, 1991, 2.

38. *Liberty Lobby, Inc.* v. *Dow Jones & Co., Inc.*, 838 F.2d 1287, 267 (U.S. App. D.C. 337, 1988).

39. Robert Eringer, "The Force of Willis Carto," *Mother Jones*, April 1981.

40. Chip Berlet, "Friendly Fascists: The Far Right Tries to Move In on the Left," *The Progressive*, June 1992, 18.

41. Chip Berlet and Matthew Lyons, *Right-Wing Populism in America: Too Close for Comfort* (New York: Guilford Press, 2000), 175.

42. Lipstadt, *Denying the Holocaust*, 162. See also George Michael, *Willis Carto and the American Far Right* (Gainesville: University Press of Florida, 2008), 47.

43. Michael, *Willis Carto and the American Far Right*, 72.

44. Willis Carto letter, quoted in Drew Pearson and Jack Anderson, "Liberty Lobby Founder's Secret Letters Revealed," *Intelligencer Journal*, February 17, 1967, 26.

45. *Robert Strange McNamara: The True Story of Dr. Strangebob* (Washington, DC: Liberty Lobby, 1967), 63.

46. *Robert Strange McNamara*, 73.

47. *Robert Strange McNamara*, 68.

48. *Robert Strange McNamara*, 84.

49. *Robert Strange McNamara*, 83.

50. *Robert Strange McNamara*, 94.

51. *Robert Strange McNamara*, 10.

52. *Robert Strange McNamara*, 112.

53. Frank P. Mintz, *The Liberty Lobby and the American Right: Race, Conspiracy, and Culture* (Westport, CT: Greenwood Press, 1985), 202.

54. *Robert Strange McNamara*, 63.

55. *Robert Strange McNamara*, 8.

56. Lipstadt, *Denying the Holocaust*, 163–164.

57. Eringer, "The Force of Willis Carto."

58. C. H. Simonds, "The Strange Story of Willis Carto," *National Review*, September 10, 1971, 978.

59. Simonds, "The Strange Story of Willis Carto," 979.

60. Lipstadt, *Denying the Holocaust*, 163.

61. Lipstadt, *Denying the Holocaust*, 165.

62. Francis Parker Yockey, *Imperium: The Philosophy of History and Politics* (Costa Mesa, CA: Noontide Press, 1962), 61.

63. Linda P. Campbell, "Liberty Lobby in the Spotlight with Duke, Buchanan in Race," *Chicago Tribune*, January 12, 1992, 4.

64. Berlet and Lyons, *Right-Wing Populism in America*, 278.

65. Jason Barry, quoted in Berlet and Lyons, *Right-Wing Populism in America*, 277.

66. David Duke, quoted in Berlet and Lyons, *Right-Wing Populism in America*, 278–79.

67. Donald J. Trump, open letter, "There's nothing wrong with America's Foreign Defense Policy that a little backbone can't cure," advertisement, *New York Times*, September 2, 1987, A28.

68. Marcellus, letter to Handman, March 27, 1991 (Lewin Papers, b7-01).

69. Lewin, "Affidavit," December 2, 1993, 16.

70. Arons, letter to Tobin, January 25, 1989 (Lewin Papers, b7-06).

71. Arons, letter to Navasky, February 8, 1989, Harold Weisberg Archive, Hood College, http://jfk.hood.edu/Collection/Weisberg%20Subject%20Index%20Files/N%20Disk/Nation%20The/Item%2033.pdf.

72. Tony Cavin, interview with author, August 2, 2023.

73. Tony Cavin, interview with author, August 2, 2023.

## CHAPTER 6: MISTER X AND THE HIGH CABAL

1. Affidavit of L. Fletcher Prouty, District of Columbia, February 1, 1980, reproduced in *Freedom*, February 1980, Radcliffe Science Library, University of Oxford.

2. "Citation to Accompany the Award of the Legion of Merit to Leroy F. Prouty, Jr.," National Personnel Records Center, Missouri.

3. Affidavit of L. Fletcher Prouty.

4. Affidavit of L. Fletcher Prouty.

5. "Understanding the CIA: How Covert (and Overt) Operations Were Proposed and Approved during the Cold War," National Security Archive, George Washington University, https://nsarchive.gwu.edu/briefing-book/intelligence/2019-03-04/understanding-cia-how-covert-overt-operations-proposed-approved-during-cold-war.

6. Chronological Listing of Service for Leroy F. Prouty, Jr., National Personnel Records Center, Missouri.

7.  L. Fletcher Prouty, letter to Bram Cavin, December 23, 1990, 4 (Lewin Papers, b7-02).

8.  L. Fletcher Prouty, *The Secret Team: The CIA and Its Allies in Control of the United States and the World* (Englewood Cliffs, NJ: Prentice-Hall, 1973), 13.

9.  Prouty, *The Secret Team*, 412.

10. Prouty, *The Secret Team* (New York: Skyhorse, 2011), 2. Prouty appears to have added the "high cabal" story at some point between 1992 and his death in 2001.

11. Prouty, *The Secret Team* (1973), 419.

12. Irving Heymont, review of *The Secret Team*, Books, *Military Review*, August 1973, 107, https://www.cia.gov/readingroom/docs/CIA-RDP88 -01350R000200460007-7.pdf.

13. Lewin, Background Information, *Report from Iron Mountain*, xviii.

14. Lewin, Background Information, *Report from Iron Mountain*, xviii.

15. Prouty, "JFK and the Thousand Days to Dallas," *Freedom*, May 1986, 37. As stated, the passage, from "War itself . . ." to "the world's total economy" is taken from [Lewin,] *Report from Iron Mountain*, 1967; these lines occur on pages 29, 30, 31, and 18.

16. Prouty, "JFK and the Thousand Days to Dallas."

17. Prouty, "JFK and the Thousand Days to Dallas."

18. Prouty, interview at National Press Club, early 1991, https://archive.org /details/l.-fletcher-prouty-1992-interview-at-the-national-press-club. In the metadata accompanying the audio recording, the interviewer's name is not given; it is dated as 1992, but as Prouty says that he has never spoken to Lewin, that U.S. troops are in the Persian Gulf, and that he has just been corresponding with Bram Cavin, it is near certain that the recording is from January or February 1991.

19. Prouty, interview at National Press Club, early 1991.

20. Prouty, letter to Cavin, June 13, 1990, 4 (Lewin papers, b7-2).

21. Prouty, interview at National Press Club.

22. Prouty, interview at National Press Club.

23. Edward Katzenbach, "U.S. Faces Arms Control Risks," *Boston Sunday Globe*, January 17, 1960, 14.

24. "Here's How You Can Hear Radio Free America and Editor's Roundtable," *Spotlight*, September 23, 1991, 4.

25. "What's Behind Collapse of Communism, End of Cold War?," *Spotlight*, January 22, 1990, 12–13 carries a transcription of the December 14, 1989 edition of *Radio Free America*.

26. "What's Behind Collapse of Communism, End of Cold War?," 13.

27. "What's Behind Collapse of Communism, End of Cold War?," 12–13.

28. "What's Behind Collapse of Communism, End of Cold War?," 12–13.

29. "Declaration of Thomas J. Marcellus," January 20, 1992 (Lewin Papers, b7-01).

30. Jim Garrison, *A Heritage of Stone* (New York, G. P. Putnam's Sons, 1970), 206, 214, 216.

31. Garrison, *A Heritage of Stone*, 31, 114.

32. Robert Wiener, "On the Trail of Dirty Tricksters," *Los Angeles Times Book Review*, April 25, 1976, 4.

33. Olmsted, *Real Enemies*, 146.

34. Olmsted, *Real Enemies*, 145.

35. See Gagné, *Thinking Critically About the Kennedy Assassination*, 81; other critical journalists and historians include Edward Jay Epstein, Kathryn S. Olmsted, George Lardner Jr., and Fred Litwin.

36. Patricia Lambert, *False Witness: The Real Story of Jim Garrison's Investigation and Oliver Stone's Film* JFK (New York: M. Evans, 1998), 201, quoted in Gagné, *Thinking Critically About the Kennedy Assassination*, 81.

37. Prouty, letter to Cavin, July 20, 1990, 3 (Lewin Papers, b7-02).

38. Stone, quoted in unsigned introductory note to transcript of a speech by Oliver Stone to the National Press Club ("Oliver Stone Discusses His Film," in L. Fletcher Prouty, *JFK: The CIA, Vietnam, and the Plot to Assassinate John F. Kennedy* (New York: Birch Lane Press, 1992) xviii.

39. Prouty, letter to Cavin, December 23, 1990, 1.

40. Prouty, letter to Marcellus, December 23, 1990, 1 (Lewin Papers, b7-01).

41. Carroll Quigley, *Tragedy and Hope: A History of the World in Our Time* (New York: Macmillan, 1966), 1309.

42. Prouty, letter to Cavin, December 23, 1990, 2.

43. Oliver Stone and Zachary Sklar, *JFK: The Book of the Film: The Documented Screenplay* (New York: Applause Books, 1992), 106.

44. *JFK*, written by Oliver Stone and Zachary Sklar, directed by Oliver Stone (Warner Brothers, 1991).

45. *JFK: The Book of the Film* (p. 112) has these lines begin: "Sometimes I think . . . "; the onscreen version is less tentative.

46. *JFK* (movie).

47. *JFK* (movie).

48. Roger Hilsman, personal papers, countries files, 1961–1964, Vietnam: "Proposal for a U.S. Policy in South Vietnam," September 30, 1963, 29–30, RHPP-004-012, John F. Kennedy Presidential Library and Museum. See Fredrik Logevall, *Choosing War: The Lost Chance for Peace and the Escalation of War in Vietnam* (Berkeley: University of California Press, 1999), 73.

49. Stone, quoted in David Baron, "Oliver's Story," New Orleans *Times-Picayune* "Entertainment Guide," May 24, 1991, 22. Stone refers to "all the CIA agent-journalists—like George Lardner."

50. Elaine Dutka, "Oliver Stone Fights Back," *Los Angeles Times*, June 24, 1991, F1.

51. George Will, " 'JFK': Paranoid History," *Washington Post*, December 26, 1991, A23.

52. Bernard Weintraub, "Valenti Calls 'J.F.K' 'Hoax' and 'Smear,' " *New York Times*, April 2, 1992, C15.

53. Oliver Stone, "Who Is Rewriting History," *New York Times*, December 20, 1991, A35.

54. "Making the Movie *JFK*," debate at the National Press Club, January 15, 1992, broadcast on C-SPAN, https://www.c-span.org/video/?23792-1/making-movie-jfk#.

55. Todd Gitlin, "The Stoning of Oliver," *Image Magazine, San Francisco*

*Examiner*, February 1992, 16 (excerpted from a speech delivered at a forum on *JFK* sponsored by *Tikkun* magazine) and reproduced in Stone and Sklar, *JFK: The Book of the Film*, 455.

56. Gitlin, "The Stoning of Oliver," 457.

57. Tom Hayden, "Shadows on the American Storybook," *Los Angeles Times*, December 30, 1991, B5, reproduced in Stone and Sklar, *JFK*, 387, 386.

58. Steven M. Gillon, "Why the Public Stopped Believing the Government about JFK's Murder," History.com, October 30, 2017, updated March 29, 2023, https://www.history.com/news/why-the-public-stopped-believing-the-government-about-jfks-murder.

59. Michael Collins Piper, "Establishment Media Has a Stake in JFK Cover-Up," *Spotlight*, January 6 &13, 1992, 14.

60. Quoted in "'Colonel X' in *JFK* Film Well Known to Spotlight Readers," *Spotlight*, February 10, 1992, 14.

61. Prouty, letter to Carto, January 27, 1992, Willis Carto Papers, box 3, folders 40–41, Kenneth Spencer Research Library Archival Collections, University of Kansas.

62. Chip Berlet, "Friendly Fascists: The Far Right Tries to Move In on the Left," *Progressive*, June 1992, 17.

63. Berlet, "Friendly Fascists," 20.

64. Alexander Cockburn, "J.F.K. and *JFK*," *The Nation*, January 6/13, 1992, 6.

65. Cockburn, "J.F.K. and *JFK*."

66. Cockburn, "J.F.K. and *JFK*."

67. Roger Hilsman, personal papers, countries files, 1961–1964; Vietnam: McNamara-Taylor Report, October 1, 1963, 4, John F. Kennedy Library; this text is from one of the sections (I B [2]) in the report detailing military recommendations which were then approved by President Kennedy in NSAM 263. The report says that it "should be possible to withdraw the bulk of US personnel by that time."

68. Fredrik Logevall, *Choosing War: The Lost Chance for Peace and the Escalation of War in Vietnam* (Berkeley: University of California Press, 1999), 399.

69. Logevall, *Choosing War*, 72.

70. Leo, "Oliver Stone's Paranoid Propaganda," *U.S. News & World Report*, January 13, 1992, available at *Frontline*, November 19, 2013, https://www .pbs.org/wgbh/frontline/article/oliver-stones-paranoid-propaganda/.

71. Sean Mitchell, "Stone, Writers Debate 'JFK' Fact, Fiction," *Los Angeles Times* Washington edition, March 5, 1992, 89.

72. The edited transcript of the debate on *JFK* at Town Hall, New York City, on March 3, 1992, from which all the quotations from the event are taken, is available at Bill Rockwood, "Hollywood & History: The Debate over 'JFK,'" *Frontline*, November 19, 2013, https://www.pbs .org /wgbh /frontline /article /hollywood-history-the-debate-over-jfk /.

73. The transcript says "maligned," which must be either a textual error or a misspeak on Mailer's part.

74. Oliver Stone, in Rockwood, "Hollywood & History: The Debate over 'JFK'" (edited transcript), *Frontline*, November 19, 2013, https://www .pbs.org/wgbh/frontline/article/hollywood-history-the-debate-over-jfk/.

75. Edward Jay Epstein, "JFK: Oliver Stone's Fictional Reality," *Atlantic*, March 1993.

76. Epstein, "JFK: Oliver Stone's Fictional Reality."

77. L. Fletcher Prouty, preface to *JFK: The CIA, Vietnam, and the Plot to Assassinate John F. Kennedy* (New York: Birch Lane Press, 1992), xxviii.

78. William Watson, *Ode on the Day of the Coronation of King Edward VII* (London: John Lane: The Bodley Head, 1902), 8.

## CHAPTER 7: BLUEPRINT FOR TYRANNY

1. Ross Hullett, quoted in Mark A. Hutchison, "Perpetrators' Membership in Organized Militia Is Doubted," *Oklahoman*, April 22, 1995, 3.

2. Robert Tomsho, "Oklahoma Militiamen See Plot by the Feds in Last Week's Blast," *Wall Street Journal*, April 24, 1995, A6.

3. Robert Tomsho, interview with the author, August 15, 2023.

4. Tomsho, "Oklahoma Militiamen See Plot by the Feds in Last Week's Blast."

5. Tomsho, "Oklahoma Militiamen See Plot by the Feds in Last Week's Blast."

6. Robert Tomsho, interview with the author, August 15, 2023.

7. Tomsho, "Oklahoma Militiamen See Plot by the Feds in Last Week's Blast."

8. Robert Tomsho, "A Cause for Fear: Though Called a Hoax, 'Iron Mountain' Report Guides Some Militias," *Wall Street Journal*, May 9, 1995, A1; as best as he recalls that period, Tomsho thinks it most likely it was these two militiamen who he remembers asking "Have you read *Iron Mountain*?" However, he is not certain.

9. Mills, *The Causes of World War Three*, 146.

10. Susan Faludi, *Stiffed: The Betrayal of Modern Man* (1999; repr., London: Vintage, 2000), 62. The US edition is subtitled *The Betrayal of the American Man*.

11. Faludi, *Stiffed*, 66.

12. "Comptroller Urges GM to Retain Arlington Plant," *Tyler Courier-Times*, December 20, 1991, 15; David Henry, "Recession Ravages Island Work Force," *Newsday* (Nassau edition), December 20, 1991, 51.

13. Dorothy Cunningham, letter to Governor Bellmon's task force, quoted in Joel Dyer, *Harvest of Rage: Why Oklahoma City Is Only the Beginning* (Boulder, CO: Westview Press, 1997), 24.

14. Arthur Kirk, quoted in Dyer, *Harvest of Rage*, 42.

15. Pat Buchanan, quoted in Berlet and Lyons, *Right-Wing Populism in America*, 280.

16. Michael Kelly, quoted in Berlet and Lyons, *Right-Wing Populism in America*, 288.

17. Marc Cooper, "A Visit with MOM—Montana's Mother Of All Militias," *The Nation*, May 22, 1995, 719.

18. Cooper, "A Visit with MOM—Montana's Mother Of All Militias," 718.

19. Tom Wayne, quoted in JoEllen McNergney Vinyard, *Right in Michigan's Grassroots: From the KKK to the Michigan Militia* (Ann Arbor: University of Michigan Press, 2011), 260.

20. 1965 California attorney general's report, quoted in David Levitas, *The Terrorist Next Door: The Militia Movement and the Radical Right* (New York: Thomas Dunne Books, 2002), 66; Levitas suggests the group never really "got off the ground" (p. 299). Gale later founded the influential far-right group Posse Comitatus.

21. Pat Robertson, *The New World Order* (Milton Keynes, UK: Word Publishing, 1992), 6.

22. Robertson, *The New World Order*, 267.

23. Robertson, *The New World Order*, back cover.

24. Quoted in Doreen Carvajal, "Onetime Political Satire Becomes a Right-Wing Rage and a Hot Internet Item," *New York Times*, July 1, 1996, D7.

25. Quoted in Tomsho, "A Cause for Fear," A15.

26. Milton William Cooper, *Behold a Pale Horse* (Light Technology Publications, 1991), 10.

27. Q clearance began as the Atomic Energy Commission's security authorization in the late 1940s. See Harold P. Green, "Q-Clearance: The Development of a Personnel Security Program," *Bulletin of the Atomic Scientists* 20, no. 5 (May 1964): 9–15. The clearance process involved is broadly equivalent to that required for a Top Secret clearance for other government agencies. See "Departmental Personnel Security FAQs," Office of Environment, Health, Safety & Security, U.S. Department of Energy.

28. Cooper, quoted in Mark Jacobson, *Pale Horse Rider: William Cooper, the Rise of Conspiracy, and the Fall of Trust in America* (New York: Blue Rider Press, 2018), 87.

29. Jacobson, *Pale Horse Rider*, 3.

30. Cooper, quoted in Jacobson, *Pale Horse Rider*, 88.

31. Michael Barkun, *A Culture of Conspiracy: Apocalyptic Visions in Contemporary America*, 2nd ed. (Berkeley: University of California Press, 2013), 60.

32. [Lewin,] *Report from Iron Mountain*, 62–63 and 66–67, reproduced in Cooper, *Behold a Pale Horse*, 465–68.

33. Cooper, *Behold a Pale Horse*, 65.

34. Cooper, *Behold a Pale Horse*, 36.

35.  Cooper, *Behold a Pale Horse*, 37.

36.  Cooper, *Behold a Pale Horse*, 37.

37.  Jacobson, *Pale Horse Rider*, 99.

38.  Jacobson, *Pale Horse Rider*, 177.

39.  *Iron Mountain: Blueprint for Tyranny*, Best Video Productions, 1993.

40.  *Iron Mountain: Blueprint for Tyranny*.

41.  *Iron Mountain: Blueprint for Tyranny*.

42.  [Lewin,] *Report from Iron Mountain*, 70.

43.  McVeigh, quoted in Jeffrey Toobin, *Homegrown: Timothy McVeigh and the Rise of Right-Wing Extremism* (New York: Simon & Schuster, 2023), 146.

44.  Lou Michel and Dan Herbeck, *American Terrorist: Timothy McVeigh & the Oklahoma City Bombing* (New York: Regan Books, 2001), 179.

45.  McVeigh, quoted in Michel and Herbeck, *American Terrorist*, 180.

46.  Cooper, quoted in James Latham "Violent Words, Violent Actions?," Far Right Radio Review in *VISTA* (Radio for Peace International), April 1996, 2, cited in Robert L. Hilliard and Michael C. Keith *Waves of Rancor: Tuning in the Radical Right* (New York: Routledge, 1999), 208.

47.  Michael Fortier, quoted in Jacobson, *Pale Horse Rider*, 258.

48.  Cooper, *Hour of the Time*, episode 530, "New World Order 3," January 19, 1995, https://www.hourofthetime.com/bcmp3/530.mp3.

49.  Samuel Sherwood, quoted in David Neiwert, *Alt-America: The Rise of the Radical Right in the Age of Trump* (London: Verso, 2017), 56.

50.  Quoted in Tomsho, "A Cause for Fear," A15.

51.  Robert Tomsho, interview with the author, August 15, 2023.

52.  Robert Tomsho, interview with the author, August 15, 2023.

53.  William Cooper, FBI file, 344.

54.  William Cooper, FBI file, 318.

55.  *Intelligence Report*, Southern Poverty Law Center, Spring 1997, 28.

56.  "Best: 'I don't associate with militia,'" *Eau Claire Leader Telegram*, April 26, 1997, 2.

57.  Advertisement by Best Video Productions, *Media Bypass*, September 1995, 61.

58. Navasky, "Anatomy of a Hoax," *The Nation*, June 12, 1995, 817.

59. Robert Tomsho, interview with the author, August 15, 2023.

60. Quoted in Tomsho, "A Cause for Fear," A1.

61. Robert Tomsho, interview with the author, August 15, 2023.

62. Lewin, afterword to *Report from Iron Mountain* (1996), 119.

63. "FC" [nom de plume of Ted Kaczynski, a.k.a. the Unabomber], *Industrial Society and its Future* (Berkeley, CA: Jolly Roger Press, 1995), 44.

64. Michel and Herbeck, *American Terrorist*, 362.

65. Kaczynski, letter, quoted Michel and Herbeck, *American Terrorist*, 363.

66. "A Lefty Reunion," *New Yorker*, May 13, 1996, 38.

67. Alexander Cockburn, "Who's Left? Who's Right?," *The Nation*, June 12, 1995, 820.

68. Cockburn, "Who's Left? Who's Right?," 821.

69. Mitch Horowitz, letter to Victor Navasky, October 26, 1995, Navasky Papers, box 110, folder on *Report from Iron Mountain*, 1967, 1987–88, 1995–2003 (1 of 2).

70. Navasky, introduction to *Report from Iron Mountain* (1996), xiv.

71. McVeigh, quoted in Gore Vidal, "The Meaning of Timothy McVeigh," *Vanity Fair*, September 2001, reproduced in Gore Vidal, *Perpetual War for Perpetual Peace: How We Got to Be So Hated, Causes of Conflict in the Last Empire* (West Hoathly, UK: Clairview Books, 2002), 109.

72. Michael Lewin, interview with the author, June 26, 2023.

73. Lewin, afterword to *Report from Iron Mountain* (1996), 120–21.

74. Carvajal, "Onetime Political Satire Becomes Right-Wing Rage and a Hot Internet Item."

75. Brad Pierce, quoted in Carvajal, "Onetime Political Satire Becomes Right-Wing Rage and a Hot Internet Item."

## CHAPTER 8: THE GHOST OF LEE HARVEY OSWALD

1. Cooper, *Hour of the Time*, episode 594, April 19, 1995, https://www.hourofthetime.com/bcmp3/594.mp3.

2. Cooper, *Hour of the Time*, episode 594.

3.  Neiwert, *Alt-America*, 59.

4.  Sen. Carl Levin, to U.S. Senate Subcommittee on Terrorism, Technology, and Government Information of the Committee on the Judiciary Militia Movement 104th Congress, 1st session, June 15, 1995, C-SPAN, video, https://www.c-span.org/video/?65722-1/us-militia-movement.

5.  Mark Koernke, quoted in Sara Rimer, "Terror in Oklahoma: The Far Right," *New York Times*, April 27, 1995, 1.

6.  Cooper, quoted in Jacobson, *Pale Horse Rider*, 256.

7.  Stephen Jones and Peter Israel, *Others Unknown: Timothy McVeigh and the Oklahoma City Bombing Conspiracy* (New York: PublicAffairs, 1995), 9.

8.  John Flores, cover illustration, *Haight Ashbury Free Press*, November 1994, http://www.johnfloresgraphics.com/HAFreePress.html.

9.  David Hoffman, "America's Militias . . . Angry White Guys or Defenders of Liberty?," *Haight Ashbury Free Press*, August 1995, 11.

10.  Hoffman, "America's Militias," 8.

11.  Meg Dixit and David Hoffman, "1984 Revisited or, How I Learned to Stop Worrying & Love the Microchip!," *Haight Ashbury Free Press*, August 1995, 13.

12.  Dixit and Hoffman, "1984 Revisited," 13.

13.  Senate Subcommittee on Terrorism, Technology, and Government Information, hearing on the militia movement, June 15, 1995, quoted in Hoffman, "America's Militias."

14.  David Hoffman, "We the People: John Mills and the Alameda County Free Militia," *Haight Ashbury Free Press*, August 1995, 17.

15.  Dixit and Hoffman, "1984 Revisited," 13.

16.  Dixit and Hoffman, "1984 Revisited, 13.

17.  Hoffman, "America's Militias," 10.

18.  Hoffman, "America's Militias," 10.

19.  Charles Key, interview with the author, September 22, 2023.

20.  Charles Key, interview with the author.

21.  Charles Key, interview with the author.

22. Larry Dellinger, interview with the author.

23. Barbara Hoberock, "Howe Tells About Informant Role," *Tulsa World*, October 9, 1997, 11.

24. John Hanchette, "New Books Look at Oklahoma Bomber," *Lansing State Journal*, May 3, 1998, 49.

25. David Hoffman, *The Oklahoma City Bombing and the Politics of Terror* (Venice, CA: Feral House, 1998), 367.

26. Hoffman, *The Oklahoma City Bombing and the Politics of Terror*, 370.

27. David Hoffman, quoted in Michael James, "Baltimore Native Faces Charge of Jury Tampering in Oklahoma," *Baltimore Sun*, January 19, 1999, 4A.

28. [Lewin,] *Report from Iron Mountain*, 81, 64, 71, quoted in Hoffman, *The Oklahoma City Bombing and the Politics of Terror*, 365.

29. Hoffman, *The Oklahoma City Bombing and the Politics of Terror*, 365–66.

30. [Lewin,] *Report from Iron Mountain*, 71, 84, quoted in Hoffman, *The Oklahoma City Bombing and the Politics of Terror*, 366.

31. Hoffman, *The Oklahoma City Bombing and the Politics of Terror*, 366.

32. Arthur M. Schlesinger, Jr. "Back to the Womb? Isolationism's Renewed Threat," *Foreign Affairs* 74, no. 4 (July/August 1995): 8.

33. Hoffman, *The Oklahoma City Bombing and the Politics of Terror*, 366.

34. Hoffman, *The Oklahoma City Bombing and the Politics of Terror*, 364.

35. Vidal, *Perpetual War for Perpetual Peace*, 119.

36. Navasky, *A Matter of Opinion*, 280.

37. Vidal, *Perpetual War for Perpetual Peace*, x.

38. Vidal, *Perpetual War for Perpetual Peace*, x.

39. Vidal, *Perpetual War for Perpetual Peace*, 67 (*fn*).

40. Vidal, *Perpetual War for Perpetual Peace*, 118.

41. Larry Dellinger, interview with the author, September 23, 2023.

42. Larry Dellinger, interview with the author, September 23, 2023.

43. David Hoffman, quoted in Tim Talley, "Book Sent to Bomb Jury, Indicated Author Says," *Daily Oklahoman*, January 8, 1999, 8.

44. Michael James, "Maryland Native Tied to Oklahoma Grand Jury Surrenders," *Baltimore Sun*, January 20, 1999, 3.

45. Quoted in James, "Maryland Native Tied to Oklahoma Grand Jury Surrenders."

46. Quoted in Diana Baldwin, "Author Surrenders on Jury Charges," *Daily Oklahoman*, January 20, 1999, 8.

47. Tim Talley, "Book Sent to Bomb Jury, Indicted Author Says," *Daily Oklahoman*, January 8, 1999, 8.

48. Associated Press, "Man Says Oklahoma City Grand Jury Indicted Him," *Fort Worth Star-Telegram*, January 2, 1999, 7. This story was widely syndicated.

49. Brian Ford, "Jury Tampering Charge for Oklahoma Conspiracy Theorist?," *Sunday Record*, Hackensack, NJ, January 3, 1999, Special from *Tulsa World*, A8.

50. Judge William Burkett, quoted in Diana Baldwin and Penny Owen, "Grand Jurors Displayed Various Backgrounds," *Daily Oklahoman*, December 31, 1998, 6.

51. Burkett, quoted in Baldwin and Owen, "Grand Jurors Displayed Various Backgrounds."

52. Larry Dellinger, interview with the author, September 23, 2023.

53. Hoffman, quoted in Judy Kuhlman, "Author of Bombing Book Says He'll Surrender Next Week," *Daily Oklahoman*, January 13, 1999, 8.

54. Hoffman, quoted in Ford, "Jury Tampering Charge for Oklahoma Conspiracy Theorist?"

55. Hoffman, quoted in Michael James, "Writer Embroils Himself in Oklahoma City Bomb Probe," *Baltimore Sun*, January 19, 1999, 1A.

56. Charles Key, interview with the author.

57. James, "Writer Embroils Himself in Oklahoma City Bomb Probe."

58. Quoted in "Conspiracy Writer Charged in Bomb Case," *San Francisco Examiner*, January 19, 1999, A9.

59. "Underwriting the Radical Right," *Intelligence Report*, Southern Poverty Law Center, March 15, 1999, https://www.splcenter.org/fighting-hate/intelligence-report/1999/underwriting-radical-right.

60. Hoffman, *The Oklahoma City Bombing and the Politics of Terror*, vii.

61. Court Order, Revell vs. Hoffman et al. before U.S. District Court for the Western District of Oklahoma (Case No CIV-99-637-C), filed 3 May, 2001.

62. Texe Marrs, "Exclusive Intelligence Examiner Report: The Report from Iron Mountain," 2001.

63. Pat Buchanan, quoted in "Buchanan Backs Demonstrators," *Spokesman-Review*, December 1, 1999, A6.

64. Joan M. Veon, "Interview with Harlan B. Cleveland (focusing on the Authenticity of the *Report from Iron Mountain*) at the Ninth Annual World Future Meeting," http://www.biblebelievers.au/veon.htm.

65. Tony Brown, *Black Lies, White Lies: The Truth According to Tony Brown* (New York: William Morrow, 1995), 95.

66. Brown, *Black Lies, White Lies*, 74; see Chapter 8.

67. Brown, *Black Lies, White Lies*, 95.

68. Brown, *Black Lies, White Lies*, 96.

69. Jim Keith, *Mass Control: Engineering Human Consciousness* (Kempton, IL: Adventures Unlimited Press), 206.

70. *Steamshovel Press*, issue 15, 59.

71. *Steamshovel Press*, issue 15, 60.

72. William F. Jasper, *Global Tyranny . . . Step by Step: The United Nations and the Emerging World Order* (Appleton, WI: Western Islands, 1992), 129.

73. Jasper, *Global Tyranny*, 131, quoting Galbraith in Times Diary, *Times* (London), February 5, 1968, 8. (See Chapter 3.)

74. Jasper, *Global Tyranny*, 130.

75. Jasper, *Global Tyranny*, 133.

## CHAPTER 9: THEY WANT TO KILL EVERYBODY

1. Cooper, *Hour of the Time*, episode 81, April 26, 1993, https://hourofthe time.com/bcmp3/81.mp3.

2. [Hartford van Dyke,] *Silent Weapons for Quiet Wars*, reproduced at https://archive.org/details/2022-4-11-exhibit-c-silent-weapons-for-quiet -wars-57-pages; all subsequent quotations from *Silent Weapons* are taken from this reproduction.

3. *Bucyrus Telegraph Forum*, March 28, 1981, 4; see also April 7, 17, and 24, 1981, 4. The newspaper still exists but its editorial policy has long since changed.

4. "The Van Dyke Letters: Letters from the author of *Silent Weapons for Quiet Wars*," *Paranoia* 11, no. 1, Issue 35 (Spring 2004), 32.

5. America's Promise newsletters for May 1983 and July 1991, Political Research Associates Records (Publications 1908–2011, box 6), Tufts University.

6. Jacobson, *Pale Horse Rider*, 119–22.

7. J. M. Berger, "Without Prejudice: What Sovereign Citizens Believe," Program on Extremism, George Washington University, June 2016, 3, https://extremism.gwu.edu/without-prejudice.

8. John Branton, "Battle Ground Man Convicted in Bogus-Bills Case," *Columbian*, December 12, 2002, C3. See also "Battle Ground Man Defiant at Federal Sentencing," *Columbian*, July 31, 2003, C3.

9. "The Van Dyke Letters: Letters from the author of *Silent Weapons for Quiet Wars*," *Paranoia* 11, no. 2, Issue 36 (Fall 2004), 33.

10. "The Van Dyke Letters: Letters from the author of *Silent Weapons for Quiet Wars*," *Paranoia* 11, no. 1, Issue 35 (Spring 2004), 32

11. "The Van Dyke Letters: Letters from the author of *Silent Weapons for Quiet Wars*," *Paranoia* 11, no. 2, Issue 36 (Fall 2004), 33.

12. Alex Jones, quoted in Jacobson, *Pale Horse Rider*, 335.

13. Cooper, *Hour of the Time*, episode 1918, September 26, 2001, https://hourofthetime.com/bcmp3B/1918.mp3.

14. Alex Jones, quoted in Neiwert, *Alt-America*, 135.

15. David Icke, *. . . and the Truth Shall Set You Free*, 421, quoted in Barkun, *A Culture of Conspiracy*, 108.

16. David Icke, *The Perception Deception or . . . It's ALL Bollocks—Yes, ALL of It* (Ryde, UK: David Icke Books, 2013), 389.

17. Icke, *The Perception Deception*, 234.

18. *Neil Oliver—Live*, GB News, February 11, 2023.

19. Matthew Sweet, post on X, February 11, 2023, https://x.com/DrMatthew Sweet/status/1624340991724453888?s=20.

20. Zack Beauchamp, "Trump Booster Alex Jones: I'm Not Anti-Semitic, but Jews Run an Evil Conspiracy," Vox, October 26, 2016, https://www.vox.com/policy-and-politics/2016/10/26/13418304/alex-jones-jewish-mafia.

21. GB News, quoted in Peter Walker, "Jewish Group Criticises GB News Host over 'Dangerous Conspiracy Theory,'" *Guardian*, July 18, 2023, https://www.theguardian.com/media/2023/jul/18/jewish-group-criticises-gb-news-host-beverley-turner-over-dangerous-conspiracy-theory.

22. Sweet, post on X. "'Kracking the Covid Ghost Code'—Mankind's Great Self-Inflicted Initiation," originally published on davidicke.com, available at Holistic Alliance for Real Ecology, https://holistic-alliance.org/articles/covid-mankinds-initiation/. Last accessed October 14, 2024.

23. *Endgame: Blueprint for Global Enslavement*, written and directed by Alex Jones (Alex Jones Productions, 2007). This is a reference to National Security Study Memorandum 200, "Implications of Worldwide Population Growth For US Security and Overseas Interests" (December 10, 1974). This noted that high population was a factor in causing wars, but not that war should be instigated to reduce population. The document displayed onscreen in *Endgame: Blueprint for Global Enslavement* at this point is not Kissinger's memorandum.

24. Stewart Best, "Jade Helm, Rumors in the Land and the Suicide of America," April 20, 2015, lightgateblogger: Lightgate with Stewart Best, https://lightgateblogger.wordpress.com/2015/04/. Last accessed October 13, 2024.

25. Dan Freisen, email to author, January 26, 2023.

26. Alex Jones, InfoWars, March 16, 2021. With thanks to Dan Freisen.

27. Jones, InfoWars, February 21, 2022. With thanks to Dan Freisen.

28. James Ball, *The Other Pandemic: How QAnon Contaminated the World* (London: Bloomsbury, 2023), 149.

29. Mike Rothschild, *The Storm Is Upon Us: How QAnon Became a Movement, Cult, and Conspiracy Theory of Everything* (London: Monoray, 2022), 41, 68, 261.

30. @midwest_mohawk, post on Thread reader, February 12, 2020, https://threadreaderapp.com/thread/1227775859647492108.html.

31. Jared Yates Sexton, quoted in Richard Ruelas and Rob O'Dell, "How William Cooper and His Book 'Behold a Pale Horse' Planted Seeds of QAnon Conspiracy Theory," *Arizona Republic*, October 1, 2020.

32. Gareth Train, quoted in Elise Thomas, "Wieambilla Shooting: Analysis of Perpetrator's Online Footprint," *Digital Dispatches* blog, Institute for Strategic Dialogue, December 14, 2023, https://www.isdglobal.org/digital_dispatches/wieambilla-shooting-analysis-of-perpetrators-online-footprint/.

33. Train, quoted in Thomas, "Wieambilla Shooting."

34. Alex Krainer, "The Crime of the Century Goes to Court," Zero Hedge, January 9, 2024, https://www.zerohedge.com/news/2024-01-09/crime-century-goes-court.

35. William F. Jasper, *The United Nations Exposed: The Internationalist Conspiracy to Rule the World* (Appleton, WI: John Birch Society, 2001), 104 (*fn*).

36. Jasper, *The United Nations Exposed*, 105.

37. Jasper, *The United Nations Exposed*, 105.

38. Jasper, *The United Nations Exposed*, 105.

39. Jasper, *The United Nations Exposed*, 105.

40. Jasper, *The United Nations Exposed*, 105–6.

41. Jasper, *The United Nations Exposed*, 117.

42. Tom DeWeese, quoted in Heidi Beirich, Mark Potok, Janet Smith, and Don Terry, "Agenda 21: The UN, Sustainability and Right-Wing Conspiracy Theory," *Intelligence Report*, Southern Poverty Law Center, April 2014, 7.

43. Michael Coffman, *Rescuing a Broken America: Why America is Deeply Divided and How to Heal it Constitutionally* (New York: Morgan James, 2000), 113.

44. Coffman, *Rescuing a Broken America*, 112.

45. Coffman, *Rescuing a Broken America*, 115.

46. Coffman, *Rescuing a Broken America*, 115.

47. Coffman, *Rescuing a Broken America*, 113.

48. Ted Cruz, interview with Glenn Beck, Glenn Beck TV [now TheBlaze], Mercury Radio Arts, January 26, 2012, https://www.youtube.com/watch?v=0JDBOaldUcE.

49. Glenn Beck TV, January 26, 2012.

50. Glenn Beck TV, January 26, 2012.

51. Beirich et al., "Agenda 21," 10.

52. Glenn Beck with Harriet Parke, *Agenda 21* (New York: Threshold Editions/Mercury Radio Arts, 2012), 121.

53. Sarah Cypher, "I Got Duped by Glenn Beck!," Salon, November 19, 2012, https://www.salon.com/2012/11/19/i_got_duped_by_glenn_beck/.

54. Alabama Senate Bill 477, quoted in George Altman, "United Nations Agenda 21 Bill Passes Legislature," AL.com, May 16, 2012, https://www.al.com/live/2012/05/united_nations_agenda_21_bill.html.

55. "The 2012 Republican National Convention Platform," *New York Times*, August 28, 2012.

56. YouTube video uploaded by "The Atlantis Report," viewed more than 200,000 times, quoted in Joey D'Urso, "An Old Conspiracy Theory Known as 'Agenda 21' Has Been Rebooted by the Coronavirus Pandemic," Buzzfeed News, April 4, 2020.

57. Heidi Beirich, "Midwifing the Militias," *Intelligence Report*, Southern Poverty Law Center, March 2020, https://www.splcenter.org/fighting-hate/intelligence-report/2010/midwifing-militias.

58. Beirich, "Midwifing the Militias."

59. Re: HIV, see Sean Easter, "Griffin: There's No Such Thing as HIV—'The Immunodeficiencies Are Caused by the Treatment,'" Media Matters, March 26, 2011, https://www.mediamatters.org/glenn-beck/who-g-edward-griffin-becks-expert-federal-reserve. Re: chemtrails, see interview with Griffin, *What in the World Are They Spraying?*, Truth Media Productions, 2010, https://www.youtube.com/watch?v=jf0khstYDLA.

60. G. Edward Griffin, *The Creature from Jekyll Island: A Second Look at the Federal Reserve*, 3rd ed. (Westlake Village: American Opinion, 1995), 536.

61. Griffin, *The Creature from Jekyll Island*, 525.

62. Griffin, *The Creature from Jekyll Island*, 526.

63. Griffin, *The Creature from Jekyll Island*, 526.

64. Griffin, *The Creature from Jekyll Island*, 516.

65. Griffin, *The Creature from Jekyll Island*, 519.

66. Griffin, *The Creature from Jekyll Island*, 558.

67. David Neiwert, "As Predicted, Beck Goes Full-Bore Bircher with Hour-Long Promotion of Griffin's Anti-Fed Conspiracy Tome, *Crooks and Liars* (blog), March 26, 2011.

68. Griffin, quoted in Beirich, "Midwifing the Militias."

69. Neiwert, *Alt-America*, 145.

70. Sam Jackson, *Oath Keepers: Patriotism and the Edge of Violence in a Right-Wing Antigovernment Group* (New York: Columbia University Press, 2020), 119.

71. Tom Boggioni, "Militia Head Warns Fed: Don't 'Waco' the Oregon Occupiers Unless You Want a 'Bloody Brutal Civil War,'" Raw Story, January 16, 2016, https://www.rawstory.com/2016/01/militia-head-warns-feds-dont -waco-the-oregon-occupiers-unless-you-want-a-bloody-brutal-civil-war/.

72. Jason Van Tatenhove, interview by the Select Committee to Investigate the January 6th Attack on the United States Capitol, U.S. House of Representatives, March 9, 2022, https://www.govinfo.gov/content/pkg/GPO -J6-TRANSCRIPT-CTRL0000051199/pdf/GPO-J6-TRANSCRIPT -CTRL0000051199.pdf.

73. Sam Jackson, Statement on "The Oath Keepers: Background and Trajectory Towards the Insurrection," to the U.S. House of Representatives, Select Committee to Investigate the January 6th Attack on the United States Capitol, March 30, 2022, https://www.govinfo.gov /content/pkg/GPO-J6-DOC-CTRL0000062418/pdf/GPO-J6-DOC -CTRL0000062418.pdf.

74. http://oathkeepers.org/oath/2011/06/21/an-empire-strikes-home-_-part -two/ (accessed August 18, 2023; link no longer functioning).

75. Lawrence Wilkerson, "Is Warfare a Human Destiny?" Responsible Statecraft, June 21, 2022, https://responsiblestatecraft.org/2022/06/21/is -warfare-a-human-destiny/.

76. Brian Knowlton, "Former Powell Aide Says Bush Policy is Run by 'Cabal,'" *New York Times*, October 21, 2005.

77. Chip Berlet, quoted in Carvajal, "Onetime Political Satire Becomes a Right-Wing Rage and a Hot Internet Item."

## CONCLUSION: AS IF

1. Appy, *American Reckoning*, 335.
2. See, for example, Matt Stoller, *Goliath: The 100-Year War Between Monopoly Power and Democracy* (New York: Simon & Schuster, 2019); Steve Fraser, *Mongrel Firebugs and Men of Property: Capitalism and Class Conflict in American History* (2019); and George Packer, *Last Best Hope: America in Crisis and Renewal* (2021; repr., London: Vintage, 2021).
3. Packer, *Last Best Hope*, 64.
4. Packer, *Last Best Hope*, 83.
5. Mike Lofgren, *The Deep State: The Fall of the Constitution and the Rise of a Shadow Government* (2016; repr., New York: Penguin Books, 2016), i.
6. Lofgren, *The Deep State*, 32–33, 39.
7. Lofgren, *The Deep State*, 24, 36.
8. Lofgren, *The Deep State*, 32.
9. Lofgren, *The Deep State*, xiv, xix.
10. Trump tweet, 11:54 a.m., May 23, 2018, reproduced in Isobel Thompson, "Trump's Fear of a Deep State Coup Has Become Full-Blown Hysteria," *Vanity Fair*, May 23, 2018, https://www.vanityfair.com/news/2018/05/trump-deep-state-coup-hysteria.
11. Whitney Phillips, interview by author, *Conspiracies: The Secret Knowledge*, "The Secret Knowledge," episode 3, BBC Radio 4, March 26, 2021.
12. Greg Myre and Rachel Treisman, "The Man Who Popularized the 'Deep State' Doesn't Like the Way It's Used," *All Things Considered*, November 6, 2019, https://www.npr.org/2019/11/06/776852841/the-man-who-popularized-the-deep-state-doesnt-like-the-way-its-used.
13. Whitney Phillips and Ryan M. Milner, *You Are Here: A Field Guide for Navigating Polarized Speech, Conspiracy Theories, and Our Polluted Media Landscape* (Cambridge, MA: MIT Press, 2021), 12.
14. "Donald Trump Hosts First 2024 Presidential Campaign Rally in Waco

Texas, Transcript," @ rev, March 27, 2023, https://www.rev.com/blog /transcripts/donald-trump-hosts-first-2024-presidential-campaign -rally-in-waco-texas-transcript#:~:text=2024%20is%20the%20final%20 battle,ones%20who%20can%20stop%20them.

15. Arlie Russell Hochschild, *Strangers in Their Own Land: Anger and Mourning on the American Right* (2016; repr., New York: New Press, 2018), 135.

16. Monica Perez, Follow-up note to "What's at the bottom of the rabbit hole? The Report from Iron Mountain" (podcast), June 7, 2014, https:// www.monicaperezshow.com/whats-at-the-bottom-of-the-rabbit-hole -the-report-from-iron-mountain-podcast-of-june-7-2014-show/ Last accessed September 30, 2024.

17. Lewin, "Report from Iron Mountain," *New York Times*, March 19, 1972.

18. E. L. Doctorow, "False Documents," in *E. L. Doctorow: Essays and Conversations*, ed. Richard Trenner (Princeton, NJ: Ontario Review Press, 1983), 16–17, 25, 26.

19. Doctorow, "False Documents," 25.

20. Navasky, *A Matter of Opinion*, 333.

21. Lipstadt, *Denying the Holocaust*, 21.

22. Lipstadt, *Denying the Holocaust*, 21–22.

23. Harry G. Frankfurt, *On Bullshit* (Princeton, NJ: Princeton University Press, 2005), 61.

24. Lipstadt, *Denying the Holocaust*, 29.

25. Stone and Sklar, *JFK: The Book of the Film*, 113.

26. Hayden, *Reunion*, 114.

27. Quoted in Emma Duncan, "Keir Starmer Must Heed Europe's Rightward Drift," *Times* (London), January 25, 2024, https://www.thetimes .com/comment/columnists/article/keir-starmer-must-heed-europes -rightward-drift-ktrc3df2l.

28. Ball, *The Other Pandemic*, 49.

29. Packer, *Last Best Hope*, 65.

30. Phillips and Milner, *You Are Here*, 197.

# BIBLIOGRAPHY

**Books, Pamphlets, and Articles Consulted**

Aaronovitch, David. *Voodoo Histories: The Role of the Conspiracy Theory in Shaping Modern History*. London: Jonathan Cape, 2009.

Acland, Charles R. *Swift Viewing: The Popular Life of Subliminal Influence*. Durham, NC: Duke University Press, 2012.

Adams, Peter. *The Insurrectionist: Major General Edwin A. Walker and the Birth of the Deep State Conspiracy*. Baton Rouge: Louisiana State University Press, 2023.

Anderson, Paul, ed. *Orwell in* Tribune: *"As I Please" and Other Writings 1943–7*. London: Politico's Publishing, 2006.

Anson, Robert Sam. "The Shooting of JFK." *Esquire,* November 1991.

Appy, Christian G. *American Reckoning: The Vietnam War and Our National Identity*. New York: Penguin Books, 2016.

Bailyn, Bernard. "The Logic of Rebellion: Conspiracy Fears and the American Revolution." In *Conspiracy: The Fear of Subversion in American History,* edited by Richard O. Curry and Thomas M. Brown. New York: Holt, Rinehart and Winston, 1972.

Ball, James. *The Other Pandemic: How QAnon Contaminated the World*. London: Bloomsbury, 2023.

Barkun, Michael. *A Culture of Conspiracy: Apocalyptic Visions in Contemporary America*. 2nd ed. Berkeley: University of California Press, 2013.

Baron, Richard, Abe Baum, and Richard Goldhurst. *Raid!: The Untold Story of Patton's Secret Mission*. New York: G. P. Putnam's Sons, 1981.

Baumgartner, Jody C., ed. *American Political Humor: Masters of Satire and Their Impact on U.S. Policy and Culture*. Vol. 2. Santa Barbara, CA: ABC-CLIO, 2019.

Beck, Glenn, with Harriet Peake. *Agenda 21*. New York: Threshold Editions/Mercury Radio Arts, 2012.

Beirich, Heidi. "Midwifing the Militias." *Intelligence Report*. Montgomery, AL: Southern Poverty Law Center, March 2010.

Beirich, Heidi, Mark Potok, Janet Smith, and Don Terry. "Agenda 21: The UN, Sustainability and Right-Wing Conspiracy Theory." Montgomery, AL: Southern Poverty Law Center, April 1, 2014.

Bell, Daniel, ed. *The Radical Right*. Garden City, NY: Doubleday, 1963.

Benoit, Emile, et al. *A Report of the Panel on the Economic Impacts of Disarmament*. Washington, DC: U.S. Arms Control and Disarmament Agency, January 1962.

Berger, J. M. "Without Prejudice: What Sovereign Citizens Believe." Program on Extremism. Washington, DC: George Washington University, June 2016.

Berlet, Chip, and Matthew Lyons. *Right-Wing Populism in America: Too Close for Comfort*. New York: Guilford Press, 2000.

Bishop, Bill, with Robert G. Cushing. *The Big Sort: Why the Clustering of Like-Minded America Is Tearing Us Apart*. New York: Mariner Books, 2009. First published 2008 by Houghton Mifflin Harcourt (New York).

Boulding, Kenneth E. "Can We Afford a Warless World?" *Saturday Review*, October 6, 1962.

Bowden, Mark, and Matthew Teague. *The Steal: The Attempt to Overturn the 2020 Election and the People Who Stopped It*. Expanded ed. London: Grove Press UK, 2024.

Bradley, Mark Philip. *Vietnam at War*. Oxford: Oxford University Press, 2009.

Brands, H. W. *American Dreams: The United States Since 1945*. London: Penguin, 2011. First published 2010 by Penguin Press (New York).

Brown, Tony. *Black Lies, White Lies: The Truth According to Tony Brown*. New York: William Morrow, 1995.

Bugliosi, Vincent. *Reclaiming History: The Assassination of President John F. Kennedy*. New York: W. W. Norton, 2007.

Burnham, James. *The Managerial Revolution or, What Is Happening in the World Now*. Harmondsworth, UK: Penguin, 1945. First published 1941 by J. Day (New York).

———. *The Struggle for the World*. London: Jonathan Cape, 1947.

Cannon, James P. "The Coming American Revolution." Speech delivered at the 12th National Convention of the Socialist Workers Party, Chicago, IL, November 15 to 18, 1946.

Case, George. *Calling Dr. Strangelove: The Anatomy and Influence of the Kubrick Masterpiece.* Jefferson, NC: McFarland, 2014.

Chomsky, Noam. *American Power and the New Mandarins: Historical and Political Essays.* Harmondsworth, UK: Pelican Books, 1969.

Churchill, Robert H. *To Shake Their Guns in the Tyrant's Face: Libertarian Political Violence and the Origins of the Militia Movement.* Ann Arbor: University of Michigan Press, 2009.

Coffman, Michael. *Rescuing a Broken America: Why America is Deeply Divided and How to Heal it Constitutionally.* New York: Morgan James, 2000.

Cohn, Norman. *Warrant for Genocide: The Myth of the Jewish World Conspiracy and the* Protocols of the Elders of Zion. Harmondsworth, UK: Pelican Books, 1970. First published 1966 by Harper & Row (New York).

Cook, Fred J. *The Warfare State.* New York: Macmillan, 1962.

Cooper, Milton William. *Behold a Pale Horse.* Light Technology Publications, 1991.

Dallek, Robert. *John F. Kennedy: An Unfinished Life.* London: Penguin Books, 2013. First published 2003 by Allen Lane (London).

Dance, Liz. *Nora Ephron: Everything Is Copy.* McFarland, Jefferson, NC, 2015.

Davison, Jean. *Oswald's Game.* New York: W. W. Norton, 1983.

Doctorow, E. L. *The Book of Daniel.* London: Penguin Classics, 2006. First published 1971 by Ballantine Books (New York).

———. *Ragtime.* London: Penguin Classics, 2006. First published 1974 by Random House (New York).

Dooley, Thomas A. *Deliver Us from Evil: The Story of Viet Nam's Flight to Freedom.* New York: Farrar, Straus and Cudahy, 1956.

Dyer, Joel. *Harvest of Rage: Why Oklahoma City Is Only the Beginning.* Boulder, CO: Westview Press, 1997.

Ellsberg, Daniel. *The Doomsday Machine: Confessions of a Nuclear War Planner.* London: Bloomsbury, 2019.

Epstein, Edward Jay. *The Assassination Chronicles: Inquest, Counterplot, and Legend.* New York: Carroll & Graf, 1992.

———. *The JFK Assassination Diary: My Search for Answers to the Mystery of the Century.* Rev. ed. New York: FastTrack Press/EJE Publications, 2014.

———. "JFK: Oliver Stone's Fictional Reality." *Atlantic,* March 1993.

Faludi, Susan. *Stiffed: The Betrayal of Modern Man.* London: Vintage, 2000. First published 1999 as *Stiffed: The Betrayal of the American Man* by Harper Perennial (New York).

Fenster, Mark. *Conspiracy Theories: Secrecy and Power in American Culture.* Rev. ed. Minneapolis: University of Minnesota Press, 2008.

Ferguson, Niall. *Kissinger.* Vol. 1, *1923–1968: The Idealist.* London: Allen Lane, 2015.

Ferry, W. H. "Masscomm as Educator." *American Scholar* 35, no. 2 (Spring 1966).

Fillerup, Steve. *Heaven's Hammers: An FBI Agent's Walk in a Dark World.* Bloomington, IN: Xlibris, 2014.

Flacks, Richard, and Nelson Lichtenstein, eds. *The Port Huron Statement: Sources and Legacies of the New Left's Founding Manifesto.* Philadelphia: University of Pennsylvania Press, 2015.

Frankfurt, Harry G. *On Bullshit.* Princeton, NJ: Princeton University Press, 2005.

Fraser, Steve. *Mongrel Firebugs and Men of Property: Capitalism and Class Conflict in American History.* London: Verso, 2019.

Freed, Donald, and Mark Lane. *Executive Action: Assassination of a Head of State.* New York: Dell, 1973.

Fryklund, Richard. *100 Million Lives: Maximum Survival in a Nuclear War.* New York: Macmillan, 1962.

Gagné, Michel Jacques. *Thinking Critically About the Kennedy Assassination: Debunking the Myths and Conspiracy Theories.* Milton Park, UK: Routledge, 2022.

Galbraith, John Kenneth. *How to Get Out of Vietnam: A Workable Solution to the Worst Problem of Our Time.* New York: Signet, 1967.

———. *The New Industrial State.* 2nd ed. Harmondsworth, UK: Pelican Books, 1974. First published in 1967 by Houghton-Mifflin (Boston).

Ganz, John. *When the Clock Broke: Con Men, Conspiracists, and How America Cracked Up in the Early 1990s.* New York: Farrar, Straus and Giroux, 2024.

Garrett, Bradley. *Bunker: Building for the End Times.* New York: Scribner, 2020.

Garrison, Jim. *A Heritage of Stone.* New York: G. P. Putnam's Sons, 1970.

———. *On the Trail of the Assassins: My Investigation and Prosecution of the Murder of President Kennedy.* New York: Sheridan Square Press, 1988.

Garson, Barbara. *MacBird!: A Sensational Parody of* Macbeth *Set Somewhere Between Dallas and Dunsinane.* Harmondsworth, UK: Penguin Books, 1967. First published 1966 by Grassy Knoll Press (Berkeley, CA).

Ghamari-Tabrizi, Sharon. *The Worlds of Herman Kahn: The Intuitive Science of Thermonuclear War.* Cambridge, MA: Harvard University Press, 2005.

Gibson, DW. *One Week to Change the World: An Oral History of the 1999 WTO Protests.* New York: Simon & Schuster Paperbacks, 2024.

Gitlin, Todd. *The Sixties: Years of Hope, Days of Rage.* 1987. Revised trade edition, New York, Bantam, 1993.

Gittleman, Edwin. "Jefferson's 'Slave Narrative': The Declaration of Independence as a Literary Text." *Early American Literature* 8, no. 3 (Winter 1974).

Goodall, Alex. *Loyalty and Liberty: American Countersubversion from World War I to the McCarthy Era.* Chicago: University of Illinois Press, 2013.

Goodwin, Richard N. *Remembering America: A Voice from the Sixties.* Boston: Little Brown, 1988.

Green, Harold P. "Q-Clearance: The Development of a Personnel Security Program." *Bulletin of the Atomic Scientists* 20, no. 5 (May 1964).

Griffin, Charles J. G. "New Light on Eisenhower's Farewell Address." *Presidential Studies Quarterly* 22, no. 3 (Summer 1992).

Griffin, G. Edward. *The Creature from Jekyll Island: A Second Look at the Federal Reserve.* 3rd ed. Westlake Village, CA: American Media, 1998.

Grove, Gene. *Inside the John Birch Society.* Greenwich, CT: Gold Medal Books, 1961.

Halberstam, David. *The Best and the Brightest.* New York: Random House, 1972.

Harrington, Michael. *The Accidental Century.* London: Pelican, 1967. First published 1965 by Macmillan (New York).

Hayden, Tom. *Reunion.* New York: Random House, 1988.

Hayes, Harold, ed. *Smiling Through the Apocalypse: Esquire's History of the Sixties.* New York: Crown, 1987.

Hitchcock, William I. *The Age of Eisenhower: America and the World in the 1950s.* New York: Simon & Schuster, 2019.

Hilliard, Robert L., and Michael C. Keith. *Waves of Rancor: Tuning into the Radical Right.* New York: Routledge, 1999.

Hochschild, Arlie Russell. *Strangers in Their Own Land: Anger and Mourning on the American Right.* New York: New Press, 2018. First published 2016 by New Press (New York).

Hoffman, David. *The Oklahoma City Bombing and the Politics of Terror.* Venice, CA: Feral House, 1998.

Hofstadter, Richard. *The Age of Reform: From Bryan to F.D.R.* New York: Alfred A. Knopf, 1955.

Hogan, Michael J. *A Cross of Iron: Harry S. Truman and the Origins of the National Security State, 1945–1954.* Cambridge: Cambridge University Press, 1998.

Horowitz, Irving Louis, ed. *Power, Politics and People: The Collected Essays of C. Wright Mills.* New York: Oxford University Press, 1963.

Icke, David. *The Perception Deception or . . . It's ALL Bollocks—Yes, ALL of It.* Ryde, UK: David Icke Books, 2013.

Jackson, Sam. *Oath Keepers: Patriotism and the Edge of Violence in a Right-Wing Antigovernment Group.* New York: Columbia University Press, 2020.

Jacobson, Mark. *Pale Horse Rider: William Cooper, the Rise of Conspiracy, and the Fall of Trust in America.* New York: Blue Rider Press, 2018.

Jasper, William F. *Global Tyranny . . . Step by Step: The United Nations and the Emerging New World Order.* Appleton, WI: Western Islands, 1992.

———. *The United Nations Exposed: The Internationalist Conspiracy to Rule the World.* Appleton, WI: John Birch Society, 2001.

Jeffreys-Jones, Rhodri. *The CIA and American Democracy.* 3rd ed. London: Yale University Press, 2003.

Jones, Stephen, and Peter Israel. *Others Unknown: Timothy McVeigh and the Oklahoma City Bombing Conspiracy.* New York: PublicAffairs, 2001.

Kaczynski, Ted [aka the Unabomber, writing as F.C.], *The Unabomber Manifesto: Industrial Society and Its Future.* Berkeley: Jolly Roger Press, 1995.

Kahn, Herman. *On Escalation: Metaphors and Scenarios.* London: Pall Mall Press, 1965.

———. *On Thermonuclear War.* London: Oxford University Press, 1960.

———. *Thinking About the Unthinkable.* New York: Horizon Press, 1962.

Kaplan, Fred. *The Bomb: Presidents, Generals, and the Secret History of Nuclear War.* New York: Simon & Schuster, 2021.

Karnow, Stanley. *Vietnam, A History: The First Complete Account of Vietnam at War.* New York: Viking Press, 1983.

Kearns, Doris. *Lyndon Johnson and the American Dream.* London: André Deutsch, 1976. First published in the U.S. by Harper & Row (New York), 1976.

Keen, Mike Forrest. *Stalking the Sociological Imagination: J. Edgar Hoover's FBI Surveillance of American Sociology.* London: Bloomsbury, 1999.

Keith, Jim. *Mass Control: Engineering Human Consciousness.* Kempton, IL: Adventures Unlimited Press, 1999.

———. *Mind Control, World Control: The Encyclopedia of Mind Control.* Kempton, IL: Adventures Unlimited Press, 1997.

Kelly, Daniel. *James Burnham and the Struggle for the World: A Life.* Wilmington, DE: ISI Books, 2002.

Kercher, Stephen E. *Revel with a Cause: Liberal Satire in Postwar America.* Chicago: University of Chicago Press, 2006.

Klein, Alexander, ed. *Grand Deception: The World's Most Spectacular and Successful Hoaxes, Impostures, Ruses, and Frauds.* Philadelphia: Lippincott, 1955.

Knight, Peter. *The Kennedy Assassination.* Edinburgh: Edinburgh University Press, 2007.

Kominsky, Morris. *The Hoaxers: Plain Liars, Fancy Liars, and Damn Liars.* Boston: Branden Press, 1970.

Kopkind, Andrew. *America: The Mixed Curse.* Harmondsworth, UK: Penguin Books, 1969.

Kort, Michael G. *The Vietnam War Reexamined.* Cambridge: Cambridge University Press, 2018.

Kurlansky, Mark. *1968: The Year That Rocked the World.* London: Jonathan Cape, 2004.

Lambert, Patricia. *False Witness: The Real Story of Jim Garrison's Investigation and Oliver Stone's Film JFK.* New York: M. Evans, 1998.

Lamont, Corliss. *The Crime Against Cuba.* New York: Basic Pamphlets, 1961.

Ledbetter, James. *Unwarranted Influence: Dwight D. Eisenhower and the Military-Industrial Complex.* New Haven, CT: Yale University Press, 2011.

Leontief, Wassily. "Alternatives to Armament Expenditures." *Bulletin of the Atomic Scientists* 20, no. 6 (June 1964): 19–21.

Levitas, Daniel. *The Terrorist Next Door: The Militia Movement and the Radical Right.* New York: Thomas Dunne Books, 2002.

[Lewin, Leonard C.] *Report from Iron Mountain on the Possibility and Desirability of Peace.* New York: Dial Press, 1967.

———. "Pirated edition" of *Report from Iron Mountain on the Possibility and Desirability of Peace.* Costa Mesa, CA: Noontide Press, c.1990. As explained in the book (p.126), this pirated (unauthorized) edition, whose date of publication is uncertain, was a photocopy of an early Dial printing, with a new cover added.

Lewin, Leonard C. *Report from Iron Mountain on the Possibility and Desirability of Peace.* New York: Free Press, 1996.

———. "'Report from Iron Mountain.'" *New York Times Book Review,* March 19, 1972.

———. *Triage.* London: Macdonald, 1972.

———, ed. *A Treasury of American Political Humor*. New York: Delacorte, 1964.

Limbaugh, Rush H. *See, I Told You So*. New York: Pocket Books, 1993.

———. *The Way Things Ought to Be*. New York: Pocket Books, 1992.

Lipstadt, Deborah. *Denying the Holocaust: The Growing Assault on Truth and Memory*. London: Penguin Books, 2016. First published 1993 by the Free Press (New York).

Lofgren, Mike. *The Deep State: The Fall of the Constitution and the Rise of a Shadow Government*. New York: Penguin Books, 2016. First published 2016 by Viking (New York).

Logevall, Fredrik. *Choosing War: The Lost Chance for Peace and the Escalation of War in Vietnam*. Berkeley: University of California Press, 1999.

———. *JFK*. Vol 1. London: Penguin Books, 2020.

Maddow, Rachel. *Drift: The Unmooring of American Military Power*. New York: Broadway Books, 2012.

Mailer, Norman. *The Armies of the Night: History as a Novel/The Novel as History*. London: Penguin Books, 2018. First published 1968 by New American Library (New York).

McCrisken, Trevor, and Andrew Pepper. *American History and Contemporary Hollywood Film*. Edinburgh: Edinburgh University Press, 2005.

McGilligan, Patrick, ed. *Backstory 5: Interviews with Screenwriters of the 1990s*. Berkeley: University of California Press, 2010.

McLaughlin, Malcolm. *The Long Hot Summer of 1967: Urban Rebellion in America*. New York: Palgrave Macmillan, 2014.

McMillan, Patricia Johnson. *Marina and Lee*. Glasgow: William Collins Sons, 1978. First published 1977 by Harper & Row (New York).

Melley, Timothy. "The Conspiracy Imaginary." *Social Research* 89, no 3 (Fall 2022): 757–85.

Melman, Seymour. *Pentagon Capitalism: The Political Economy of War*. New York: McGraw-Hill, 1970.

Merlan, Anna. *Republic of Lies: American Conspiracy Theorists and Their Surprising Rise to Power*. London: Arrow Books, 2020. First published 2019 by Metropolitan Books (New York).

Michael, George. *Willis Carto and the American Far Right*. Gainesville: University Press of Florida, 2008.

Michel, Lou, and Dan Herbeck. *American Terrorist: Timothy McVeigh & the Oklahoma City Bombing*. New York: Regan Books, 2001.

Mills, C. Wright. *The Causes of World War Three.* London: Secker & Warburg, 1959.

———. *Listen, Yankee: The Revolution in Cuba.* New York: Ballantine Books, 1960.

———. "Listen Again, Yankee." Typescript, 1961. General Manuscript Collection, Box 38, Rare Book & Manuscript Library, Columbia University, New York.

———. *The Power Elite.* New York: Oxford University Press, 1956.

———. *The Sociological Imagination.* New York: Oxford University Press, 1959. First Evergreen Edition, 1961.

———. *White Collar: The American Middle Classes.* New York: Oxford University Press, 1951.

Mills, C. Wright. *Letters and Autobiographical Writings.* Edited by Kathryn Mills, with Pamela Mills. Berkeley: University of California Press, 2000.

Milne, David. *America's Rasputin: Walt Rostow and the Vietnam War.* New York: Hill and Wang, 2008.

Mintz, Frank. *The Liberty Lobby and the American Right: Race, Conspiracy, and Culture.* Westport, CT: Greenwood Press, 1985.

Minutaglio, Bill, and Steven L. Davis. *Dallas 1963: The Road to the Kennedy Assassination.* London: John Murray, 2014. First published 2013 by Twelve (New York).

Mitchell, Greg. *The Campaign of the Century: Upton Sinclair's Race for Governor of California and the Birth of Media Politics.* New York: Random House, 1992, 2011.

Morris, Christopher D., ed. *Conversations with E. L. Doctorow.* Jackson: University Press of Mississippi, 1999.

Morris, Dick, and Eileen McGann. *Here Come the Black Helicopters!: UN Global Governance and the Loss of Freedom.* New York: Broadside Books, 2012.

Mueller, Brian S. *Democracy's Think Tank: The Institute for Policy Studies and Progressive Foreign Policy.* Philadelphia: University of Pennsylvania Press, 2021.

Mulloy, D. J., ed. *Homegrown Revolutionaries: An American Militia Reader.* Norwich, UK: University of East Anglia, 1999.

Nachman, Gerald. *Seriously Funny: The Rebel Comedians of the 1950s and 1960s.* New York: Pantheon, 2003.

Navasky, Victor S. "Anatomy of a Hoax." *The Nation,* June 12, 1995.

———. "The Happy Heretic." *Atlantic,* July 1966.

———. *A Matter of Opinion.* London: New Press, 2005.

Neiwert, David. *Alt-America: The Rise of the Radical Right in the Age of Trump*. London: Verso, 2017.

Oklahoma Bombing Investigation Committee. *Final Report on the Bombing of the Alfred P. Murrah Federal Building, April 19, 1995*. Oklahoma City: Oklahoma Bombing Investigation Committee, 2001.

Olmsted, Kathryn S. *Real Enemies: Conspiracy Theories and American Democracy, World War I to 9/11*. New York: Oxford University Press, 2009.

Orwell, George. *Nineteen Eighty-Four*. Penguin, 1989. First published 1949 by Secker & Warburg (London).

Packer, George. *Last Best Hope: America in Crisis and Renewal*. London: Vintage, 2022. First published 2021 by Farrar, Straus and Giroux (New York).

———. *The Unwinding: Thirty Years of American Decline*. Faber & Faber, London, 2014. First published 2013 by Farrar, Straus and Giroux (New York).

Parker, Richard. *J. K. Galbraith: A 20th Century Life*. London: Old Street, 2007.

Patterson, James T. *Restless Giant: The United States from Watergate to Bush v. Gore*. Oxford: Oxford University Press, 2007. First published 2005 by Oxford University Press (New York).

" 'Peace Is Hell': reviews of *Report from Iron Mountain*." *Trans-action* 5, no 3 (January–February 1968): 7–20.

Perlstein, Rick. *Before the Storm: Barry Goldwater and the Unmaking of the American Consensus*. New York: Nation Books, 2009. First published by Hill and Wang (New York), 2001.

———. *Nixonland: The Rise of a President and the Fracturing of America*. New York: Scribner, 2008.

Phillips, Whitney, and Ryan M. *You Are Here: A Field Guide for Navigating Polarized Speech, Conspiracy Theories, and Our Polluted Media Landscape*. Cambridge, MA: MIT Press, 2021.

Piel, Gerard. "Can Our Economy Stand Disarmament?" *Atlantic*, September 1962.

Polsgrove, Carol. *It Wasn't Pretty, Folks, But Didn't We Have Fun?: Esquire in the Sixties*. New York: W. W. Norton, 1995.

Posner, Gerald. *Case Closed: Lee Harvey Oswald and the Assassination of JFK*. Warner, London, 1994. First published 1993 by Random House (New York).

Prouty, L. Fletcher. *JFK: The CIA, Vietnam, and the Plot to Assassinate John F. Kennedy*. New York: Birch Lane Press, 1992.

———. "JFK and the Thousand Days to Dallas." *Freedom* 18, no. 9 (May 1986).

———. *The Secret Team: The CIA and Its Allies in Control of the United States and the World.* Prentice-Hall, London, 1973. First published 1973 by Prentice-Hall (Englewood Cliffs, NJ).

———. *The Secret Team: The CIA and Its Allies in Control of the United States and the World.* Rev. ed. Costa Mesa, CA: Institute for Historical Review, 1992.

———. *The Secret Team: The CIA and Its Allies in Control of the United States and the World.* New ed. New York: Skyhorse, 2011.

Quigley, Carroll. *Tragedy and Hope: A History of the World in Our Time.* New York: Macmillan, 1966.

Reiterman, Tim, with John Jacobs. *Raven: The Untold Story of the Rev. Jim Jones and His People.* New York: Jeremy P. Tarcher, 2008. First published 1982 by E. P. Dutton (New York).

Richardson, Peter. *A Bomb in Every Issue: How the Short, Unruly Life of Ramparts Magazine Changed America.* New York: New Press, 2009.

Robertson, Pat. *The New World Order.* Milton Keynes, UK: Word Publishing, 1992.

*Robert Strange McNamara: The True Story of Doctor Strangebob.* Washington, DC: Liberty Lobby, 1967.

Ronson, Jon. *Them: Adventures with Extremists.* London: Picador, 2015. First published 2001 by Picador (London).

Rothschild, Mike. *The Storm Is Upon Us: How QAnon Became a Movement, Cult, and Conspiracy Theory of Everything.* London: Monoray, 2022. First published 2021 by Melville House (Brooklyn, NY).

Sahl, Mort. *Heartland.* New York: Harcourt Brace Jovanovich, 1976.

Schaller, Tom, and Paul Waldman. *White Rural Rage: The Threat to American Democracy.* New York: Random House, 2024.

Schelling, Thomas C. *The Strategy of Conflict.* Cambridge, MA: MIT Press, 1960.

Seligman, Ben B. "Disarmament & the Economy." *Commentary,* May 1963.

Shapley, Deborah. *Promise and Power: The Life and Times of Robert McNamara.* Boston: Little, Brown, 1993.

Simonds, C. H. "The Strange Story of Willis Carto." *National Review,* September 10, 1971.

Smoot, Dan. *The Invisible Government.* Belmont, MA: Western Islands, 1962. Americanist Library edition, 1965.

Snow, Captain Robert L. *Terrorists Among Us: The Militia Threat.* Oxford: Perseus, 2002. First published 1999 as *The Militia Threat: Terrorists Among Us* by Perseus (Cambridge, MA).

Southern Poverty Law Center. "Underwriting the Radical Right." *Intelligence Report,* March 15, 1999.

———. *Intelligence Report,* Spring 1997.

Sparrow, James T. *Warfare State: World War II Americans and the Age of Big Government.* Oxford: Oxford University Press, 2011.

Stoller, Matt. *Goliath: The 100-Year War Between Monopoly Power and Democracy.* New York: Simon & Schuster, 2019.

Stone, Oliver, and Zachary Sklar. JFK: *The Book of the Film: The Documented Screenplay.* New York: Applause Books, 1991.

Talbot, David. *Season of the Witch: Enchantment, Terror, and Deliverance in the City of Love.* New York: Free Press, 2013. First published 2012 by Free Press (New York).

Terry, Megan. *Viet Rock: Comings and Goings; Keep Tightly Closed in a Cool Dry Place; The Gloaming, Oh My Darling: Four Plays.* New York: Touchstone, 1967.

Thomas, Evan. *The Very Best Men: The Daring Early Years of the CIA.* New York: Simon & Schuster, 2006.

Tomsho, Robert. "A Cause for Fear: Though Called a Hoax, 'Iron Mountain' Report Guides Some Militias." *Wall Street Journal,* May 9, 1995.

Toobin, Jeffrey. *Homegrown: Timothy McVeigh and the Rise of Right-Wing Extremism.* New York: Simon & Schuster, 2023.

Trenner, Richard, ed. *E. L. Doctorow: Essays and Conversations.* Princeton, NJ: Ontario Review Press, 1983.

Treviño, A. Javier. *C. Wright Mills and the Cuban Revolution: An Exercise in the Art of Sociological Imagination.* Chapel Hill: University of North Carolina Press, 2017.

Trillin, Calvin. "The Buffs: Was Lee Harvey Oswald Innocent?" *New Yorker,* June 2, 1967.

Troy, Gil. *The Age of Clinton: America in the 1990s.* New York: Thomas Dunne Books, 2015.

Tye, Larry. *Demagogue: The Life and Long Shadow of Senator Joe McCarthy.* New York: Houghton Mifflin Harcourt, 2020.

Varon, Jeremy. *Bringing the War Home: The Weather Underground, the Red Army Faction, and Revolutionary Violence in the Sixties and Seventies.* London: University of California Press, 2004.

Vidal, Gore. *Perpetual War for Perpetual Peace: How We Got to Be So Hated, Causes of Conflict in the Last Empire.* West Hoathly, UK: Clairview Books, 2002.

Vinyard, JoEllen McNergney. *Right in Michigan's Grassroots: From the KKK to the Michigan Militia*. Ann Arbor: University of Michigan Press, 2011.

Vonnegut, Kurt. *Player Piano*. London: Vintage Classics, 2022. First published 1952 by Delacorte Press (New York).

Wakefield, Dan. *Supernation at Peace and War: Being Certain Observations, Depositions, Testimonies, and Graffiti Gathered on a One-Man Fact-and-Fantasy-Finding Tour of the Most Powerful Nation in the World*. Boston: Little, Brown, 1968.

Walker, Jesse. *The United States of Paranoia: A Conspiracy Theory*. New York: Harper, 2013.

Ward, James A. *Ferrytale: The Career of W. H. "Ping" Ferry*. Stanford, CA: Stanford University Press, 2001.

Waskow, Arthur I. *The Limits of Defense*. Garden City, NY: Doubleday, 1962.

———. *Toward a Peacemakers Academy: A Proposal for a First Step Toward a United Nations Transnational Peacemaking Force*. The Hague: W Junk, 1967.

———. "Toward the Unarmed Forces of the United States." Pamphlet, 1965. Waskow Papers. University of Wisconsin, Madison.

Watson, William. *Ode on the Day of the Coronation of King Edward VII*. London: John Lane: The Bodley Head, 1902.

Weidenbaum, Murray L. "Obstacles to Conversion." *Bulletin of the Atomic Scientist* 20, no. 4 (April 1964): 10–14.

Wilson, Andrew. *War Gaming*. London: Pelican, 1970. First published 1968 as *The Bomb and the Computer: A Crucial History of War Games* by Barrie & Rockcliff (London).

Yockey, Francis Parker. *Imperium: The Philosophy of History and Politics*. Costa Mesa, CA: Noontide Press, 1962.

Zipperstein, Steven J. *Pogrom: Kishinev and the Tilt of History*. New York: Liveright, 2019.


**Audio and Video Resources Consulted**

Best, Stewart. *Iron Mountain: Blueprint for Tyranny*. Best Video Productions, 1993.

Cooper, Milton William. *The Hour of the Time*, 1992–2001.

Jones, Alex. *Endgame: Blueprint for Global Enslavement*. Alex Jones Productions, 2007.

Koernke, Mark. *America in Peril*, parts 1–3, 1995.

Lewin, Leonard. Interview by Matt Biberfeld. *Listen!*, WRVR Riverside Radio, March 25, 1968, American Archive of Public Broadcasting.

Prouty, L. Fletcher. Interview at National Press Club, early 1991.

*Public Broadcast Laboratory;* episode 102, WNET, November 12, 1967, American Archive of Public Broadcasting.


## Archives Consulted

Bodleian Libraries, University of Oxford.

Carto, Willis. Papers. Kenneth Spencer Research Library Archival Collections. University of Kansas, Lawrence.

General Manuscript Collection. Rare Book & Manuscript Library, Columbia University, New York.

Hayes, Harold T. P. Papers. Wake Forest University, Winston-Salem, NC.

Lewin, Leonard. Papers. University of Massachusetts, Amherst.

Lewin, Leonard. Unpublished journal, 1965. Leonard Lewin Papers, University of Massachusetts, Amherst.

Lewin, Leonard. Unpublished journal, 1967. Leonard Lewin Papers, University of Massachusetts, Amherst.

Lewin, Leonard. Unpublished journal, "1968" [1966 to 1970]. Leonard Lewin Papers, University of Massachusetts, Amherst. Lewin's "1968" journal actually covers 1966 to 1970.

Lyndon Baines Johnson Presidential Library, University of Texas at Austin.

Mills, C. Wright. Papers. University of Texas at Austin.

National Personnel Records Center, St. Louis, MO.

Navasky, Victor. Papers. New York University.

Political Research Associates Records. Tufts University, Medford, MA.

Radcliffe Science Library, University of Oxford.

Rothermere American Institute, University of Oxford.

*Spotlight.* University of Texas at Austin.

Waskow, Arthur. Papers. University of Wisconsin, Madison.

Weisberg, Harold. Archive. Hood College, Frederick, MD.

# INDEX

communism
    Cuba and, 14
    domino theory, 12, 14
    global communist plot, 65
    McCarthyism and, 6–7, 11, 29, 39,
        40, 141
    Oswald and, 32–33
    post–World War II expansion of, 14
    right-wing opposition to, 28–29
conspiracy theories, xiv–xv, xvi, 1, 2,
        109, 238, 242
    "Agenda 21," 228–31
    bombing of Pan Am Flight 103,
        210–11
    centralized military power, 102, 192,
        213
    "deep state," xvi, 2, 239–40
    depopulation, xvi, 223–26, 229, 231
    Federal Reserve, 123, 124, 136, 178,
        217, 232
    global communist plot, 41, 65
    Gregory and, 123
    Gulf War, motive behind, 129
    Hofstadter and, 37–38, 110–11
    Israel and American foreign policy,
        132
    Japanese attack on Pearl Harbor,
        105–6, 124, 217
    Jewish, 105, 126, 128, 136, 174, 178,
        223, 248
    Johnson caught up in, 55
    Kennedy assassination, xiv, xvi,
        38–39, 106–11, 131, 132, 141, 145,
        147–48, 153, 157–61, 164–67, 246
    King assassination and, 131
    "merchants of death" theory, 105,
        106, 110, 124, 142, 160, 239
    Mills's disciples and, 39–40
    mind control, 9, 28, 140–41, 224–25
    New Left's views and, 24

Oklahoma City bombing, 197–98,
    200–202, 205–6, 208–9, 211
omnipotent power elite, 107, 152,
    153, 154, 155, 159
one-world, globalist domination,
    102, 122–23, 170, 197–98, 211, 234
Pizzagate, 247–48
POWs and MIAs left behind, 173
Report from Iron Mountain cited as
    proof of, xv, xvi, 2–3, 107, 178–79,
    186–87, 189, 195, 211, 231, 247,
    248
right-wing conspiracism, 28, 134,
    135, 222
satire overlapping with, 107–9
Conversations with Americans (Lane),
    130
Cook, Peter, 70
Cooper, William, 179–83, 202, 220, 221
    Behold a Pale Horse, 180–81, 225–26
    death of, 215
    The Hour of the Time talk show, 180,
        186, 188, 197
    military service of, and time in
        Naval Intelligence, 179–80,
        289n27
    Oklahoma City bombing and, 197,
        198
    Report from Iron Mountain and, 181,
        182
    "sheeple," 180, 186, 192
    Silent Weapons for Quiet Wars and,
        215, 216
Council on Foreign Relations, 122, 162,
    178, 233
Covid pandemic, 223, 224, 225, 231
Creature from Jekyll Island, The
    (Griffin), 232–33
Cronkite, Walter, 62, 98–99
Cruz, Ted, 229, 231